THE APPALACHIAN NATIONAL SCENIC TRAIL

D1568291

THE APPALACHIAN NATIONAL SCENIC TRAIL

A Time to Be Bold

Charles H.W. Foster

ISBN 0-917953-20-7

Contents

Preface

At the intersection of Horse Pond and Parker roads in the highlands of north-central Massachusetts lies the small village of Shirley Center. In the middle of the triangular green, a Civil War soldier leans pensively on his rifle butt, reflecting upon Shirley's role in suppressing the great rebellion. Across the street, a glacial boulder, purportedly sold to the town for one dollar by 19th-century farmer M. W. Longley, [1] commemorates an earlier engagement in which the men of Shirley responded to the Lexington alarm sounded by Paul Revere.

Shirley Center seems prototypically New England, displaying what Harvard curator Harley P. Holden has termed the five Yankee "senses": the homestead, the town hall, the meeting house, the school house, and the country store. [2] Picture perfect in colonial white and yellow, and immaculately preserved in a special historic district, Shirley Center still manages to illustrate that other special Yankee quality—pragmatism. An elderly maple on the village green, witness to at least a hundred years of history, is pressed into service to guy up a modern Massachusetts Electric Company light pole. Not far from the village center, a line of new houses marches like militiamen toward the green, notwithstanding the best efforts of the Shirley Historical Society and the Shirley Conservation Commission to contain such intrusions. [3]

To this idyllic spot in 1889 came the eight-year-old son of author, playwright, and inventor Steele MacKaye, first to vacation and later to reside. [4] Benton MacKaye was to become a renowned forester, planner, and perhaps the Northeast's first practicing bioregionalist. From MacKaye's early exposure to Shirley's fields, hills, orchards, forests, streams, and swamps came the inspiration for some of his earliest, natural-resource-based, regional planning, [5] supremely manifest in his conception of the two-thousand-mile Appalachian Trail, a wilderness footpath destined to interlink urban and hinterlands from Maine to Georgia. [6] By 1975, well into the ninth decade of a remarkable life, MacKaye was surveying the universe from the "Sky Parlor" (study) of his beloved "Empire," [7] the family's modest frame house and adjacent meadows just up the street from Shirley's historic green. His outlook was "overall," an admirer later declared, [8] for as MacKaye himself had remarked, paraphrasing Thoreau, he had "travelled much in Shirley." [9]

The account to follow describes what came to be called the Appalachian National Scenic Trail, the first of the so-called long trails officially designated by Congress. Like all such projects, the Appalachian Trail is truly bioregional in character, traversing as it does the central mountain spine of fourteen eastern states. More particularly, this volume charts the history of its various institutions. One in particular, the Appalachian National Scenic Trail Advisory Council (ANSTAC), was a bioregional institution specifically created by section 5(a)(3) of the National Trails System Act for the purpose of overseeing its implementation. ANSTAC started full of promise, dwindled to the point of becoming virtually nonfunctional and then was born again. With a mixed constituency of landowners, Trail club members and state and federal officials, ANSTAC's role has always been problematical. Nevertheless, without its active involvement and influence, the Appalachian Trail would not now be approaching the goal of full establishment and protection,an extraordinary accomplishment for a park of these dimensions and complexities.

Benton MacKaye followed the progress of the Appalachian Trail literally to his dying day. He reminded one and all, upon every possible occasion, that its purpose was cultural as well as recreational, terming the through-hikers "stunt-men" and chiding them about not spending more time savoring the natural experience.[10] He once advocated a prize for the individual who traversed the Trail in the slowest, not the fastest time. MacKaye was also a firm believer in retracing and viewing from a new perspective a path already trodden.[11] It is in that spirit that this retrospective look is taken of the Appalachian National Scenic Trail and its Advisory Council, with special attention to those who have been part of its living history.

Many people have contributed to the account to follow, clothing the bare bones of minutes and records with the flourish and color of personal experience and recollection.[12] Every modern chairman of ANSTAC consented to be interviewed, as did many of its members. The Trail's trail led from Harpers Ferry, West Virginia, to Olympia, Washington; from Milwaukee, Wisconsin, to the Old Custom House in Boston, Massachusetts; from Atlanta, Georgia, to Concord, New Hampshire.

Special acknowledgments are due the Eastern National Park and Monument Association, which awarded the author one of its first Herbert E. Kahler Research Fellowships to assist with travel and other expenses, and the Appalachian Trail Conference, the National Park Service and the Fund for New England, which enabled the publication of this book.

The research began at the time of the 1985 Appalachian Trail Conference, held at Green Mountain College in Poultney, Vermont. The findings are scheduled to be released at the 1987 session scheduled for Lynchburg College, Lynchburg, Virginia. These now-biennial events draw a thousand Trail enthusiasts to a long weekend of meetings, workshops, and recreational and inspirational events. It is here that the true spirit of the Appalachian Trail is apparent, for outdoor enthusiasts of all ages, backgrounds, and persuasions come together from many different regions of the country to exchange ideas, experiences, and convictions.

Throughout it all, the man most responsible for bringing Benton MacKaye's dream to final fruition, a low-key National Park Service professional named David Arthur Richie, blessed with a special blend of tact, patience, and commitment, has been in the forefront of the effort, noticeable as usual by his deliberate lack of prominence. I trust that the account to follow will give him as much satisfaction as it has me.

Needham, Massachusetts   C.H.W.F.
January, 1987

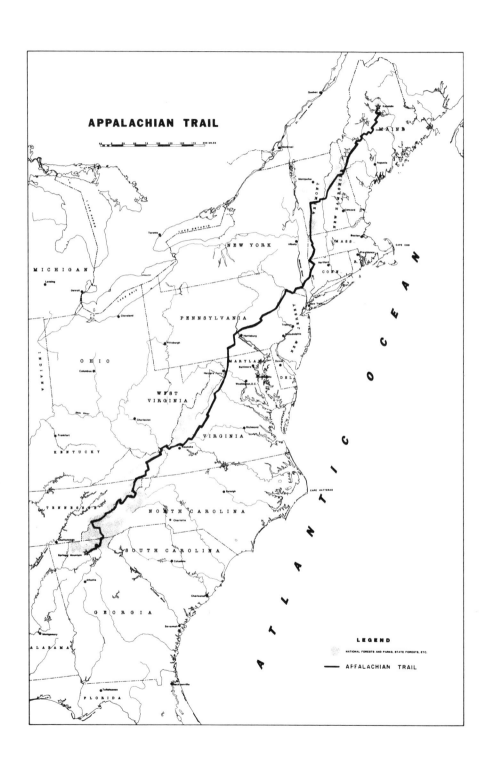

APPALACHIAN TRAIL

LEGEND

NATIONAL FORESTS AND PARKS, STATE FORESTS, ETC.

APPALACHIAN TRAIL

THE APPALACHIAN NATIONAL SCENIC TRAIL

Introduction

Less than a day's drive from 150 million Americans lies the great eastern mountain range called the Appalachians. Extending some three thousand miles from the Canadian border to the very edge of Mississippi in the Deep South, this most ancient of North American mountain ranges touches a deep vein of the history and culture of the entire United States. In the beginning, it *was* America.[13] To this region came the first waves of European immigrants—the Anglo-Saxons, the Scotch-Irish, the Germans, and the Dutch. It was in the Appalachians that many of the decisive moments in American history took place. Control of the region had first to be wrested from the Iroquois Indian Confederation and their French allies to the north, and then from the British at the time of the Revolutionary War. By the time of the Civil War, divisive sectionalism had begun to rack the new nation.[14]

Beyond all these events, the Appalachians remained a formidable physical barrier that had to be breached if the settlers were to reach the fertile lands of the Midwest and, eventually, the uncharted territory of the West. The "gaps" and "notches" through the mountains, products of glacial action, river erosion, and weathering, became the initial capillaries of an overland circulatory system, converted subsequently from Indian footpaths and trading routes into the major highway and rail arteries they represent today.

The Appalachians are marked by extraordinary variety in both natural and human terms—what former Appalachian Regional Commission director Ralph Widner has characterized "a country for Everyman."[15] Small wonder that Benton MacKaye, in his seminal article in the October 1921 *Journal of the American Institute of Architects*, saw both a need and an opportunity to interlink this extensive natural and cultural region with the burgeoning metropolises lying both east and west. His solution was a primitive footpath, extending from Maine to Georgia, to be called the Appalachian Trail, with tributary connectors to civilization along the way.

Many existing treatises today describe the region and its resources.[16] Only a brief overview will be offered here. Yet, some sense of the diversity of the Appalachians is a prerequisite for understanding the complexities of the project that would later implement MacKaye's dream. For the Appalachian National Scenic Trail merely mirrors the larger Appalachian experience, with its own band of visionaries, sets of conflicts, cultural and regional differences.

1

Like the Appalachians themselves, the Trail has worn well over the years. Its story, too, deserves a charted footpath.

Now why on earth would a rational human being want to travel on foot two thousand miles from Maine to Georgia? More than a thousand have already done so, and others are certain to join them in the future.[17] Part of the answer is a genuine sense of adventure—a challenge to both body and soul. Like the classic response of the mountaineer, the Trail is traversed simply because it is there. But another reason is the opportunity to experience a wide range of natural environments.

Peter Farb, in *Face of North America*, eloquently describes the cataclysmic events that produced the present backbone of the Appalachians. It was volcanic action more than two hundred million years ago that first formed Maine's Blue Mountains and New Hampshire's majestic White Mountains, ranges that endure today as sharp peaks of erosion-resistant granite. Vermont's Green Mountains just to the south are even more ancient—among the oldest rocks on the entire North American continent. Composed of bands of mineralized material, and worn down over time to rounded and verdant ridges, they are both literally and figuratively "gneiss." The Appalachians south of New England, for the most part, escaped the great ice sheets that molded and sculpted much of the northern landscape. The results are gentle, rounded slopes surrounded by pockets of rich and fertile soil. In Pennsylvania, the Indians' so-called Endless Mountain,[18] the Kittatinny Range, serves a dual function as footpath for the hiker and flight path for migrating birds of prey.

The central Appalachians are the wrinkled and troubled brow of this eastern mountain chain. A buckling of the earth's crust millions of years ago resulted in a series of parallel ridges—in essence, a set of "folded mountains." Climbing to the top of such mountains, the traveler encounters a vista of what are popularly called hogbacks—ridges of essentially the same height broken only by the occasional cuts of the riverine water gaps. Farther south, the mountain mood changes again. Rather than petering out to obscurity, the Appalachians rise to renewed prominence in the form of the Great Smokies, named for the wisps of haze that invariably wreathe the mountains. Here lie the highest peaks east of the Mississippi River, a unique landscape nurtured by natural processes of great antiquity.[19]

Less immediately noticeable but equally profound have been the effects of water in shaping the face of the Appalachian region.[20] For example, the mountains traversed by the Appalachian Trail form the headwaters of sixteen major rivers that drain toward the Atlantic Ocean. The great glacier of the Pleistocene epoch stretched its icy fingers southward into northern Pennsylvania and New Jersey a mere twenty thousand years ago, leaving behind a legacy of depositional channels (eskers) and ice-gouged ponds (kettle holes) that are still visible today.[21] But water marks the Trail in countless other ways as well.

Standing water, held in once-crystalline mountain lakes (tarns), enhances the outdoor experience. Running (lotic) water lends infinite variety to the landscape, both intercepting and servicing the Trail user. Water and ice-derived landforms bestrew the Appalachian realm—glacial cirques (basins) and erratics (boulders) to the north, gorges and eroded formations both north and south—all remnants of a bygone era. More subtle are the continuing effects of water—foliation and weathering of rock from constant freezing and thawing, microscopic changes from chemical action, and the steady erosion of the landscape, millimeter by millimeter, through the wearing action of brooks, rivulets, and streams. The latter can produce sudden and profound changes at times of heavy rainfall and runoff for, as water doubles in velocity, it increases its carrying capacity sixty-four fold. There is constant warfare between water and land in the Appalachians, and sometimes between adjacent water basins. Rivers can literally "steal" headwaters from one another as the process of erosion progresses upstream.[22] All of these effects can be seen readily in the Appalachians by the environmentally aware traveler.

The region is also marked by life zones that convert climatic and physiographic characteristics into distinct aspects of plant and animal geography.[23] The Appalachian Trail, for example, crosses four of the seven transcontinental life zones in North America: the *Canadian*, with its dominant spruce-fir forest; the *Transition* zone, marked by northern hardwoods; the *Upper Austral* (Carolinian), whose central hardwood forests contain possibly the greatest number of tree species of any forest in the world; and the *Lower Austral*, marked by stands of pine and oak and assorted species.

For the botanically inclined, the Appalachian Trail, throughout its length, is a treasure trove of natural history. Change is evident both horizontally and vertically for, as Peter Farb has observed, an ascent of one thousand feet along the Trail is roughly equivalent to the changes encountered driving north at sea level a distance of six hundred miles. Heading from Maine to Georgia, the hardy terrain of birch, spruce, and balsam of the Blue and White Mountains gives way to beech and maple in the higher elevations of southern New England, the great oak forests of the central Appalachians, and the incomparable "cove" forests of the Great Smokies.[24] At the right season of the year, the hiker may pass through unbroken fields of mountain wildflowers, or stands of shrubs and trees in full bloom. The Trail, for most of its length, is marked by what the Cherokees called their "seven sacred trees"—red cedar, pine, spruce, balsam, hemlock, mountain laurel, and rhododendron.[25]

A profusion of natural features also greets the through-hiker. In the New England Appalachians, he may encounter Screw Auger Falls near Maine's "Gulf Hagas"; view the rock face of the "Old Man of the Mountain" in New

Hampshire's historic Franconia Notch; or visit the hemlock-clad boulders, pools, and waterfalls of Connecticut's Dark Entry Ravine. In the central Appalachians are found the looming highlands of the Hudson River, the fifteen-hundred-foot gorge of the Delaware Water Gap on the border of New Jersey and Pennsylvania, and the wild and scenic peaks of the Allegheny Highlands.[26]

South of the Potomac River, the Appalachians have been described as a "long, wide, and lonesome country" of rolling mountains and deep river "runs." Between the Blue Ridge Range in North Carolina and the Unakas of Tennessee lie forty-six peaks above the six-thousand-foot elevation, and some three hundred ridges above five thousand feet. Here is found the Great Smoky Mountains National Park, encompassing six hundred square miles of incomparable landscape and containing more than thirty-five hundred known species of plants and animals. The key to all the southern mountains, as Thomas Connelly has observed, is their over-powering sense of isolation. "These are a mountain man's mountains—wide, tall, and awesome.[27]

The Appalachians are a *region* in the accepted sense of the term. Their resources and environment constitute a distinct *bioregion*. The Appalachian National Scenic Trail is, thus, a *bioregional project*. And the various organizations and agencies concerned with the prosecution of the Trail program can properly be termed *bioregional institutions*.

The account to follow chronicles the course of events leading to the establishment of the Appalachian National Scenic Trail. It is an administrative history of that effort in some detail, faithfully recorded through documentary evidence and supplemented by human recollection. But the Appalachian National Scenic Trail is also a bioregional experiment of sufficient significance to warrant thoughtful review and analysis, for the lessons learned here are potentially applicable elsewhere. To pour the foundations for that later analysis and to frame the underlying premises, a general discussion of both *regionalism* and *bioregionalism* is in order at this time.

REGIONALISM

There are no mystical properties associated with *regionalism*. As one observer has stated, regions do not have truth—they have only utility. Some, in fact, have almost an enigmatic quality about them, for regions can be defined in many different ways.[28]

They can have distinct *spatial* configurations, for example, predicated upon such obvious geologic, geomorphic, or biotic characteristics as have been mentioned earlier. The Appalachians have a rich history of such definitions, dating back to Hernando de Soto in the sixteenth century. The conventional physiographic divisions are the six provinces set forth by Fenneman in 1913 and modified by Atwood in 1940. Hunt's so-called natural regions (1974) are a composite of modern geographic theory. They include an Appalachian Highlands division subdivided into seven distinct physiographic provinces: the Piedmont, the Blue Ridge, the Valley and Ridge, the Appalachian Plateaus, the New England, the Adirondack, and the St. Lawrence Valley.[29] All but the last two are traversed by the Appalachian Trail.

Regions can also be circumscribed in *economic* terms. Much like water, goods and services frequently flow in definable systems. In recognition of that fact, Congress in 1965 established two economic development regions for the Appalachians: the six-state New England Regional Commission area in the north, and the twelve-state Appalachian Regional Commission jurisdiction in the south.[30] While they lasted, the commissions were curious regional institutions, a hybrid between federal and state agencies. They were chaired by a presidential appointee, but the co-chairmen were the governors of the affected states. The commissions were charged generally with encouraging economic growth and development in their respective regions.

Regionalization in *political* terms is a familiar phenomenon. Elected representatives serve designated districts, and governmental functions generally follow established political boundaries. Experimentation with multi-jurisdictional arrangements has occurred throughout the nation's history with mixed results.[31] Multistate agencies, for the most part, simply fall through the cracks of federal and state jurisdictions.[32] Substate regionalization has been more successful, but the resultant agencies are frequently held hostage by their state progenitors. Less formal political institutions can be successful and influential, however. An Appalachian example is the organization of the states into loose confederations termed governors conferences. Three such conferences embrace the Appalachian Trail states: the New England Governors Conference in that region; the Mid-Atlantic Governors Conference, which includes the Trail states of New York, New Jersey, and Pennsylvania; and the Southern Governors Conference representing the seventeen states of the middle and Deep South, six of which harbor the Appalachian Trail.[33]

Administrative regionalization, for planning and management purposes, is another commonly used device for organizing large territories into meaningful units. Governmental regionalization for the Appalachians has taken many forms. The National Park Service and the former Bureau of Outdoor Recreation, for example, have traditionally operated through regional offices located in Boston, Philadelphia, and Atlanta, respectively. The Forest Service, by way of contrast, functions through but two regions east of the Mississippi River: an eastern region headquartered in Milwaukee, and a southern region based in Atlanta.[34] The principle of administrative regionalism is manifest in private sector organizations as well. For example, the Appalachian Trail

Conference (ATC), the confederation of Trail clubs responsible for Trail oversight and maintenance, operated for many years through six districts, split north and south at the confluence of the Potomac and Shenandoah rivers at Harpers Ferry, West Virginia. Each of the three regions was represented by a vice-chairman elected to the ATC's Board of Managers.[35]

Sociocultural regions have been recognized since the days of the original colonies. In 1940, sociocultural and administrative realities came together in the division of the Appalachians into so-called rural cultural regions by the Works Progress Administration.[36] Howard W. Odum's pioneering sociological studies of the next decades gave added credence to this form of regional definition, especially in the South.[37] More recently, the term *Appalachia* has come into widespread usage less as a prescribed region than as a general descriptor of an area with underdeveloped resources, cultural isolation, and rural poverty[38]—what Peirce has termed the "outback" of eastern America.[39]

There is also what might be termed a *cognitive* regionalization[40]—the simple perception by those living within a geographically discrete area that they belong to a given region. This sense may be validated by economic, political, physical, or social realities. It is often reinforced by media outreach (e.g., newspaper or television coverage) or by pragmatic association with a regional activity or cultural facility (e.g., the New England Patriots football team).

What makes a region viable may be directly related to how its boundaries have been drawn.[41] One suspects that a combination of the elements listed above is required. In the best of worlds, the boundaries of a given region should be as coincident as possible with its functional components. But even then, hard choices may have to be made between nonconforming parts. Experience suggests that some of the elements are more important than others. For example, if a job is to be done, the region must certainly have political integrity, for that is how most programs and projects are carried out. But, even so, the region must consist of whole political units—an entire state, county, or municipality—and the membership should be organized in approximate power parity. In order to have the means to get the job done, the region must be able to draw upon an adequate economic base. The overarching requirement of all is a public constituency that has a sense of belonging to the region. Whether the region is so in fact is immaterial, for a regionally aware citizenry will usually provide the political and economic support necessary to get the job done regardless of the legitimacy of the chosen boundaries.

Ironically, the most tangible definitional elements of all—the physiographic and ecological characteristics of a region—are often the least important. The futile efforts in history to harness the energies of the nation in prescribed river basin or valley authorities bear witness to this fact. There are simply limits to the human willingness to reach beyond conventional jurisdictions. Many a well-deserved regional effort has foundered upon the determination to include every portion of an ecologically defined area within the organizational framework. The result is often a mix of actors who feel only a marginal sense of relationship to one another and, correspondingly, contribute only discontinuity to their organization. Under such circumstances, it is unfamiliarity that most often will breed contempt.

Matters of scale also come into play. If the human elements of regionalization are indeed the most important, then a region should be no larger than the public perception of that region, and preferably contain the smallest political and economic base necessary to sustain the effort. In regionalization, smaller tends to be better.

BIOREGIONALISM

The portion of regionalism that concerns itself with elements of natural resources and environment has come to be called *bioregionalism*.[42] The term derives from the Greek *bios* (mode of life) and the Latin *regio* (territory). *Bios* conveys the flavor of living systems, including human beings. *Regio* furnishes the geographic context—a specified area of activity or interest. Thus, *bioregional resources* are life forms and related activities that occur within distinct regions. They are typically transboundary in nature. *Bioregionalism* is variously the state or condition of a bioregional resource, and the concept or theory associated therewith. Bioregionalism is thus very old and very new.

As a state or condition, bioregional influences date back literally to the beginnings of recorded time. Take the Rift Valley in East Africa, for example. Here a naturally distinct bioregion was host to the earliest ancestors of modern man. So too was the so-called Fertile Crescent—the confluence of the Tigris and Euphrates rivers in Asia—where civilization achieved some of its earliest accommodations with nature. The Minoan Island kingdom in the Mediterranean is a third example of a once-flourishing human endeavor shaped inexorably by bioregional forces.[43]

In our time, bioregionalism is so new a concept that it has yet to appear in most computer data bases, but there are two discernible and one emerging thrust to modern bioregionalism. An example of the first category is the effort of biologists such as Raymond F. Dasmann (University of California at Santa Cruz) to define life forms in regional terms, thereby encouraging their conservation and management as whole systems. The other wing of the discernible movement is more populist in character and, at times, almost metaphysical. It is illustrated by the efforts of Peter Berg and his colleagues at the Planet Drum Foundation (San Francisco) to stress human/land interdependencies, encourage appropriate technologies, and emphasize an ethical sense of belonging to a particular region. Manifestations of this movement are the series of popular bioregional congresses springing up across the country and the lively journal *Co-Evolution Quarterly.*[44]

The emergent facet of bioregionalism is more institutional. It addresses the quandary created by the clash of two hard realities: the reality that the most significant natural resource and environmental problems are frequently transboundary in character; and the concurrent reality that doing something about bioregional problems depends largely upon fixed political jurisdictions. Victims of these realities, the few attempts to manage resources bioregionally have been either marginal successes or abject failures. Yet, if we are to deal with the environment as a whole system, as many would advocate, it is essential that new kinds of management institutions be developed that can succeed even within a dispersed, participatory, political system. From the limited case experience available to date, one can begin to speculate upon what might constitute a successful bioregional institution once its territory has been properly bounded.[45]

The right timing for creation is particularly crucial, for successful bioregional institutions are more likely to be the products of fortuitous or compelling circumstance than of careful design. A formal instrument of some sort is usually helpful because it provides a sense of legitimacy to the venture. A specific mission can bring clarity and direction to the program. But a fixed mandate may also carry with it the seeds of future difficulty, for the institution can become so engaged in its own program interests that it fails to respond to a changing set of needs within its region. If the institution is to endure over time, it must have self-correcting mechanisms built into its operating structure to ensure that it remains relevant.

As a rule of thumb, a bioregional institution must do something for its region over and above what the existing entities can do for themselves. Its functions must be performed in noncompetitive, nonthreatening ways—good enough to be effective, yet not so good that they show others up. An adequate, dependable, independent means of support can avoid a sense of competition with component jurisdictions.

Careful distinctions must be made between the exercise of authority and the employment of influence. Here is where trouble usually begins. Contrary to the prevailing wisdom, authority is not essential for an institution to be viable. In fact, in the case of a bioregional institution, conventional power may actually countervail its ability to work well with component jurisdictions and achieve supportive constituencies. Perceived to be a competitor and a threat, the bioregional institution will, in time, be put out of business. Conversely, without direct authority but with access to channels of significant influence, the institution can become—de facto—enormously powerful.

Once bounded and constituted, the fledgling bioregional institution will typically start out strong with a crisp and definitive mission and a body of alert and committed members. Budgetary support will be provided and professional staff hired. Over time, its goals and tasks will become more diffuse. The early leaders will depart, and their successors will either be indifferent or have other agendas in mind. If the work goes well, the original mission will be substantially complete and a process of program invention will ensue to justify a continuing organization. A good professional staff can help fill the void here, but at some risk of substituting their own agendas and outreaching the goals of their constituency. At that point, the bioregional organization can become manifestly suspect. If it does a poor job, or has fulfilled its circumscribed mission, it is often termed obsolete. On the other hand, if there is evidence of a high level of activity and energy, particularly by staff, the organization is often perceived to be a threat and a competitor. More often than not, a bioregional organization will follow a path of flourish and flounder. If it enjoys a broad mandate to inquire and advise, and avoids restrictive, functional empowerments, then the organization stands a good chance of being captured by new leadership and reinvigorated as new program needs emerge.[46]

In short, the tendency to regard bioregional institutions as fixed and stable entities ignores the reality that their operating environments are changing constantly. Thus, the institutions with the built-in flexibility to adjust their activities, modify their memberships, and remain truly responsive to bioregional concerns are the ones most likely to succeed over time. In the final chapter of this book, we will see how well these principles are reflected in the Appalachian Trail experience. But before doing so let us trace in some detail the history of the Trail, its advocates, and its predominant institutions.

Prospect

THE EARLY YEARS

In October of 1921, the *Journal of the American Institute of Architects* published an article by Benton MacKaye entitled "An Appalachian Trail: A Project in Regional Planning."[47] The nation has enormous undeveloped power in the spare time of its population, MacKaye observed. For the most densely populated portion of the United States, its eastern region, the skyline along the main divides and ridges of the Appalachians could and should serve as a strategic base for utilizing this untapped resource in "recreation, health and recuperation, and employment." MacKaye's Appalachian Project was to consist of four elements: (1) a "long trail" over the full length of the Appalachian skyline from Mount Washington in New Hampshire to Mount Mitchell in North Carolina, "each section to be in the charge of a local group of people"; (2) a series of "shelter camps" for users, built by volunteers, operated in the fashion of the Swiss chalets and guarded, in MacKaye's words, "against the yegg-man and against the profiteer"; (3) scattered "community camps" consisting largely of private domiciles, again on a nonprofit basis, for "recreation, recuperation, and study"; and (4) largely self-sustaining "food and farm camps" to encourage individuals "to get back to the land." Such a project, MacKaye declared, would "appeal to the primal instincts of fighting heroism, of volunteer service, and of work in a common cause." Care of the countryside, he observed, was consistent with the highest goals of protecting home and country.

MacKaye's proposal reflected his earlier Forest Service assignment exploring New Hampshire's White Mountains for the newly authorized eastern national forests, and a two year stint as a specialist in land colonization for the Department of Labor. But MacKaye had also fallen under the spell of two persuasive urban planners and social critics, Lewis Mumford and Clarence Stein, founders with MacKaye of the New York–based Regional Planning Association of America. It was on July 10, 1921, MacKaye recalled, that he, Clarence Stein, and Charles Whitaker, the editor of the AIA *Journal*, sat down for a talk at the Hudson Guild Farm in Netcong, New Jersey: "then and there the Appalachian Trail was born."[48]

The first of MacKaye's four elements, the long trail, found instant favor with local, volunteer, trail clubs throughout the Northeast.[49] At the time, the

concept of a regionwide trail system was in its infancy. Trails were locally inspired endeavors, such as the efforts of the Green Mountain Club, formed
in 1910, to establish and sponsor the Long Trail in Vermont.[50] Only New
England's Appalachian Mountain Club, founded in 1876 to "explore the
mountains of New England and adjacent regions both for scientific and ar-
tistic purposes, and in general to cultivate an interest in geographical studies,"
had any vestiges of program, structure, and status—qualities that resulted
in a generally patrician attitude toward the younger Appalachian Trail Conference.[51] A New York–New Jersey Trail Conference had come into being in
1920, subsuming an earlier Palisades Interstate Park Trail Conference which
had been formed to develop a system of trails for Harriman Park.[52] This new
confederation of local trail interests promised to augment the voices of the
established AMC chapters in the mid-Atlantic region. But it would be the
better part of a decade before other strong trail consortia, such as the Potomac
and Georgia Appalachian Trail Clubs, would emerge to serve other
regions.[53]

The first mile of the Appalachian Trail was cut and marked in 1922 in New
York's Palisades Interstate Park; the last was opened on the south slope of
Mount Sugarloaf, Maine, on August 14, 1937.[54] A driving force behind the
accomplishment of this unprecedented volunteer effort was Myron H. Avery,
a native of Maine and a resident of Hartford, Connecticut, when first enlisted
in the cause by Judge Arthur Perkins.[55] Avery later became the chief ad-
miralty officer for the Navy Department in Washington and, for many years,
served as the president/chairman of the Appalachian Trail Conference. In a
remarkably successful, though not always agreeable alliance, Avery "the doer"
joined forces with MacKaye "the dreamer" to bring about the two-thousand-
mile Appalachian Trail.[56] From then on, MacKaye's regional planning concept would be set aside in favor of the establishment of a continuous footpath.

By 1925, there had been sufficient progress to warrant consideration of a
formal organization for the Trail as a whole. To expedite its development and
maintenance, the Federated Societies on Planning and Parks sponsored a conference in Washington on March 2 and 3, 1925,[57] and a confederation of
clubs was formed, the Appalachian Trail Conference. Maj. William A. Welch,
general manager for the Palisades Interstate Park Commission and a steadfast supporter of the trails movement, served as the presiding officer for the
first meeting and later as the first president of the Conference.[58] The
presidents of the American Civic Association, the American Institute of Park
Executives, the National Conference on State Parks, and the director of the
National Park Service lent credence to the occasion by attending the event
personally.

At the 1937 Appalachian Trail Conference, held in Gatlinburg, Tennessee,[59] it was reported that the Trail was initially open throughout its

length. But the job was far from over, delegate Edward B. Ballard warned. He proposed a protective zone on either side of the Trail, to be termed the Appalachian Trailway, to preserve the larger Trail surroundings. The suggestion was received warmly and adopted officially by the Conference. The first target would be the federal agencies—the National Park Service and the Forest Service—whose holdings in the South encompassed seven-hundred miles of the Trail. By 1938, formal Appalachian Trailway Agreements had been signed with each of the agencies.[60] There would be a zone one-mile wide on either side of the Trail within which incompatible developments would be barred. The Conference then began a similar missionary effort with the states, enlisting the help of a young Park Service recreation and land planner, Conrad Wirth,[61] in organizing meetings of state officials north and south "to procure the adherence of the states" to the Appalachian Trailway Agreement.[62] By 1940, all of the states but Maine were signatory, the latter uncertain only because of possible conflicts with its strong Maine Guide statute. In his report to the 1939 Appalachian Trail Conference,[63] held under the shadow of Katahdin, Chairman Myron Avery observed that the concept of the Appalachian Trailway "marks the beginning of the second era . . . a distinct epoch in Appalachian Trail history." The emphasis had now moved from the placement and construction of a physical trail to the creation of an entire conservation zone. In recognition of this significant development, the Conference entitled the first issue of its newsletter *The Appalachian Trailway News*.

But events in other portions of the globe dictated that the new era would have to wait. World War II intervened, and Trail leaders were enlisted in the defense effort. Sections of the Trail adjacent to sensitive military installations, power plants, and strategic transportation routes were closed.[64] Maintenance efforts dwindled. Editor Jean Stephenson of *Trailway News*, a close friend of Avery's, master of five different professions, and the real driving force at Conference headquarters for nearly a quarter of a century,[65] did her best to keep the movement alive with periodic status reports, but the crucial Trail Conferences had to be suspended for the duration of the war. Then–Lt. Comdr. Myron Avery penned his 1943 chairman's report from the Judge Advocate's office in Washington, closing with the words, "Yours for a short war and a long, long trail."[66]

By mid-1945, the war was over and efforts on behalf of the Trail could be resumed. Portions of the Trail were found to be in significant disrepair. So also was the structure of Trail-maintaining clubs. In key sections, such as northern Virginia, land ownerships and attitudes had changed, necessitating relocations into friendlier hands. The effects of the 1938 hurricane still remained unrepaired in many parts of the New England region.[67] But, even more ominous, the lean wartime years had produced a pent-up demand for development. A lead editorial in the May 1945 *Trailway News* entitled

"Conservation" warned of the coming flood of projects "to provide for war-shock absorption."[68] They promised to "vitally affect the few remaining wilderness areas we have in the east."

One such example was the proposed extension of the Blue Ridge Parkway south, favored by the National Park Service and authorized by Congress, which promised to impact some fifty of the seventy-five miles of Trail in Georgia. Another was the Federal-Aid Highway Act, rushed through Congress in 1944, which authorized a nationwide interstate highway system. The latter measure prompted D. K. Hoch, president of the Blue Mountain Eagle Climbing Club and the Blue Mountain Wilderness Association, and a freshman member of the Pennsylvania congressional delegation, to introduce H.R. 2142 on February 13, 1945.[69] Hoch proposed to amend section 10 of the Federal-Aid Highway Act to authorize a National System of Foot Trails ten thousand miles in length. The Appalachian Trail "shall be included as a trail of the National System of Foot Trails," Congressman Hoch's bill declared. The House Committee on Roads remained unmoved. After a courtesy hearing, where the measure was opposed by both the Bureau of Public Roads and the Bureau of the Budget, the legislation languished and died in committee. Hoch himself failed to be reelected to a second term. But the idea of public ownership for the Trail had awakened once and for all. Even Myron Avery, the staunchest of proponents for volunteer action, was convinced. "Any Trail route which is to survive must be in public ownership," he wrote in the January 1946 issue of *Trailway News*. "This objective, that of carrying the Appalachian Trail into public ownership, is the primary and fundamental problem of the Conference."[70]

One other postwar development preoccupied the Conference—the hunger by seemingly all America for outdoor recreation. For many, military experience had provided the first real taste of the outdoors, and they liked it. Moreover, a revolution of sorts had occurred in the development of lightweight materials suitable for hiking and camping; the discovery of dehydrated and anhydrous foods; the advances in waterproofing, insect repellents, maps, and compasses; and the widespread availability of war surplus equipment.[71] The Appalachian Trail, proximate as it was to population centers, became a good place to practice these new outdoor skills, and national feature articles began to proclaim the merits of such an experience.[72] With public interest in the Trail never higher, the Conference leadership felt that it was a good time to enlist government in its cause. "After a day on the Appalachian Trail (August 20, 1963)," ATC chairman Stanley Murray recalled, "four of us sat down by lantern light (at the Chairback Mountain Camps on Long Pond in central Maine) and discussed the need for federal protection and how the ball might be set in motion."[73] The serious business of protecting the Trail had begun. The Trail was so unique that federal designation seemed to be warranted. But other straws were in the wind too. Confronted by the heavier-use impacts of the recreation revolution, landowner attitudes were changing dramatically along the route of the Trail. The informal handshake agreements with landowners were beginning to fall apart. The good old days were about over.

In October of 1963, a strategy session was held in Washington.[74] Former congressional staffer W. Harley Webster, involved in the discussions by the Nature Conservancy's Walter Boardman, a longtime Trail activist, was charged with drafting legislation.[75] The Potomac Appalachian Trail Club's "D.C. Crowd," virtual professional citizens because of their familiarity with the bureaucracy and the congress, would take the political role of leadership, it was decided.[76] But, late in 1963, Wisconsin senator Gaylord Nelson attended a congressional fund-raiser in the northwest section of Washington.[77] A member of the Potomac Appalachian Trail Club, Dr. Cecil Cullander, came up and introduced himself. "He knew I was interested in conservation, and we got to talking," Nelson recalled. "He was concerned about permanently protecting the Appalachian Trail because so much of it was on private lands. I thought, well, hell, I might as well introduce a bill to preserve the Appalachian Trail." In the early 1960s, Nelson had developed a personal interest in hiking trails and had proposed a fifteen-hundred mile system for his native state of Wisconsin. He called Dr. Edward Crafts, the head of Interior's Bureau of Outdoor Recreation (BOR), for help in drafting the legislation. By happy circumstance, the ATC's chairman, Stanley Murray, was visiting the BOR just when Senator Nelson's call came in and obliged Crafts with the particulars.[78] Murray and Nelson's legislative assistant, Fred Madison, then began collaborating, and, in June of 1964, S. 2862 was introduced into Congress. As Senator Nelson told the Senate Interior Subcommittee on Parks and Recreation at its hearing on September 16, 1965, "There is no hope of maintaining the present 2,000 mile continuous foot trail through a primitive environment close to our eastern cities without public protection of the route and adjoining lands."[79] By May of 1966, eight House members from Trail-related districts had filed companion bills, and the prospect for Appalachian Trail legislation looked promising indeed.

But another significant action was also underway that would preempt Senator Nelson's initiative. Although the Nelson bill did not pass, it attracted considerable attention. Pres. Lyndon B. Johnson, on February 8, 1965, delivered a special message to Congress on natural beauty.[80] "In the back country," he said, "we need to copy the great Appalachian Trail in all parts of America." He directed the secretary of the interior to prepare a cooperative program to encourage a national system of trails. Interior secretary Stewart Udall was more than happy to oblige. Udall was enamored of the concept. He knew the Appalachian Trail and had walked it personally.[81] The resultant report, *Trails for America*,[82] prepared by the Bureau of Outdoor Recreation, contained a special chapter on the Appalachian Trail drawn up by agency specialist Donald Shedd following close consultation with Stanley Murray and other Conference officials.[83] Legislation was subsequently introduced by Rep. Roy Taylor (North Carolina) and Sen. Henry Jackson (Washington) on behalf of the administration,[84] and, within a month, the bills were scheduled for hearings in both the Senate and the House. Earlier versions of the legislation had been flawed, ATC chairman Stanley Murray advised his membership,[85] but the proposed National Trails System Act merited the Conference's wholehearted support. The Conference provided that support with one minor complication. Massachusetts congressman Philip Philbin, with the backing of New England's Appalachian Mountain Club (AMC), had filed trails legislation of his own[86] and there were divided loyalties within the Trail community. However, exercising collegial courtesy, the House Committee on Interior and Insular Affairs made certain that much of Philbin's language was included in the final draft. The ATC was consulted too. When the idea of an Advisory Council was questioned in committee, Chairman Murray responded supportively—as long as the legislation made it plain that the Conference would be adequately represented on the Council.

On October 2, 1968, in the presence of many conservation notables, President Johnson signed the legislation.[87] After his January retirement, the president remarked, he would have plenty of time for walking. Richard Droege, the Forest Service's eastern regional forester, was in charge of arrangements, not the Park Service, the AMC's C. Francis Belcher recalled.[88] So many dignitaries were present that President Johnson ran out of pens. Benton MacKaye, physically unable to attend the ceremonies in the Blue Room of the White House, was sent one of the pens used in the signing.[89] He was pleased.

Public Law 90-543, the National Trails System Act,[90] was a comprehensive document providing, generally, for increased outdoor recreation opportunities near urban areas and within established scenic areas. Three types of trails were authorized: *national recreation trails*, capable of a variety of outdoor recreation uses; *national scenic trails*, for recreation and for the conservation and enjoyment of the areas through which the trails would pass; and *connecting or side trails*, to link up the recreational and scenic trails and provide additional points of public access. Only Congress could designate a national scenic trail. The legislation, therefore, specified two initial national scenic trails: the Pacific Crest Trail in the West and the Appalachian Trail in the East, to be administered by the secretary of agriculture and the secretary of the interior, respectively. The appropriate secretary was required to select an official right-of-way for each trail which would minimize adverse effects upon adjacent landowners or users. Subsequent relocations would be permitted administratively, but substantial relocations would require the consent of Congress. Facilities for users, such as campsites and shelters, would be allowed but, except in special cases, motorized vehicles would be barred.

Only limited authority was provided to acquire lands or interests in lands. For example, not more than twenty-five acres per mile (an average two-hundred-foot corridor) could be acquired by condemnation, and acquisition was to proceed only after state and local governments, two years after the official route had been published, had failed to protect the trail on their own initiative. Even then, only $5 million was authorized for Appalachian Trail acquisitions. Additional provisions of the bill, and the accompanying legislative record, made it plain that less-than-fee approaches, cooperative agreements, and volunteer services should be utilized wherever possible.

Section 5(a)(3) of the legislation called for the establishment of a formal advisory council for each national scenic trail to consist of not more than thirty-five members drawn from the involved federal agencies, the states, and private landowners or organizations with "an established and recognized interest in the trail." The advisory council was to be consulted "from time to time" with respect to the selection of the right-of-way, its marking and maintenance, and the general administration of the trail. Members were given five-year terms and were required to serve without compensation. The ATC leadership was heartened by a special provision of the legislation relating to the Appalachian Trail. "The Appalachian Trail Conference shall be represented by a sufficient number of persons to represent the various sections of the country through which the Appalachian Trail passes," Congress had decreed. About the first thing to expect, Chairman Stanley Murray advised his 1969 membership, was the appointment of the advisory council.[91]

1969

After many delays, the inaugural meeting of the Appalachian National Scenic Trail Advisory Council (ANSTAC) took place in the Penthouse Conference Room of the Interior Department in Washington, D.C., on November 3, 1969.[92] The presiding officer was Robert B. Moore,[93] assistant director of the National Park Service, the individual chosen by Park Service director George F. Hartzog, Jr., with Interior secretary Stewart Udall's approval, to serve as chairman of ANSTAC. Moore's job as director of planning activities for the Park Service made him the logical professional to serve in such a capacity. He was well liked by the Trail community.[94] Nevertheless, those fresh from the legislative wars of the new National Trails System Act could not help but wonder whether the level of representation was high enough to reflect real commitment by Interior toward the Appalachian Trail.[95]

Thirty-two ANSTAC members were on hand for the session, including representatives of thirteen of the fourteen states involved in the Trail. The

New England contingent was particularly strong. There was C. Francis Belcher, the executive director of the Appalachian Mountain Club, the oldest conservation organization in the region. Arthur W. Brownell, commissioner of the Massachusetts Department of Natural Resources, and a chairman-to-be of ANSTAC in later years, represented his state. Other New England state government colleagues included Joseph E. Hickey of the Connecticut Department of Agriculture and Natural Resources; George T. Hamilton, then assistant planning director and later state park director for New Hampshire; Austin H. Wilkins, the veteran forest commissioner for the state of Maine; and Commissioner Robert B. Williams of the Vermont Department of Forests and Parks. The New England contingent was rounded out by two other nongovernment members: Arthur R. Koeber, longtime Trail club leader and enthusiast from Pittsfield, Massachusetts and a designee of the Appalachian Trail Conference, and John T. Maines, the respected vice president for woodlands of the Great Northern Paper Company, a major landowner in the state of Maine.

After a welcoming statement from the chairman and the showing of a new film about the Trail produced in conjunction with the Appalachian Trail Conference,[96] Chairman Moore turned the session over to Richard L. Stanton, the Park Service's designated project director for the Trail, who discussed the relationship of his agency to the states and the Trail Conference, and layed out the initial mapping and descriptive assignments needed to conform with the requirements of the act. The Park Service would operate through two regional coordinators, he said, one each for the northern and southern sections of the Trail. Their job would be to work cooperatively with the state and Trail Conference designees for those respective regions. Stanton then turned to Elmer V. Buschman, the Park Service's legal expert,[97] for a discussion of the official right-of-way for the Trail.

Buschman explained that a comprehensive set of maps and descriptive materials would be assembled by the regional coordinators with the assistance of the Washington office of the Park Service, state officials, and members of the Trail Conference. Supporting information would be on file regionally and nationally, but a summary of the material, involving both the centerline of the Trail and an accompanying running description of the line, would be published in the Federal Register for public review and comment. Once the Trail route had been established officially, the conditions of the act and the particular provisions of agency regulations could begin to be applied and enforced, he said.

ANSTAC members broke in to question whether motorized vehicles would be permitted on the Trail as is often the case on state and federal properties. Buschman reminded the group of the specific prohibition in the act against motorized vehicles on designated national scenic trails. But the report of the Conference Committee of Congress should also be heeded,[98] he observed, for provision was made for motorized-vehicle use on or across the national scenic trails under specified conditions, such as fire suppression or law enforcement. The Conference Committee report also reflected Congress's effort to accommodate other kinds of recreational uses (horseback riding, for example), and the distinction it was trying to make between scenic trails (primarily wilderness footpaths) and a tributary system of recreational trails. Buschman promised to distribute to ANSTAC members copies of the Park Service's current policies and regulations governing trail use in the National Park system and the Forest Service's comparable regulations for the eight national forests crossed by the Trail.[99]

Discussion then turned to the desirability of written cooperative agreements between the federal government and the states. The states should be encouraged to acquire land and interests in land to protect the Trail once officially designated, it was generally agreed. Stanton reminded the group that the provision for federal land acquisition was severely limited and that the sense of the act was to regard the states as the primary acquisition vehicles. The reaction of ANSTAC's state representatives was decidedly mixed. Most welcomed the states' rights flavor of the National Trails System Act but, pragmatically, wondered how they could justify acquiring land for a national project in the face of their own need for parks at the state level.[100] Looking after a Trail corridor once acquired seemed to be less of a problem, particularly if the associated Trail clubs were still willing to carry the burden of patrol and maintenance activities. To ensure this objective, ANSTAC encouraged the National Park Service to negotiate a set of cooperative agreements with state jurisdictions along the entire length of the Trail. What Benton MacKaye had described as the "third lap" of the Trail's development—government aid— was ready to get underway.[101]

ANSTAC then turned to the manner of its own organization and operation. State and Trail Conference representatives pressed for a formal vice chairman of the Advisory Council who could speak for the nonfederal interests. It was further suggested that an executive committee be formed to enable ANSTAC to keep track of progress between full meetings of the Council. An executive committee of ten members was ultimately settled upon: the chairman and vice chairman, a representative of the Forest Service, three of the Trail Conference's six district vice-chairmen, and four members at large. Chairman Moore invited nominations and promised to appoint such an executive committee without delay.

At the close of the meeting, a few of the New Englanders present—Belcher of Massachusetts, Hickey of Connecticut, and Hamilton of New Hampshire—held a rump session at National Airport on the way home. Despite the official pronouncement of unanimity, there was a shared sense of frustration and a mutually felt need to "get a handle on ANSTAC."[102] One state official remembered asking himself, "Why are we here?"[103] Interior's domination of the meeting had clearly flawed ANSTAC and proven troublesome to many of the members, particularly those from the Trail clubs who were anxious to maintain their traditional sphere of influence. If nothing else, Interior's dominance made it plain that the states and the Trail clubs would have to work closely with one another. Otherwise, ANSTAC "would have no teeth to bite with".[104] The Park Service's present view of the Advisory Council appeared to be that it was too cumbersome to be useful.

1970

On May 29, 1970, the newly constituted ANSTAC executive committee convened in Washington for its first meeting.[105] In Chairman Robert Moore's absence, Vice-Chairman Stanley Murray, chairman of the Appalachian Trail Conference, presided. Eight of the ten executive committee members were present, including its two state representatives, Conrad Lickel of Pennsylvania and George Hamilton of New Hampshire. The first item of business was a progress report on the definition of the official Trail route.

Elmer V. Buschman, the staff assistant to Chairman Moore for Appalachian Trail matters, distributed sample descriptions and maps. ANSTAC members were encouraged to review the draft material carefully, noting relocations that could be identified with certainty. In turn, the Park Service's regional coordinators were encouraged to share information and correspondence freely with ANSTAC members within an affected state, particularly in the northeastern region where the Trail's route would take it principally across nonfederal ownerships.

The status of cooperative agreements was then discussed. It was reported that an Appalachian Trail Conference–National Park Service Cooperative Agreement had been signed by Acting Director Edward A. Hummel on May 19, 1970.[106] A revised draft of an agreement between the National Park Service and the Forest Service was in the works. Exception was taken to the discretionary language of the new Forest Service agreement regarding zones to be designated and managed to enhance the Trail environment. Executive Committee members insisted that the Forest Service keep in mind the earlier Trailway zones and consult with the Appalachian Trail Conference before any changes were made.[107]

This triggered a general discussion about the latitude allowed for relocations once the Trail route had been promulgated officially. It was the consensus of the group, concurred in by the federal officials present, that departures from the centerline of twenty feet or less would not need to be reported officially.

A draft National Park Service–State Cooperative Agreement was also distributed for discussion. The earlier state agreements had stipulated a quarter-mile zone on either side of the Trail where incompatible developments or uses should be avoided,[108] but several states (Virginia and Pennsylvania, for example) preferred less restrictive language. Under certain circumstances, they argued, the surrounding zone might properly vary in width. The term *suitable zone* was recommended by the Executive Committee in place of a zone of fixed dimensions, with the determination of the actual boundaries left to consultation with the Appalachian Trail Conference.

Committee members also urged careful attention to federal-aid highway proposals in planning for the Trail.[109] Given advance notice, highway officials might make provision for safe pedestrian crossings, grade separations, or route relocations. The state cooperative agreements should include a clause encouraging such consultations, the executive committee agreed.

John DeLay of the National Park Service's Eastern Service Center then presented a proposed set of guidelines for the planning, design, management, and public use of the Appalachian Trail. It was decided that the draft was so central to the program that it should be submitted to the full membership of ANSTAC for review and comment. Buschman similarly reviewed the revised regulations being drafted by both the National Park Service and the Forest Service for publication in the Federal Register. These would supplement the general and special regulations then in effect but would pertain only to the Trail lands administered by the adopting agency. But what about use and enforcement on nonfederal lands, the executive committee asked? The consensus was that the state cooperative agreements should provide for the use of state enforcement powers within any nonfederal, designated rights-of-way.

An immediate, practical problem was the matter of how the Appalachian National Scenic Trail would be marked on the ground. Park Service and Forest Service land managers had estimated that as many as five-thousand markers and possibly five-hundred road signs might be required. There was much sentiment in favor of retaining the historic, diamond-shaped, galvanized, trail marker first designed by Maj. William A. Welch of the Palisades Interstate Park Commission.[110] The proposed rearrangement of the lettering on the sign also received some criticism. A further question was how far a landowner could go in objecting to the placement of a marker on his property.

Executive committee member Edward B. Garvey of Washington, newly retired from government service and in the process of hiking the full length of the Trail, urged a concerted effort to identify water sources available to users. The motion was approved, but with recognition that caution would have to be exercised in order to avoid liability for the acceptability or potability of such water supplies.

1971

On June 1, 1971, ANSTAC assembled in Washington, D.C., for its second full meeting.[111] After welcoming remarks by Assistant Director Edward A. Hummel of the National Park Service, Chairman Moore moved the discussion to a series of status reports on the Appalachian Trail program.

Richard L. Stanton, now the Park Service's full-time field administrator for the Trail,[112] introduced his principal assistant, Edgar L. Gray, and the two regional coordinators, Robert L. Burns for the Northeast and William Holloman for the Southeast, each working out of their respective NPS regional offices. The principal event since the last meeting had been the publication of the proposed Trail route in the February 9 Federal Register, Stanton reported. Accompanying press releases in local newspapers along the Trail had helped alert landowners and land users to the pending route selection.

ANSTAC members wondered whether use of the Federal Register had been either advisable or necessary. Chairman Moore replied that the Solicitor's Office had strongly favored such action in compliance with section 7(a) of the National Trails System Act. About thirty responses had been received, half of them from northern Virginia where private landowners were generally supportive of the Trail—but on someone else's property! State park director Ben H. Bolen was reportedly hard at work resolving the situation. Several ANSTAC members expressed the hope that the solution would not be the placement of more of the Trail's route on public roads.[113] Once questions like these had been resolved, the Park Service would move promptly to publish the final route in the Federal Register, Chairman Moore promised.

Turning to the states, it was evident from the reports offered that progress had been spotty. Maine's forest commissioner Austin H. Wilkins spoke positively of events in his state. Ten "memoranda of agreement" had been signed between the state, private landowners, and the Maine Appalachian Trail Club covering 130 miles of the Trail; another 60 miles were under negotiation. The question of liability was the only likely obstacle to cooperative agreements along the full length of the Trail, he reported. In New Hampshire, home of the greatest concentration of trails in America, including the historic Crawford Path, the Appalachian Trail was just one of many. Nevertheless, a study of the Trail had been completed by George Macinko of Dartmouth College, George Hamilton reported,[114] and state legislation had been introduced generally endorsing the concept of protection. A similar situation was reported for Connecticut, where the state's recently enacted landowner liability law promised to eliminate many of the problems reported in Maine. In Massachusetts, Trail relocations were under intensive consideration in line with a recently completed study and special state legislation enacted soon after the National Trails System Act became law.

South of New England, New York's Taconic Park Commission had received a gift of 650 acres, and an additional portion of the Appalachian Trail had thereby been placed on public land. Other relocations to public lands were reportedly under consideration. In New Jersey, special legislation had been introduced to secure the Trail permanently by easement or fee purchase. Pennsylvania's situation was more conjectural. Although 60 percent of its section of the Trail was already on public land, the state had no funds available for either acquisition or maintenance. In Maryland, forest and parks director Spencer Ellis predicted that the necessary acquisitions would be completed within two years' time. Virginia's new state law authorizing a walking trail across the entire length of the commonwealth came in for detailed discussion. The legislation relieved the landowner of liability under written, cooperative agreements and authorized the acquisition of lands, rights-of-way, and easements by the Division of Parks.[115] Virginia had become the first state to execute a written cooperative agreement with the National Park Service.

Farther south, Tennessee was reported to have new authority and ample funds for Trail protection following passage of a Comprehensive Trail Systems Act in April of 1971. Special legislation was under consideration in North Carolina for the small amount of Trail mileage lying outside of federal lands. And in Georgia, a legislative resolution had been adopted urging full cooperation with the Appalachian Trail protection effort.[116]

From the private sector as well, the news continued to be positive. Reporting for the Appalachian Trail Conference, Chairman Stanley A. Murray confirmed the appointment of ATC coordinators in each of the fourteen states traversed by the Trail. The Conference had also reviewed the proposed route published in the Federal Register which, with a few minor corrections, had fully met its specifications. Chairman Murray further advised the group of a sign plan being prepared by the Conference for the entire length of the Trail pursuant to a request by the Park Service for accurate information on needed sign locations and numbers.[117]

Next on the agenda was John G. Parsons, the Park Service specialist responsible for preparation of the draft guideline material governing Trail management and use. Following his presentation, many questions arose. The need for interpretation of the Trail experience drew several supportive comments, but the idea of a series of roadside visitor centers drew widespread opposition, even from the Park Service's own professionals.[118] Quality hiking should be more than a physical experience, all agreed. Signing and marking the Trail continued to be a sensitive subject. The concept of a natural "greenway" along highways seemed worth pursuing,[119] but only where road locations for the Trail were clearly inevitable. A family of maps for the Trail, first suggested by the Forest Service, would be a cooperative venture with the Trail Conference once the official route had been established, Chairman Moore promised.

Field administrator Richard L. Stanton then outlined the range of acquisition techniques available to the states and others, including landowner agreements, permits, easements, fee acquisition, and variations thereof. Many would materially reduce the costs of protecting the Trail, he observed. ANSTAC member C. Francis Belcher of Massachusetts wondered whether the Park Service had explored an assertion of the public rights acquired by adverse use or possession over the years, a situation common to much of the Trail.[120] Stanton pointed out the obvious legal uncertainties, the length of time required for such proceedings, and the adverse publicity likely to ensue. In fact, until such time as legal agreements had been negotiated, Trail users should brace themselves for additional closures of private property, Chairman Moore warned.

Park Service legal specialist Elmer V. Buschman then brought up the matter of user regulations to be published in the Federal Register once the official Trail route had been selected. He hoped that comparable regulations would be adopted thereafter by the Forest Service, the states, and local agencies. ANSTAC members again mentioned likely conflicts with horseback users, and the draft regulations were revised accordingly. Buschman also reported that the National Park Service and the Forest Service had recently executed a revised cooperative agreement governing the Trail. All parties were urged to cooperate in compiling an up-to-date "bank" of map records and information describing the overall progress toward protection of the Trail right-of-way.

In closing comments, ANSTAC members reminded the Park Service that the Appalachian Trail was to be a conservation, not a recreation project.[121] Promotional literature should be phrased accordingly. It was suggested that other conservation organizations should be enlisted in the Trail protection effort, since their support and influence could be of significant benefit.[122]

1972

For its third official meeting, ANSTAC traveled to Plymouth, New Hampshire, convening at Plymouth College on June 19, 1972.[123] A number of surprises greeted the twenty-five members in attendance. Since its last meeting, the ANSTAC chairmanship had rotated among three different Park Service officials:[124] Robert B. Moore, the original designee; Richard L. Stanton, now the assistant director for cooperative activities of the National Capital Parks; and Edgar L. Gray, former assistant to the field administrator for the Appalachian Trail program. Gray was now the official chairman of ANSTAC. He was not a strong leader in the eyes of many members of the Council.[125]

With some apologies for the unsettled state of events, Stanton offered welcoming remarks. In so doing, he also sounded a genuine note of concern for the Trail program. While the Park Service was in a position to receive the authorized appropriation of $5 million for land acquisition in the budget cycle starting October 1, 1973, it was a long way from applying these resources to actual projects and had no formal plan to present to the Office of Management and Budget in support of any such appropriation request. Furthermore, environmental impact analysis requirements,[126] now mandated under provisions of the National Environmental Policy Act of 1970, were likely to create up to a year's delay in any land purchases, he warned, and condemnation actions could take as much as three years' time for settlement.

But from Stanton's remarks, it was evident that the Park Service was also fundamentally undecided on how to proceed with the Trail. Should it come into a state that had an active acquisition program of its own underway? If it did, how would the other states feel that were spending their own money for Trail protection projects? And what about the management of any lands so acquired when they might be hundreds of miles from the nearest National Park Service facility? It was clear from Stanton's remarks that he continued to regard the states as the first and, possibly, the only line of assault on the problem. His own view, and one shared by his superiors, was that NPS acquisitions should be limited to a connecting corridor between its existing holdings at Shenandoah National Park and Harpers Ferry.[127]

The execution of eight formal agreements governing the Trail demonstrated that state interest in the project was still alive. But progress at that level was slow too. For example, although three of the New England states (New Hampshire, Massachusetts, and Connecticut) were actively engaged in site planning, ownership surveys, and cost evaluations, their legislatures still remained reluctant to commit any funds for acquisition. The Vermont effort appeared to be of minimal priority in light of the federal authorization for the Trail.[128] In Maine, a one-hundred-foot corridor appeared to be the maximum the industry landowners would consider even for a Trail easement.

New York's proposed environmental bond issue, containing $4 million in matching funds for the Appalachian Trail, was scheduled to go before the voters in November, Taconic Park manager Harold J. Dyer reported, but he felt that at this pace a hundred years would be required to establish a decently protected corridor for the Trail in New York. In New Jersey, special legislation for the Appalachian Trail had failed to pass the General Assembly. Progress in Pennsylvania had been slow too, ANSTAC's members were told, the result of a massive reorganization of state government and the continued absence of a state trails bill. The Maryland program was reported as authorized and funded, but the actual purchases were not making much progress.

An observer present for the state report session was Sally K. Fairfax,[129] then a doctoral degree candidate in political science at Duke University. It was her first experience with Trail advocates. Going into the ANSTAC session, her central thesis was that the most cooperative states would be the ones with the most Trail mileage. Not so, however. Later on, she was forced to conclude that no particular pattern distinguished states that would be active from those that would not be.

A small state appropriation had been received in Virginia for the purchase of lands, and new positions of coordinator and field representative were approved for the state trails program. Negotiations with northern Virginia landowners were reported as continuing but proceeding slowly. In West Virginia, the Trail program still remained at an embryonic stage. Tennessee's policy would be one of supplemental assistance only to the federal agencies, Joseph Gaines advised, limited to key tracts lying outside the bounds of the authorizing legislation. Although Georgia had enacted a trails system act, no funding was available to implement the program. In North Carolina, neither funding nor legislation was at hand.

Reporting for the Appalachian Trail Conference, Chairman Stanley Murray touched on a number of other subjects of growing significance to the Trail. Despite the new emphasis on acquisition, he said, it is important to maintain friendly relations with landowners and other people along the Trail. Also, Murray felt, the time horizon for planning should be at least fifty years into the future. This suggested a need for supplemental protection zones adjacent to the formal Trail corridor to offset the impact of likely private development. And, in his opinion, it was only a question of time before the basic Appalachian Trail act would need to be enlarged to provide expanded condemnation authority and, possibly, ten times as much money for acquisition.[130]

Russell McRorey, speaking for the Forest Service, picked up on the subject of condemnation. Unlike Interior, the Department of Agriculture favored its use and frequently filed declarations of taking. This helped avoid an escalation of values and settled cleanly negotiations with private landowners that might otherwise extend over a period of years, he said. Edward Hay, representing Interior's Bureau of Outdoor Recreation, observed that the states do not have the federal agencies' statutory limitations on acquiring Trail acreage. And they can use general Land and Water Conservation Funds for any Trail project as long as the acquisition is consistent with the state's Comprehensive Outdoor Recreation Plan.

In general discussion, ANSTAC members brought up a number of bothersome items. What had happened to the executive committee, they asked? Chairman Gray reported that several of the original members had been lost due to state administrative changes, but he assured the group that a new committee would be appointed soon. With a quarter of its members unable to attend meetings, ANSTAC wondered whether some kind of travel expense assistance might not be possible.[131] The chairman agreed to pursue this matter in Washington, although the legislation seemed clearly to forbid compensation or expense allowances of any kind.

When pressed to define a "substantial relocation" under section 7(b) of the act (one that must be approved by Congress), Chairman Gray expressed his reluctance to do so, citing the need to retain a measure of managerial discretion.[132] However, he was willing to seek the advice of the executive committee of ANSTAC before making any such decisions. Similar managerial discretion had been exercised already in the matter of Appalachian Trail signs, he reported. A nine-inch sign was to be used to mark Trail heads, and an eighteen-inch sign for approach warnings on traveled roads. The smaller three-and-a-half-inch sign which was, regrettably, pocket-sized would not be used at this time, Moore stated.

1973

On April 27, 1973, ANSTAC assembled twenty-seven members strong at the Mather Training Center of the National Park Service for its fourth official meeting.[133] The location was historic Harpers Ferry, where the Potomac and Shenandoah rivers, as Thomas Jefferson once observed, "rush together against the mountain, render it asunder, and pass off to the sea."[134] Rainy weather prevented all but the hardy from making the steep descent from Jefferson Rock to the river, crossing, and ascending to the panoramic view from Split Rocks on the Virginia side, the first section of the Appalachian Trail to be completed south of the Hudson River.[135]

Chairman Gray began by presenting a graphic account of the status of the Trail in each of the fourteen states, four national parks, and eight national forests. He reported that each governor had been alerted to the unprotected areas in his state, and all governors had been given a target date of August 1, 1973, for the initiation of a protection program. By that time, the National Park Service should have a comprehensive picture of the funds needed, both federal and state, to complete the Trail protection program, and could tailor its appropriation requests accordingly.

The chairman reported two specific problem situations along the Trail. Using managerial discretion, he had decided to retain the original Trail route in Georgia, rather than the relocation published in the Federal Register. A proposed extension of the Blue Ridge Parkway south threatened to impact the new route of the Trail.[136] And in the Green Mountains of Vermont, the Forest Service was proposing to limit the size of hiking groups to ten in order to minimize the cumulative environmental impact on the Trail.

Gray was followed by Maurice D. ("Red") Arnold, the northeast regional Director of Interior's Bureau of Outdoor Recreation.[137] Arnold's agency was a key position to help, for it administered the distributions from the Land and Water Conservation Fund (LAWCON), the principal source of money for state and federal acquisitions. Arnold spoke first about the steady and inevitable urbanization of the East Coast, and the contributions to be made by a linear park such as the Trail at a time of national energy supply limitations. He discussed the use of LAWCON funds, not just for recreational projects, but for scenic and aesthetic preservation as well. But, like all such federal programs, there were procedural hurdles to overcome. In the first place, allocations within a given state were the primary responsibility of a designated state liaison officer, who might or might not be the ANSTAC member for that particular state. Second, the funds were available only on a matching basis. Finally, a prerequisite for any such grants was that a project be fully consistent with a State Comprehensive Outdoor Recreation Plan. In all candor, Arnold observed, some states would be hard-pressed to accord the Appalachian Trail a higher priority than an intensively used urban park.

Efforts to contain management problems were illustrated by Forest Service regional engineer John Adams's report on litter removal along a pilot section of the Trail in Georgia. Eleven sites, near but out of view of the highway, had been selected as depositories, and arrangements had been made with the state's highway agency to service them regularly. It was evident from the views of Trail club members that the litter problem along the Trail had decreased dramatically in recent years, hopefully the result of extensive educational efforts by the Trail Conference and others.

Chairman Gray also provided an updated picture of the sign program for the Trail. The chief difficulty appeared to be the eighteen-inch elliptical marker at highway crossings which encouraged overuse at these locations. Upon motion of the representative from Georgia, ANSTAC recommended that the more modest, standard pedestrian crossing sign be used to mark such Trail/highway intersections in the future.

The matter of expense reimbursement and other forms of compensation, prohibited by the National Trails System Act, came up for renewed discussion. Chairman Gray reported that he had filed a request within Interior seeking to have the appropriate section of Public Law 90-543 amended accordingly.[138]

ANSTAC members were urged to use the language of the draft cooperative agreement contained in the guidelines document approved by the Interior Solicitor's Office as the basis for all subsidiary agreements. The only exception might be some reference to the matter of landowner liability. A growing number of states were electing to hold the owner harmless in return for public recreational privileges.

Chairman Stanley Murray of the Appalachian Trail Conference spoke again of the need to think of the Appalachian Trail as a "greenway," not just a recreational facility.[139] In so doing, the Trail could remain faithful to Benton

MacKaye's founding concept. It was evident from Murray's remarks, and the ensuing discussion, that the matter of zoning would require detailed consideration at subsequent meetings.

The final portion of the session dealt again with land acquisition. Russell McRorey of the Forest Service presented an encouraging picture of the Trail's right-of-way through the national forests.[140] Better than sixty-two miles of Trail had been acquired during the last three quarters, he reported. ANSTAC members argued the respective cases for fee versus easement acquisitions with state representatives, observing that the costs are not appreciably different. But for certain owners, it was agreed, a limited right to use their property might be easier to accept than loss of the entire tract.

By September 28, 1973, the date of a meeting of the reconstituted executive committee,[141] storm clouds were on the horizon for ANSTAC. Nevertheless, Chairman Gray greeted warmly the six committee members in attendance and expressed his pleasure at being able to meet with them at the Appalachian Trail Conference's new headquarters in Harpers Ferry, West Virginia.[142] He reminded the group that the statutory five-year terms of ANSTAC members were scheduled to expire in 1974 but, until then, it would be business as usual. He told the group that his annual report to the secretary of the interior, timed to coincide with the anniversary date of the publication of the official route of the Trail on October 19, 1973, would observe that of all the delegated responsibilities under the National Trails Systems Act, only the code of managerial responsibility remained unaccomplished. To complete that obligation, Gray proposed to appoint a special committee consisting of a representative of each federal agency plus three members from each state (a planner, manager, and law enforcement specialist). The Appalachian Trail Conference would be asked to supply a chairman. The target date for a discussion draft of such a managerial code would be March 1, 1974.[143]

Gray further urged the Trail Conference to accelerate its efforts to build an educational awareness of the Trail generally among landowners and users. With land acquisition to be substantially complete within five years' time, the emphasis would necessarily shift to management activities. As the "bone and sinew" of the Trail protection effort, he said, the Trail Conference and state representatives must be in the forefront of transferring to others a sense of the "sacred spaces" of the Trail.[144]

A panel of speakers was then enlisted to review the concept and status of wilderness proposals and to spark a discussion in open forum of their applicability to the Appalachian Trail.[145] National wilderness legislation could affect significant portions of the Trail in New England and the South. The speakers included Superintendent Robert R. Jacobsen of Shenandoah National Park, West Virginia outdoor recreation planner Robert Mathis, and Assistant Director Owen Jamison of the Forest Service. Most of the discussion centered on possible restrictions on public use within designated wilderness areas. What about Trail development, Trail facilities such as shelters, and the use of equipment such as backpacker stoves, ANSTAC members asked? It was apparent that if wilderness principles were to be applied without modification, traditional Trail programs would have to be modified drastically: no route signs, for example, no overnight use of shelters, use of heat sources without residual by-products, and possible abandonment of Trail maintenance in its entirety. How would such restrictions be enforced, the public officials were asked? Ultimately, some form of permit system might have to be instituted, the panelists responded. To prepare for such an eventuality, Appalachian Mountain Club executive director C. Francis Belcher urged the federal government and the states to initiate a program of cooperative research on wilderness problems.[146] He felt that private organizations such as his would gladly join in such an effort.

The matter of Trail relocations reappeared on the agenda. Under provisions of the National Trails System Act, ANSTAC members were reminded, all substantial relocations required the specific consent of Congress, a process that could involve as much as three years' time. The only recourse, Chairman Moore observed, was an administrative determination by the secretary of the interior that the proposed relocation was not substantial. Even this would require the publication of a notice in the Federal Register. A case in point had arisen. It had been suggested that the Trail be moved laterally four to six miles from its present location over a distance of about forty-four miles. Chairman Gray expressed the opinion that a relocation affecting 5 percent or more of the Trail's total mileage could be construed as the dividing line between what was marginal and what was substantial.[147] He encouraged ANSTAC to attempt an official definition so that future relocations, such as those in the complex southern region of the Trail, would not be subject to challenge. The Trail Conference representatives present noted that a systematic, rather than arbitrary, process of relocation would greatly facilitate Trail use and maintenance. Upon motion of ATC chairman Stanley Murray, the ANSTAC executive committee went on record as recommending that the secretary of the interior publish in the Federal Register a complete list of the relocations that had been approved by the Trail Conference to date, and the future relocation procedures, as a preliminary step to amending the official Trail route. In further action, the executive committee voted to return seventy-seven miles of Trail in Georgia to its original location—technically a reversion, not a relocation. The proposed extension of the Blue Ridge Parkway in that state was not likely to occur in the near future.

ANSTAC's reaction to the new Park Service folder for the Appalachian National Scenic Trail was far less cordial. It objected strongly to the promotional tone of the material, and even more to the cavalier way in which it had been developed.[148] Despite the presence of the Conference's headquarters two blocks away, designers at the NPS Service Center in Harpers Ferry had failed to consult ATC specialists before proceeding with the brochure. It was the expressed sense of the executive committee that although the need for any brochure at all seemed questionable, if found desirable, it should be produced in revised form. In the meantime, it was recommended that the offensive leaflet be recalled from distribution by the National Park Service.

A variety of management issues then occupied ANSTAC's attention. Problems of vandalism were reported, not at roadside as heretofore, but increasingly in the back country. The abolition of the permit required for camping, mandated by the new general recreation passes authorized by the Land and Water Conservation Fund legislation,[149] was believed to be at least partially responsible for this lack of control. The states should continue to be reminded of the need to coordinate Trail and highway planning, ANSTAC members agreed. Use of the Trail by Boy Scouts to meet their fifty-mile hiking requirement had created problems in some locations, ATC executive director Lester Holmes reported. On the other hand, the army engineering facility at Fort Devens, Massachusetts, had expressed interest in assisting with Trail construction projects in the New England region. The 1973 Maine State Trails System Act had become law. The number of executed state cooperative agreements had now reached nine, Chairman Gray reported, and he was hopeful that others would follow. Horseback riding within Great Smoky Mountains National Park continued to bother Trail users in the southern region, it was observed. Upon motion of executive committee member Francis Belcher, the Forest Service was urged to renew, beyond the expiration date set by law, its special $500,000 authorization for acquisition of Trail lands.[150]

Discussion then ensued about the effects of the nation's Bicentennial celebration, scheduled for 1975–76. Groups such as the Appalachian Mountain Club had been approached to furnish hiking guides and services for foreign visitors during this period. An increased visitation of 20 percent to 25 percent was predicted for accessible sections of the Trail. State and federal officials were urged to become directly involved in Bicentennial planning in order to avoid problems of overuse of Trail facilities.[151]

Not until two years and three months later, on June 20, 1975, would ANSTAC again reassemble. A number of events were responsible for this unfortunate hiatus.

Federal legislation had passed Congress in 1973 clearing the decks of all previously established advisory committees,[152] the result of Congress's concern for the proliferation of such agencies and the elevation of some to de facto management status. Even advisory committees created by statute were not immune from the sweep of the new act. Hereafter, they too would have to be chartered officially and renewed at two-year intervals. The Office of

Management and Budget, the fiscal watchdog of the administration, was certain to cast a skeptical eye on any moves toward wholesale reinstitution.

For the Appalachian Trail, never a priority undertaking for the National Park Service, the Federal Advisory Committee Act made an already poor situation even more untenable. There were many advisory bodies within Interior warranting administrative enthusiasm, but ANSTAC was not one of them. With some relief, the Park Service could allow the Council to lapse, claiming no other recourse under the directives of the new act.

Within the National Park Service, musical chairs was still the order of the day for the Appalachian Trail program. After a rare year of managerial stability, ANSTAC chairman Gray had been transferred to the Federal Energy Office late in 1973. Before leaving, he had drafted an inaccurate and rather self-serving report stating that the Trail protection job, in essence, had been completed.[153] Trail club leaders were outraged. They began a steady drumbeat of protest, intended first for the National Park Service and later for members of Congress. The old guard leadership was joined by a new breed of young, well-meaning trail enthusiasts who felt that the Appalachian Trail should be accorded greater visibility.[154] And along the route of the Trail, landowners were beginning to stir too. Passage of the National Trails System Act, and the establishment of the official Appalachian National Scenic Trail, meant that something was going to happen to their land, prior reassurances to the contrary.[155]

THE TRANSITION YEARS

1974

By mid-1974, David A. Richie, a career professional and the deputy director of the North Atlantic Regional Office of the National Park Service, was assigned to spend 10 percent of his time overseeing what was left of the Trail program—the efforts of a staff Trail coordinator and a group of generally dispirited Trail clubs and states. Richie was appalled by the state of affairs and campaigned vigorously with Regional Director Jerry Wagers and the Washington office of the Park Service for a greater commitment to the Trail. There was neither interest nor opposition in these quarters, Richie recalled— simply, "if Richie wants it that way, we'll do it." During 1975, Richie was enabled to spend a quarter of his time on the trail program, and by January 1976 he had won acceptance of the project on a full-time, staffed basis.[156]

By later 1974, it was evident to Richie that a reconstituted ANSTAC was of critical importance to the Trail. After persistent overtures to the new Park Service director Gary E. Everhardt, and repeated representations within the

Interior Department hierarchy, an administrative charter was finally approved for ANSTAC under the provisions of the Federal Advisory Committee Act. A Council of thirty-five members was provided for with appropriate representation from the states, affected federal agencies, and the Trail club community. The long, drawn-out process of identifying prospective members, and arranging for their nomination and appointment by Interior secretary Rogers C. B. Morton, occupied much of Richie's attention at the turn of the year.

But the most central question of all was who would chair the reconstituted ANSTAC. Richie was determined to avoid the mistakes of the past and pressed for a chairman independent of the federal managing agency. His candidate was Dr. Charles H. W. Foster, former Massachusetts secretary of environmental affairs and private consultant at Arthur D. Little, Inc.[157] Richie had come to know Foster in two capacities: his early service as the first chairman of the Cape Cod National Seashore Advisory Commission, and his current position as chairman of the National Park Service's North Atlantic Region Advisory Committee. Richie had found himself genuinely stimulated by the association with this broader group and their different perspectives. In addition to his long experience with advisory bodies, Foster's background as a former state official, and his predisposition toward citizen involvement, seemed to fill the bill in terms of Appalachian Trail needs. But there was one problem with Foster—just whom would he represent? While favorably disposed to his appointment, the Trail club community did not want to use up one of its own precious nominations. And now out of office, Foster could no longer serve as a state representative. The matter was resolved by Stanley Murray, chairman of the Appalachian Trail Conference, who was in the process of resurrecting a moribund Appalachian Highlands Association to plan and implement an Appalachian "greenway" embracing the Trail. Foster would be advanced as the representative of the Association on the Council.[158]

1975

By April of 1975, sufficient appointments had been made to permit firm plans for the first meeting of the reconstituted ANSTAC. The location was assured, for the biennial Trail Conference was scheduled to meet in the South in 1975. A one-day meeting of ANSTAC would be held the day before the Trail Conference convened. This would ease travel burdens for many of the members and permit ready reporting to the Trail community as a whole. Richie was also able to persuade National Park Service Director Gary Everhardt to address the Conference and talk about the initiatives his agency was prepared to take.[159] One rumored commitment was the NPS's willingness to contract with the Appalachian Trail conference to develop a network of cooperators at state and local levels, an event that would bolster the stature and capabilities of the Trail's primary volunteer organization.

Thus, six years after the first Council was established, ANSTAC gathered around an open rectangle of tables at the· Holiday Inn in Boone, North Carolina, to resume the business of the Appalachian Trail.[160] The room was warm and the conversation increasingly animated. In his welcoming remarks, Richie hailed the new membership and the new leadership as symptomatic of what lay ahead for the Trail. Twenty-two of the thirty-five appointed members were present, but several key states could not attend due to out-of-state travel restrictions and budgetary limitations. As the official federal officer present, Richie expressed the hope that the Council would assist the National Park Service in three areas: provide guidance on policy, stimulate public interest in the Trail, and encourage action by the states and the federal government in seeking protection for the Appalachian Trail.

Chairman Foster characterized Richie's appointment as coordinator as one of the few good things that had happened to the Trail recently.[161] The record otherwise was dismal. There had been not much in the way of follow-through on the National Trails System Act, little real leadership on the federal end, and a singular lack of accomplishment on the states' part. Ironically, he observed, the strong private movement for the Trail may have had the effect of making the Trail less of a priority for government. Resuscitation of the Advisory Council seemed to be a good way to start remedying the defects. Beginning with this meeting, he hoped that ANSTAC would address itself regularly to three subjects: reporting, policy, and action. Of them all, he regarded action as the most important.

To initiate a discussion of land protection, the chairman turned to soft-spoken Virginia state park director, Ben H. Bolen, a man born and reared in the mountains of southwest Virginia.[162] After the state's General Assembly passed a Trail protection bill in 1971, Bolen had been persuaded to hike sixty miles of the Trail in northern Virginia where, in his own words, "I lost six pounds, gained a lot of knowledge, and met some of the finest people ever." Bolen ran down the list of requirements for a successful state program—enabling legislation, authority to acquire land and adopt and enforce rules and regulations, full background information on ownerships and, of course, funds. He talked about the problems of negotiating with landowners, the steady encroachment of civilization upon the Trail, and the increasing volume of Trail users. "I think the time is rapidly approaching when we are going to have to take a very firm position if the Appalachian Trail program is to be successful," he concluded. Would that include direct federal acquisition, he was asked? Not now, but soon, was his response.

How soon was to become more clear toward the end of the Boone meeting. As chairman of a special ANSTAC subcommittee charged with recommending steps for Council action, Bolen laid out a sweeping, seven-point proposal.[163] The National Park Service should play a role "far more active and positive" than before, he said, including acquiring land itself in those states that had not secured legislation or initiated an acquisition program within a maximum of two years' time. Delinquent states would find their regular apportionment of Land and Water Conservation (LAWCON) funds reduced by the federal funds spent on their behalf. The state park director clearly had ANSTAC's full attention.

Was he aware that approval of the resolution would be a reversal of ANSTAC's previous policy position opposing federal land acquisition outside of federal boundaries? He was.

Was Bolen also aware that the resolution would be viewed with particular skepticism by the Park Service itself? He was under no illusions. The new policy would be a tough one to sell within the present establishment.

Had the Bolen committee considered incentives, rather than sanctions, for the states? Indeed it had, for other parts of the resolution recommended an earmarked allocation of LAWCON funds, over and above the regular apportionment, at a 70:30 rather than 50:50 federal/state cost-sharing ratio, to encourage Trail-related acquisitions.

Bureau of Outdoor Recreation specialist William Rennebohm reminded the group that a policy of this sort would require congressional approval.[164] A special allocation of contingency reserves, available at the secretary of the interior's discretion, seemed a more promising route to take, Virginia's Bolen and New Jersey's Joseph Truncer observed.

To further sweeten the pot for the states, the Bolen committee urged the National Park Service to seek an appropriation within its existing $5 million Trail authorization to accelerate the surveys, title work, and appraisals necessary for any acquisition, federal or state. The same advance legwork would have to be done regardless of the agency involved.

ANSTAC's discussion of the Bolen resolution was thoughtful and thorough. The state representatives present, surprisingly, did not object to the approach. Some even felt that a tougher federal stance would make it easier for them to elevate the Trail to a position of priority in their states.[165] And veteran ANSTAC members argued that a call for federal leadership was not really inconsistent with previous policy.[166] ANSTAC had merely said that it was not timely at that earlier date. Now it was. However, Vermont's John Nuffort strongly urged removing the sanctions element in order to keep the resolution entirely positive. By mutual agreement, a statement encouraging preacquisition by private organizations, such as the Nature Conservancy and the Appalachian Trail Conference, was inserted in place of the sanctions provision. With these clarifications and amendments, the resolution relating to land protection was passed without a dissenting vote.

Action subcommittee number two, chaired by ATC chairman Stanley Murray, continued the pathbreaking tradition. The National Park Service should immediately establish a program to provide guidance in designating a continuous, variable width right-of-way and a broad, corridor protection zone, it advised.[167] To ensure that this would be done, the Murray committee attached a short fuse to its recommendations. Within one year's time, the National Park Service was to deliver a full status report to ANSTAC. Though not opposed to the resolution, the Park Service's David Richie observed that the designations contemplated were dependent upon general agreement on the location of the corridor and some understanding in depth of the values to be protected. This could take time. But in earlier comments on the draft management objectives of the National Park Service's Trail program,[168] part of the federal government's new management-by-objective thrust, Richie had expressed his personal commitment to the organization and mobilization of a cooperative planning effort to identify on the ground where the actual corridor should be.

ANSTAC members contributed other useful thoughts and suggestions. They urged Richie to canvas the states individually along the Trail, establishing firm points of contact and preparing an accurate assessment of prospects and needs. Clearer organizational relationships were also needed with the Trail community, especially the Appalachian Trail Conference. There was further consensus that uniform procedures for relocating portions of the Trail should be developed and followed by all parties. ANSTAC continued to insist upon an action timetable for what Richie termed these "beacons" of the Trail management program.[169] It was agreed that efforts toward improved communication would be reviewed at the next meeting; all memoranda of agreement between the states, the federal government, and the Trail Conference would be on ANSTAC's agenda two years' hence; and the Trail corridor definition issue would be subject to review within three years' time. Regular progress reports were to be prepared and distributed in the interim.

The final item of discussion was equally sensitive—the matter of construction standards for the Trail.[170] Russell McRorey of the Forest Service argued that the federal government had a responsibility to build the Trail for every citizen who wanted to use it. Not so, said the Appalachian Mountain Club's executive director Thomas Deans, recalling the historic and legislative conception of the Appalachian Trail as that of a primitive footpath. It clearly should not be overbuilt. Other ANSTAC members agreed with him.

Hiking the Trail is not like going to a movie where you come in at the beginning and go out at the end, the ATC's Stanley Murray argued.[171] The physical path, rather than an end in itself, should be merely a means of sojourning in the primeval wilderness, New Hampshire's Arthur Morrill observed. Chairman Foster characterized the Forest Service's construction policy as seemingly that of the least common denominator. The answer could be the tributary system of recreation trails also provided for in the National Trails

System Act, thereby ensuring a range of hiking experiences from expert to beginner.[172]

Questions of cost arose during the discussion. The Forest Service has an obligation to be prudent with the taxpayer's money, Russell McRorey observed. But high construction standards could place maintenance beyond the reach of the smaller, volunteer Trail organizations, Deans responded. The matter of liability could also be a factor, McRorey advised, for the federal government seemed to be fair game for most people. A national standard of posted warning signs for difficult sections of the Trail could actually increase the probability of such liability cases, Trail club members asserted. With the management issues well defined but consensus still elusive, Chairman Foster promised to try his hand at drafting a policy position for ANSTAC's consideration at its next meeting.[173]

The final matter of business was consideration of the Council's own structure and method of operation. Responding to a suggestion set forth by John Oliphant of the Potomac Appalachian Trail Club,[174] ANSTAC approved a decentralization of its activities. Three trial regional Council meetings would be held during the coming year to fine-tune the discussions to particular Trail segments. Each would be chaired by a vice-chairman appointed by the chairman. A fourth vice-chairman would serve at large to represent nonfederal interests. He should be Ben Bolen of Virginia, the Council concluded. The five officers of ANSTAC would serve as an informal executive committee between annual meetings of the full Council. With this extended set of activities on the horizon, it would obviously be important for the National Park Service to provide travel expense reimbursement. David Richie promised to see what he could do to expedite a resolution of this still-troublesome matter.[175]

With the landmark ANSTAC meeting safely behind him—"a lively and productive session," as the official minutes so reported, but also one in which all the principals met face to face for the first time in years and became intellectually engaged—Chairman Foster had one other responsibility ahead. An ad hoc committee of the Potomac Appalachian Trail Club, consisting of three past presidents of the organization, Grant Conway, Edward Garvey, and John Oliphant, had set in motion prior to the ANSTAC meeting an official vote of the Appalachian Trail Conference decrying the lack of progress on the Trail. Despite the best efforts of ATC's leadership, the motion had prevailed at the official business meeting.[176] To counter this negative development, Foster was invited to offer reflections and retrospections on the Trail program at the concluding convocation of the Trail Conference held in the outdoor amphitheatre of Appalachian State University. Here Foster spoke candidly of the disarray that had marked the efforts of the past several years, but said that matters had taken a definite turn for the better, listing the actions taken at the recent ANSTAC meeting as examples. "The Council is clearly reinvigorated; it has set ambitious goals for itself; and it has given the National Park Service a demanding assignment to fulfill in the months ahead," he reported.[177] Foster pledged his personal commitment to the Trail and his willingness to work cooperatively with the ATC and Park Service leadership to accomplish its objectives.

The efforts would come none too soon, for word of the Park Service's delinquency had begun to spread on Capitol Hill.[178] Congressman Roy Taylor (North Carolina), the respected chairman of the Interior Committee's Subcommittee on National Parks and Recreation, urged on by ATC spokesmen, was reportedly considering oversight hearings for the entire National Trails System Act. Representatives of the Potomac Appalachian Trail Club, for years the political arm of the Trail movement due to its knowledge of the federal bureaucracy and its proximity to Congress, was in the forefront of such representations.[179]

Less than a week after the Boone session, Foster and Richie got together in Boston to review the Trail situation and plan future strategy.[180] It was agreed that the first order of business should be to exchange a list of ANSTAC members and key state contacts to expedite the renewed interest in intercommunication. An up-to-date assessment of the status of the Trail was next in priority, to be accomplished by letter request to the states, but also by staff field visits to each of the states over the next several months. New York, New Jersey, and Pennsylvania were particular trouble spots, and Richie urged Foster to try to clear his personal schedule for such visits. But the most urgent need of all was to advance the resolutions adopted at the Boone meeting. These would warrant face-to-face meetings in Washington with key Interior officials. The first step would be a session with National Park Service director Gary Everhardt which Richie would try to set up.

The meeting with Everhardt came off on July 21, 1975. Foster again spoke candidly of the poor record of performance by NPS, and the urgent need for new leadership and action, terming the present a "threshold situation."[181] He asked for prompt action by the NPS in seeking appropriations for land acquisition and preacquisition services, a heightened personnel commitment to the Trail (perhaps a formal superintendency), special funds to encourage cooperative planning with the states and Trail groups, and Park Service support for a special LAWCON allocation to the states for Trail protection projects. Although Everhardt remained noncommittal throughout the meeting, his key staff advisers were less restrained.[182] Former ANSTAC chairman Richard Stanton and chief of land acquisition Philip Stewart openly opposed the initiatives, arguing that a more direct role would create management headaches for the NPS and cause the states to discontinue their own acquisition programs. Stewart was especially emphatic in his opposition, fearing acquisitions to put out brush fires, not a well-thought-out protection program.

Nevertheless, Everhardt instructed his staff to prepare a plan of action for the protection of the Trail with the NPS's responsibilities spelled out in detail.[183]

The second Washington foray took place on July 30, 1975.[184] It was a session with Interior's Interagency Task Force on Trails to pursue ANSTAC's recommendations relating to Land and Water Conservation Fund allocations. By happy circumstance, the presiding officer was the Bureau of Outdoor Recreation's associate director A. Heaton Underhill—like Foster, a former executive secretary of the Massachusetts Fish and Game Association.[185] Here again the ANSTAC chairman spoke candidly of the problems facing the Appalachian Trail, many the direct result of a default of responsibility by the Department of the Interior. Foster and Richie, supported by the BOR's William Rennebohm, advised the group of a heightened sense of commitment following ANSTAC's Boone meeting and urged prompt action on its recommendations. Although Underhill could make no formal commitments, the Trail situation obviously had his interest and attention. The states were encouraged to prepare a joint application for a special allocation from the secretary's LAWCON contingency fund, emphasizing cases where threats of commercial development were imminent and the Trail could not be relocated without significant loss of quality.[186] For this and other reasons, it was now time to visit the key states along the Trail to offer both moral and financial encouragement. The situation was much worse than many had expected.

Circumstances in Pennsylvania were especially grim. At the Boone meeting,[187] Robert Pritchett of the Delaware Valley Chapter of the Appalachian Mountain Club had received special permission to address ANSTAC from the floor, describing bulldozers already at work in portions of Little Gap. Richie and Foster decided to make a special effort to encourage action in Pennsylvania, a state that some felt should be leading the pack.[188] Foster's personal relationship with Secretary of Environmental Resources Maurice Goddard would be used as the entering wedge.[189] But New Jersey and New York were also placed on the priority list of states to visit personally. The strategy would be to try to secure the "portals" of the Trail at state boundaries.[190] This meant that Massachusetts, Connecticut, and Maryland would also be included.

By October of 1975, Foster could report an encouraging amount of progress on several fronts. As he told the annual meeting of the Potomac Appalachian Trail Club (PATC) in Washington,[191] the National Park Service was moving to provide a strengthened administrative commitment to the Trail and was likely to receive $500,000 in preacquisition funds in its Fiscal Year 1977 budget. The Bureau of Outdoor Recreation would reportedly look kindly upon a LAWCON appropriation of $1.25 million to enable the Forest Service to complete its Trail-related acquisition program. The idea of a special $1 million contingency reserve allocation to the states had also been received warmly. The states, in turn, had all been circularized for up-to-date information on the status of the Trail. In states where there was trouble (e.g., Pennsylvania), the new Trail leadership was "rifling" its energies to get an effective protection effort underway. The Appalachian Trail Conference, too, was becoming a major cooperator in many of the initiatives, thanks to its $25,000 contract with the National Park Service to improve coordination and encourage cooperative planning.[192]

Foster could also report that the regional Councils, authorized at the recent ANSTAC meeting, were scheduled to meet during the first quarter of 1976. In sum, he said, the Trail's process of drift appeared to have been checked, and a new sense of purpose and direction had emerged. For the two hundred Trail Club members present, the news was welcome indeed. As PATC chairman John Oliphant reported later,[193] they were especially glad to hear that the National Park Service was coming to realize the Trail's importance and taking more of an interest in its protection.

In the meantime, ANSTAC's new vice-chairman, Ben Bolen, had been tackling the sensitive matter of Trail relocations. His special committee would be ready with suggested procedures for the consideration of the three regional Councils, he reported.[194] After much discussion, three Council regions had been agreed upon. The southern region would extend northward to Rockfish Gap in Virginia and include the states of Virginia, West Virginia, Tennessee, North Carolina, and Georgia. Virginia and West Virginia would also have seats on the mid-Atlantic Council, which would be bounded to the north by the Delaware Water Gap, and include Pennsylvania and Maryland. The northern region, by default, would cover an immense area including five of the New England states plus New York and New Jersey. In light of their own backgrounds in state government, Bolen and Foster had agreed to turn to the private sector for the initial regional Council chairmen. Three respected ATC leaders had consented to serve: Stanley Murray in the South, Ruth Blackburn in the mid-Atlantic region, and Francis Belcher in New England.[195]

1976

The first region to meet was the southern Council, which assembled in the downstairs training room at Great Smoky Mountains National Park on January 30, 1976.[196] All twelve ANSTAC members from that region were in attendance. After general reports on the status of the Trail, state by state, four items of official business were considered: the Bolen committee draft on uniform relocation procedures, current problem relocations within the southern region, control of vehicular use on the Trail, and a review of the criteria for corridor definition. Chairman Murray had wisely scheduled the Council meeting to precede a two-day session on corridor definition sponsored by the Appalachian Trail Conference,[197] thereby making it more likely that members would attend. A thorough exchange of information and views occurred. Formal action was taken to alert ANSTAC to conflicts with highway construction agencies throughout the South and to flag a potential new problem, that of the reservation of subsurface mineral rights on properties acquired by the Forest Service and others for Trail protection purposes.[198]

The mid-Atlantic meeting was held in Washington, D.C., two weeks later at the "N" Street headquarters of the Potomac Appalachian Trail Club.[199] Chairman Ruth Blackburn had followed Murray's practice of scheduling the meeting to precede the ATC's own corridor planning sessions. As Blackburn privately confided to ANSTAC chairman Foster,[200] the Trail community was "on cloud nine" with the news of David Richie's recent appointment as full-time Appalachian Trail Project Manager, a move facilitated by Assistant Secretary Nathaniel Reed's growing insistence that the Trail project be given an established priority within the National Park Service.[201] Richie would be assisted by Steven Golden, a recent master's program graduate of the State University of New York's College of Forestry, whom he had literally run into during a morning jog at a Land-between-the-Lakes (Kentucky) National Trail Conference. Golden's experience as a former truant officer was also likely to stand him in good stead with delinquent members of the Trail community.[202]

The mid-Atlantic regional Council focused on several matters of current concern: the uniform relocation procedures suggested by the Bolen committee, vehicle usage on the Appalachian Trail, overuse of shelters at Shenandoah National Park, corridor planning, on-the-Trail educational programs, and special action areas. Among the latter, a resolution of commendation was offered to the commonwealth of Pennsylvania where the deputy secretary for enforcement and general counsel, William M. Eichbaum, was personally negotiating with developers to try to save portions of the Trail at Smith Gap and Fox Run.

Nearly two months later, the final regional Council meeting took place. With some misgivings about the unwieldy nature of a group covering seven states and 852 miles of Trail, Chairman Francis Belcher assembled the northern region Council at Quinsigamond State College, Worcester, Massachusetts, on April 2, 1976.[203] Eleven official ANSTAC members and fourteen observers were present. The discussions were lively and wide ranging. With the exception of New Jersey, where Environmental Protection commissioner David Bardine had pledged $1.5 million in Green Acres bond funds to acquire a permanent Trail corridor, the reports from the states were generally pessimistic. It was hoped that the prospect of federal contingency funds would turn some of them around. In formal action, the Council urged the Forest Service to add the Bog Pond tract to the White Mountain National Forest, commended the

Maine Department of Conservation for its efforts to protect the Trail by acquiring public lands at Bigelow Mountain and the Mahoosuc Range, and served notice that it would recommend to the next ANSTAC meeting action by the National Park Service to acquire a connecting link for the Trail between the Green Mountain and White Mountain national forests in the vicinity of Hanover, New Hampshire.[204]

In the meantime, the Washington end of the Trail program had advanced on two important fronts. One was the continuing campaign for contingency funds to encourage the states to acquire key tracts of land. The other was the decision by Congressman Roy Taylor, chairman of the Subcommittee on National Parks and Recreation of the House Interior and Insular Affairs Committee, to schedule oversight hearings on the entire National Trails System Act.[205]

In the course of their personal visits to the states late in 1975 and early in 1976, Foster and Richie were growing confident that a package of Trail protection projects could be assembled to buttress the case for an allocation of special funds from the secretary's contingency reserve. They had also managed to enlist the active interest and cooperation of two key Bureau of Outdoor Recreation professionals, William Rennebohm of the Washington staff and Maurice ("Red") Arnold, the BOR's northeast regional director. At a strategy session held on January 19, 1976,[206] Arnold recommended a preemptive announcement by the secretary inviting state submissions. Money should be no problem, he said, because in addition to the statutory reserve of 5 percent of the regular Land and Water Conservation Fund appropriation, the secretary was likely to have substantial underruns of state projects to reallocate. It was decided that Foster and Richie would seek meetings with both Assistant Secretary Nathaniel Reed and the new director of the Bureau of Outdoor Recreation, John Crutcher, the former lieutenant governor of Kansas. Their goal would be an allocation of $1.4 million for projects in Pennsylvania, New Jersey, New York, Connecticut, and Massachusetts.

True to his promise, Arnold had a long and supportive memorandum on Director Crutcher's desk when Foster and Richie came to call on February 5, 1976.[207] Secretarial action, he advised, "offers high promise of success" and would be popular throughout the region. "The Secretary has here a high gain, low risk potential," Arnold wrote. The more the states and the private sector commit to the Appalachian Trail, the less federal investments will be needed, he observed. Moreover, if the states fail to respond, the stage will be set for a larger federal initiative. Foster's remarks at his cordial meeting with Crutcher hammered home four key points:[208] "The program is needed, the projects are sound, the timing is good, and a substantial support base is at hand."

In a meeting with Assistant Secretary Reed later that afternoon,[209] there were grounds for further optimism. Reed and Foster had worked together on Nature Conservancy projects in Florida, and both knew and respected one another. Reed's assistant, Douglas Wheeler, had gone to school with ATC executive director Paul Pritchard's wife, Libba,[210] and readily abetted the ATC's tireless pursuit of the Nixon bureaucracy. The idea of a special LAWCON allocation for the Appalachian Trail appealed to Reed, but he was impatient that an even more positive program had not emerged from his agencies, and he was forcing the Park Service to be more responsive.[211] At his suggestion, the contingency fund matter was brought formally to the attention of Interior secretary Thomas S. Kleppe in correspondence from both ANSTAC chairman Foster and the Appalachian Trail Conference's Paul Pritchard. It was, therefore, with relief rather than surprise that the official news of a special $1 million contingency reserve allocation reached the Trail community on March 6, 1976[212]—an action, in Secretary Kleppe's words, to "rekindle enthusiasm among the Trail states." The announcement was timed to commemorate the birthday of Benton MacKaye, who had died on December 13, 1975, at the age of ninety-six.[213]

During the same Washington excursion, Richie had been asked to attend a session with Cleveland Pinnix and Clay Peters of Congressman Taylor's subcommittee staff. Pinnix and Richie were already well acquainted from their prior service together at Mount Rainier National Park.[214] After visits from representatives of the Trail community, Taylor had become convinced that all was not well with the Trail. He authorized Pinnix and others to investigate the situation. Pinnix, a North Carolina native and career Park Service professional until his assignment to Taylor's staff under Interior's intensive management program, was well fitted to the task. He knew that Taylor was close to NPS director George Hartzog, had constituency interests in the Great Smokies and Blue Ridge Parkway regions, but, as a low-key, principled, consensus-type politician and a conservationist in the old sense of the term, would be scrupulously fair. The investigation promised to give Taylor an agenda he could operate on. The evidence turned up documented the many shortcomings of Interior's administration of the Appalachian Trail program. Based on the staff research and recommendations, a decision was made to hold oversight hearings on the National Trails System Act—as Pinnix described it, to confront the Park Service and get its full attention.[215] The Washington session served notice on the NPS that the subcommittee would be interested in the agency's views on the adequacy of present legislation and any changes needed.[216] To the Park Service, the legislation was adequate; the real problem was fitting a national trails program into the structure of the agency itself. At the suggestion of specialists such as Richard Stanton,[217] recalled from his National Capital Parks assignment to help prepare the case for the oversight hearings, the NPS's official stance would be that the states were the ones that had fallen down on the job.

At 10:02 A.M. on Thursday, March 11, 1976. Congressman Roy Taylor called the Subcommittee on National Parks and Recreation to order.[218] Ten years ago, he said, in response to a joint Interior-Agriculture report, *Trails for America*, Congress began the process of authorizing a system of national trails. It was now time to ask whether the act was providing what Congress intended and, if not, what changes in the act might be warranted.

The first official witness was Interior assistant secretary Nathaniel Reed, flanked by supporting staff from the National Park Service, Bureau of Outdoor Recreation, and Forest Service. In eight years' time, Congressman Taylor asked, why did not Interior acquire even one foot of the Trail outside of the existing federal areas? We lost contact with this project, Reed answered honestly. What happened to the nine mandated trail studies in the 1968 act? Some were discontinued administratively, Secretary Reed replied, but most had been held up by the president's Office of Management and Budget. He was clearly embarrassed. Would you say that much of the federal interest and spirit in the Trail has taken place rather recently, subcommittee member Robert Lagomarsino (California) asked? The leadership changes in the Park Service and the Department of the Interior, which were responsible for much of the delay, are now behind us, Secretary Reed responded. Is it true that most of the Trail protection work has been done by volunteers, Congressman John Seiberling (Ohio) asked? Indeed so, Reed acknowledged, but volunteers alone cannot save the Trail from encroachment. Congressman Goodloe Byron (Maryland) observed that he had attended the twentieth Appalachian Trail Conference in Boone as a member of the Trail community and had been struck by the fact that the next fifty years will require major land acquisition efforts.[219] If so, is the Interior Department prepared to use the powers given it to protect the Appalachian Trail and to exercise the leadership role that the statute lays out, asked Congressman Seiberling? "Absolutely, sir," Secretary Reed responded. Congressman Taylor concluded the first part of the hearing by expressing his sense of disappointment in the small amount of progress with the Trail to date. Perhaps the hearings will provide the department a needed sense of momentum, he observed dryly. The subcommittee's intentions were fortified by two rounds of specific questions posed to the principal governmental agencies, which were made an official part of the oversight proceedings. Lee McElvain, the full committee's general counsel, wise in the ways of bureaucracy, had suggested this method of building an indelible record.[220]

Later in the day, a panel of witnesses from the Appalachian Trail Conference presented their views. Edward Garvey of Washington, a past member of the Board of Managers of the Conference, and one of the backdoor instigators of the oversight hearings,[221] expressed the opinion that the National Park Service had been hiding behind the permissive language of the authorizing legislation, despite the fact that Congress clearly intended the agency to undertake direct acquisition if the states failed to do so. Garvey was followed by Stanley A. Murray, current chairman of the Appalachian Trail Conference, who presented a section-by-section evaluation of the act. The most serious weakness, Murray observed, was the limitation of condemnation authority to not more than twenty-five acres per mile, a corridor that would extend only one hundred feet in either direction from the centerline of the Trail. The Trail Conference's executive director, Paul C. Pritchard, drew on his previous coastal zone experience to advocate a similar federal/state cooperative effort in managing the Trail.[222] The costs of such a program could be reduced appreciably if a significant role for the volunteer is retained, he observed. Congressman Taylor asked whether the Advisory Council had been serving a useful purpose. Since 1975, Pritchard replied, the Conference had seen a great turnaround in ANSTAC and a great change in commitment. But why has so little been accomplished, Taylor asked the witnesses? Seven years of inactivity by Interior, was Garvey's answer. No project is a reality until the money is appropriated to get to work, Chairman Taylor observed. "I think we have learned that, sir," Garvey replied, "I think we have learned that."[223]

With spring just around the corner, it was time to begin thinking of the next full meeting of ANSTAC. The year 1976 was an off year for the biennial Trail Conferences, so ANSTAC could meet when and where it wished. Richie's choice was Overlook Lodge, Bear Mountain State Park, in New York's Hudson River Highlands. He and Foster agreed that meeting in a problem state would help encourage concerted attention to the solutions needed. Richie had a measure of good news to report. Interior secretary Kleppe had signed the charter amendments permitting reimbursement of expenses for attendance at ANSTAC meetings. And after much bureaucratic wrangling, a formal Trail project office had been opened in the Boston National Historic Park complex at the Charlestown Navy Yard, evidence that the Appalachian Trail had received heightened status within the National Park Service.[224]

Richie and Foster had one other matter pending. The ATC for several years had been exploring the concept of an Appalachian "greenway," a corridor of varying width (up to ten miles on either side of the Trail), patterned after the British countryside zone. Long concerned about what might happen adjacent to the footpath itself, and faithful to Benton MacKaye's founding concept of a larger, protected, mountain environment "to provide vicarious benefits to the American people,"[225] the Appalachian Trail Conference in 1972 had endorsed the greenway concept in principle and had authorized the preparation of a feasibility study. Ann Satterthwaite, a versatile and well-connected Washington consultant—as much an artist as a planner—had been engaged to undertake the study. Her report, submitted in October of 1974, was accepted by the ATC's Board of Managers and later by the membership as a whole. A New York–based organization, the Appalachian Highlands Association (AHA), had been enlisted to help implement the program.[226] Former ATC chairman Stanley Murray, grappling with the preservation of the Roan Mountain "balds" on the North Carolina–Tennessee line, had proved an eager and willing chairman of AHA. With assistance from the Andrew W. Mellon Foundation,[227] the Association convened a workshop for some forty leadership individuals in Washington, March 19–20, 1976, to consider how best to implement the greenway proposal. The response from the participants was enthusiastic but guarded in its prognosis. A greenway simply could not be imposed at will upon the social and natural landscape of the twenty-million-acre Appalachian mountain region. At a time of widespread distrust of land-use planning, and a general wariness about governmental ventures of any sort, a greenway would come about only if local people became convinced of its merits and involved in its implementation, the workshop concluded.[228] Despite subsequent efforts to organize a working Appalachian Highlands Association, the greenway program never really got off the ground. It was way ahead of its time, supporter George Zoebelein recalled,[229] and never attracted the single charismatic leader in the tradition of Benton MacKaye. But the basic concept of viewing the Trail as more than a physical hiking experience would stick, coming to the fore again once the basic task of laying out and protecting the footpath had been accomplished.

There was no shortage of business to be transacted when ANSTAC assembled at Bear Mountain on May 24, 1976, for its next meeting.[230] Twenty-six members were present, and all but one of the fourteen Trail states were represented. "It has been quite a year for the Appalachian Trail," Chairman Foster observed in his opening remarks. He cited fifteen program accomplishments in the eleven months since the last meeting, including tangible accomplishments in inventory, planning, the development of standards and guidelines, and the securing of new funds for land acquisition. But by far the greatest accomplishment was the active and positive leadership now being provided by the Park Service, he said. The years of marking time were about over.

For the coming year, Foster set forth a number of target objectives for ANSTAC. It must come to grips with the two items scheduled for review at the 1977 meeting: Trail user education and the existing cooperative agreements. Two other policy issues need to be opened up for discussion, preferably in the open forum of regional Council sessions: the matter of Trail standards, and possible revisions of the management guidelines promulgated by the predecessor Advisory Council. ANSTAC should try to assist the states in other ways too, Foster argued. He suggested sending requests for special grant funds to regional agencies such as the Appalachian Regional Commission and the New England Regional Commission.[231] Finally, the matter of a careful examination of research interests and objectives relating to the Trail seemed particularly timely. In his new position as dean of the Yale University School of Forestry and Environmental Studies, Foster had been exposed to students and faculty with research interests in the recreational and environmental aspects of long-distance trails and had been persuaded of the merits of a comprehensive review of research needs.

After much fine-tuning, Vice-Chairman Ben Bolen was also ready to present the final recommendations of his committee on Trail relocations. The job of reconciling differences had not been an easy one, for placement of the Trail on the ground was potentially threatening to the role of volunteer maintenance groups. As ATC executive director Paul Pritchard had pointed out, any removal of the Conference as the central authority, or any attempt to make its involvement a token one, would weaken the very reason for the existence of the Trail itself.[232] There was little Trail club sentiment in favor of a role for the states, particularly states that had not even taken the simple step of signing a cooperative agreement with the Trail Conference and the Park Service.

Echoing the sentiment of the larger Trail community, ANSTAC member Arch Nichols urged that the relocation procedures include a substantive role for the regional ATC coordinators, who, close as they were to local conditions, might exercise the review authority for the Conference in the case of relocations of one thousand feet or less.[233] Reconvening over lunch, the Bolen committee agreed to support a strengthening of the coordinator's role as suggested. However, ANSTAC member Stanley Murray felt that the committee's recommendations did not go far enough. The Trail-maintaining clubs were not given the opportunity to participate directly in Trail relocation decisions.[234]

ANSTAC members were then exposed to the results of two studies of Trail protection strategies: one sponsored by the Department of Landscape and Regional Planning at Pennsylvania State University;[235] the other by the Allagash Institute in Maine.[236] Despite their differing approaches, the results were surprisingly complementary, for as Pennsylvania's William Eichbaum observed, the use of simple "jawboning" to protect the Trail was simply not viable in the face of increasing development pressure.[237] The basic problem, Connecticut's Joseph Hickey commented, was the fact that Trail advocates were trying to preserve land without buying it. ANSTAC chairman Foster encouraged the Park Service to continue to serve as a switchboard and conduit for appropriate protection strategies and to make every effort to see that the Trail's location appeared on every official governmental map regardless of the level of jurisdiction.

ATC executive director Paul Pritchard then reviewed the progress of his organization's corridor planning, a project being advanced under contract with the National Park Service. The Trail's alignment had been transferred onto standard topographic sheets, and the scenic, cultural, historical, and natural resource inventories were in full swing in the fourteen affected states, he reported. A revised set of guidelines for Trail management and use was in preparation with the help of a network of ATC volunteers.

Picking up on the management concerns, the AMC's Thomas Deans noted that management and corridor protection were closely interrelated. Recalling the discussions at the 1975 ANSTAC meeting, he felt strongly that management concerns should receive high priority in the coming year. The Forest Service's Raymond Housley, a newcomer to ANSTAC affairs, although continuing to stress the need for proper attention to visitor safety and resource protection, did feel that in some places there was a need to hold down Trail construction standards.[238] Privately, he had spoken of a "moment of real heartburn" when the heavily engineered standards for the Pacific Crest Trail had crossed his desk.[239] Recent correspondence between Zane Smith of the chief's office and Raymond Fadner of the ATC Trail Standards Committee seemed to confirm the movement on the Forest Service's part toward consensus on this sensitive issue.

Maine ATC representative David Field then presented a proposal for a research symposium on the needs of the Appalachian Trail, including the compilation of a complete bibliography of Trail research completed or underway. The Park Service was reportedly prepared to enter into a small contract with the Yale School of Forestry and Environmental Studies to organize the symposium and publish a proceedings. Yale forest sociologist William R. Burch had long been interested in the recreational user and had helped prepare the first outdoor recreation plan for the state of Connecticut. Burch was also an active adviser to the AMC's modest research program in the White Mountains. Though wary of being studied like laboratory animals, the Trail community had no real objection to the project.[240] A seconding motion was made by ATC representative Stanley Murray, and ANSTAC voted to endorse the idea of a research symposium. However, it was suggested that the symposium include land managers among the participants so as to prevent the occasion becoming one of researchers merely talking to other researchers.

ANSTAC then moved to a series of reports from the three regional Councils. It was evident from the enthusiasm expressed that the idea of decentralization had been well received by the ANSTAC membership.

Stanley Murray, chairman of the southern regional Council, characterized his session as a great success. Meetings of this sort are useful forums for complex and sensitive matters that will ultimately come before the full ANSTAC, he observed. Without dissent, all five matters recommended by the southern Council received ANSTAC's endorsement. For the mid-Atlantic region, the dominant problem continued to be the protection of the Trail on private land,

Chairman Ruth Blackburn reported. ANSTAC agreed to support the regional Council's commendation of Pennsylvania for its efforts in this regard. For the northern regional Council, much the same sentiment was expressed by chairman C. Francis Belcher. Resolutions commending the state of Maine and urging Forest Service action in the White Mountains were accepted by ANSTAC without dissent. Vermont's John Nuffort added a footnote of warning to Belcher's report by expressing pessimism about the proposed connector across the Connecticut River valley. Lack of funds and landowner tensions promised to make this a difficult acquisition project, he observed.[241]

ANSTAC agreed to hold another round of regional Council meetings in 1977, but to modify the northern region boundary to the Connecticut–New York state line. After much discussion, it was further agreed that the regional Councils, with the concurrence of the designated ANSTAC officer present, would be empowered to adopt their own resolutions on regional matters in addition to forwarding recommendations for action by the full ANSTAC.

ANSTAC then turned its attention to the status of Trail protection efforts and the priorities for future action. It had before it the results of the first comprehensive inventory, assembled by David Richie and his staff from state reports and visits.[242] ANSTAC agreed that the new reporting arrangements were a good start. The ensuing discussions spotlighted how well each state was doing. Matters were still touch-and-go in problem states, the representatives from New York, New Jersey, Pennsylvania, Virginia, and West Virginia reported. Four states—Massachusetts, New Jersey, Pennsylvania, and Virginia—were virtually certain to use their new contingency fund allocations; two other states, Connecticut and New York, would try hard but the required match might have to be raised from private sources. ANSTAC made it plain to the states that expenditures of less than the full amounts available would be a great embarrassment to the Council.

But in addition to the matching fund requirements, BOR had placed other strings on the contingency allocations, it was discovered. An October 1, 1976, deadline had been imposed for all expenditures to reflect the reality of a true acquisition emergency. Beyond that date, any state in addition to those specified could apply for the funds. Furthermore, the states were required to have used up their regular apportionment of LAWCON funds in order to be eligible for the contingency reserves. ANSTAC was not unduly troubled by these bureaucratic assertions, for it was rapidly becoming expert at unraveling administrative red tape.

In final action, a smattering of other resolutions were enacted, sensitive to particular problems along the course of the Trail. Despite its success in LAWCON apportionments specific to the Trail, ANSTAC continued to feel that a higher federal/state cost-sharing ratio was warranted for projects designated as having national significance, and Chairman Foster was authorized to continue to press the point in Washington.[243] And, prompted by the sentiments of the private Trail community, ANSTAC lent its official support to all reasonable efforts to protect the home of Benton MacKaye in Shirley Center, Massachusetts, through public or private means, as a historic site.[244]

So crowded was the agenda that AT project manager David Richie offered to postpone his own report on priorities to a subsequent mailing, which went out to ANSTAC members on June 11, 1976.[245] Perfecting Trail status information was number one on his list. Without an adequate data base, the project could not be properly responsive to hot-spot situations. Monitoring the use of the $1 million contingency reserve allocation was another obvious priority. Beyond these immediate needs, the AT project staff planned to turn its attention to a number of special issues identified by ANSTAC. Dartmouth College's venerable Outing Club would be asked to help develop a workable strategy for providing a Trail connector between the Green Mountain and White Mountain national forests. Putnam and Dutchess counties in New York, and Wantage Township in New Jersey, were places where the Trail needed to be relocated from roadsides. And Fox Gap in Pennsylvania was a thorny but high-priority problem area warranting continued attention, Richie reported.

Indeed, the Pennsylvania situation had achieved some prominence after Robert Pritchett's eloquent plea for help at the Boone ANSTAC meeting. Reading about Pennsylvania's alleged shortcomings later in the editorial columns of the *Philadelphia Inquirer,* deputy secretary of Environmental Resources William M. Eichbaum, an occasional user of the Trail in New England, Pennsylvania, and Virginia, called a departmental meeting to find out whether the assertions were true.[246] He discovered that the Appalachian Trail had fallen between the cracks of agency responsibilities and was not deemed central to its mission. Much of the Trail's route lay on State Game Commission lands, an agency outside the direct jurisdiction of Pennsylvania's cabinet-level environmental agency. Still other portions involved separate park and forest agencies. Ninety miles remained in private hands, much of it threatened by development. The commonwealth, unlike many of its sister states, lacked comprehensive state trails legislation.

Eichbaum's interest was especially fortuitous, for AT project manager David Richie and ANSTAC chairman Foster, a longtime colleague of Secretary Goddard, were planning a special trip to Harrisburg to stir up interest in a Pennsylvania trail protection program. Removed though it was from his regular enforcement responsibilities, Eichbaum agreed to set up an initial meeting of state agency representatives and invite federal and ATC officials as a means of buying into their special expertise.[247] By this stroke of good fortune, the Trail community acquired a creative and aggressive advocate of the protection program,[248] unafraid to negotiate head to head with developers for key sections of the Trail. As an example, Eichbaum remains proud of the fact that a hiker can stand on Wolf Rocks today and still not see any houses. He recalled the first of a long series of strategy sessions held in 1975–76 and attended by Secretary Goddard, ANSTAC chairman Foster, AT project manager Richie, and BOR regional director Arnold. As a relative newcomer to the natural resources business, with environmental advocacy rather than conservation credentials, Eichbaum found himself bemused by "the old geezers sitting around swapping conservation war stories." State trails legislation, initially the excuse for organizing on behalf of the Trail generally, later took on a political life of its own.[249]

Nevertheless, Eichbaum's subsequent exposure to protection problems in Pennsylvania led to his conviction that the Trail community was failing to convey a proper perception of the threat in its fullest dimensions. This led him to turn to Pennsylvania State University's School of Landscape Architecture for a professional assessment of corridor requirements, a project enabled by a special grant from the state Department of Community Affairs.[250] Eichbaum credited the Pennsylvania State University study with eventually "turning the entire protection program around." The contribution was a crucial one, but the broad-corridor approach did have two precedents to draw upon:[251] the earlier Trailway agreements in the South, and the quarter-mile corridor across South Mountain authorized by the Maryland legislature. He testified to this effect at House hearings in Washington,[252] an occasion made memorable by the fact that the caucus bell rang just as he was about to speak. Only the delegate from Guam remained for his presentation.

By the end of 1976, the House Subcommittee on National Parks was ready to move ahead with amendments to the National Trails System Act, including those favorable to the Appalachian Trail, but political change dictated a measure of delay. Former governor James Earl Carter of Georgia had been elected to the White House, and a Democratic administration would replace the Republicans for the next four years. Among Jimmy Carter's particular priorities was the advancement of the nation's environmental agenda. To do so, he had discarded much of the Nixon/Ford administration's seasoned bureaucracy and had brought into government, many for the first time, a cadre of young environmental advocates and state natural resources officials—what his critics referred to as an "infestation of termites."[253] There had been leadership change in the Congress as well. Veteran congressman Roy Taylor had retired to North Carolina after many years of distinguished public service. The new chairman of the House Subcommittee on National Parks and Recreation would be Congressman Phillip Burton of California, a personally ambitious legislator still smarting from his close loss of the majority leadership position as the new Congress convened.[254] Burton was determined to make something of the subcommittee business. His favorite project was a proposed national park for the redwoods in his native California. Thus, all legislation was put on hold until Burton could consolidate his power base and balance the competing interests for new parks both West and East. Very early on, Burton could sense that the Appalachian Trail made sense politically. Moreover, it could serve as trading ammunition to garner votes from eastern congressmen for important parks in the West.[255] Burton was not averse to practicing the politics of intimidation to get what he wanted, and he had the capacity to follow through. But underneath the bravado, Burton seemed to sense that there was something special about the Appalachian Trail and later came to regard the legislation as among the most significant he had been associated with.

1977

Only partially cognizant of these national developments, ANSTAC had been proceeding with its regular business. On January 22, 1977,[256] the southern region Council assembled in the conference room of the Forest Service in Asheville, North Carolina, for a full day's meeting. Ten of the twelve ANSTAC members were present or represented, and more than forty observers were on hand to witness the proceedings. There was much to report and debate.

Preacquisition funds had been released to the Park Service, David Richie advised the group, and contingency fund allocations were now available to the states. Uniform relocation procedures had been accepted by all of the states except Massachusetts and Maryland, and the managing federal agencies had agreed to utilize the procedures from now on. At the state level, a host of specific issues had arisen, ranging from development problems adjacent to Max Patch Mountain in North Carolina and Roan Mountain in Tennessee to prospective highway encroachments in North Carolina, Tennessee, and Georgia.

The Forest Service reported continued, steady progress in securing the two hundred miles of Trail earmarked for acquisition in 1971. The Forest Service was utilizing whole tract purchases wherever possible. Much discussion ensued over the seemingly narrowed protection zones from those of the earlier Trailway agreements.[257] But the larger zones were never really implemented, the federal park managers argued. Nevertheless, there was consensus among the southern region Council to utilize the one mile Trailway corridor as a starting point in defining the geographic area within which protection should take place.

AT project manager David Richie also reported significant progress in defining the limits of a desirable Trail corridor. Two prototype studies were underway using acoustical and visual variables: one derived from the Forest Service's experience in North Carolina and Tennessee;[258] the other from

Pennsylvania State University's special planning project.

On February 4, 1977, chairman Ruth Blackburn brought the mid-Atlantic region Council to order at Skylands Manor, Ringwood State Park, New Jersey.[259] Thirteen of the seventeen ANSTAC members were present or represented, and thirty-five observers sat in on the discussions. Once again, the official business was wide ranging.

AT project manager David Richie reported up to $500,000 available for preacquisition activities such as mapping, surveying, and title searches, which could be contracted out in a manner consistent with state procedures. The $1 million contingency reserve now made it possible for eligible states to buy land in key locations. The Park Service had also contracted for other special studies, Richie advised the group.[260] The Conservation Law Foundation of New England would look into ways of strengthening the existing cooperative agreements; the Appalachian Mountain Club had agreed to help relieve the acquisition bottleneck in western Massachusetts; the Institute for Man and Environment at the University of Massachusetts (Amherst) would look into aspects of the Trail corridor affecting the user's experience; and the Yale School of Forestry and Environmental Studies was moving steadily toward an October symposium on Trail research.

Judging from the reports of mid-Atlantic Council members, protection efforts were also moving forward. Northern Virginia had been targeted for initial activity, but the lack of interest in nearby West Virginia was hampering efforts. A special "Save the Trail" organization had arisen in Pennsylvania where massive housing developments were threatening the most scenic portions of the Trail. Real estate transfer taxes were supporting the state program in Maryland—Green Acres bond issue funds in New Jersey. New York had utilized its contingency allocation to pry out matching funds from the state treasury, Ivan Vamos reported.

Discussion then focused on corridor planning, especially the citizen role in such efforts. ATC's Hank Lautz spoke of the inventories necessary for the proper definition of a right-of-way. Pennsylvania's Caren Glotfelty introduced the Pennsylvania State University study, describing the test application of the approach in Monroe County where twenty miles of actual Trail had been examined. Over half of the townships had agreed to cooperate, and two towns had volunteered to be the first to initiate local zoning and subdivision controls geared for protection of the Trail. In New York's Putnam and Dutchess counties, too, the value of local and citizen participation was becoming evident. However, zoning was more likely to be successful in urban and suburban areas than in rural locations, the ANSTAC planners agreed.

More touchy was the matter of an increased federal presence in land acquisition pursuant to the provisions of the National Trails System Act. The artificial, twenty-five acres per mile corridor mentioned in the act was a serious impediment, William Eichbaum remarked. Too active a federal presence could also upset already fragile relations with landowners, others observed. The representatives from New York and New Jersey stated that they would reconsider their own commitments to the protection of the Trail if federal intervention occurred. If states approached the Department of the Interior with their own problems and solutions properly defined, it might be possible to arrange a cooperative effort in land acquisition, the Council concluded.

The matter of the federal government's role in Trail protection returned to the agenda at the New England Council meeting, held at the Appalachian Mountain Club's headquarters in Boston on March 4, 1977.[261] Chairman C. Francis Belcher presided over a crowded gathering of fifteen official ANSTAC members (only New Hampshire was unrepresented) and twenty-eight observers. The discussion was timely because Congress was rumored to be considering an augmented authorization for the Trail protection program. With the exception of the Forest Service's efforts within the Green Mountain and White Mountain national forests, not much seemed to be occurring in land acquisition. At the state level, planning and preacquisition were under way, but land purchases had encountered difficulties. Special legislation in Connecticut was described as having a slim chance of passage; the Governor's Council in New Hampshire could not be counted upon for support; Vermont's participation was limited to a survey of landowners outside the national forest boundaries; and Maine's principal hope rested on possible action by the Land Use Regulation Commission to restrict the use of corridor lands and carry out strategic land trades in the Mahoosucs and other key regions.

Other Trail protection strategies were discussed in detail, such as the role of corridor planning, the use of landowner agreements, the provision for tax write-offs for donated lands and easements, and the missionary efforts of volunteers and other locals influential with private landowners. A tie-in with the National Registry of Historic Places was also possible, David Richie observed. The Bureau of Outdoor Recreation's regional director Maurice ("Red") Arnold discouraged talk of a second $1 million contingency reserve allocation to Appalachian Trail states. While fully supportable in terms of need, a renewal of this sort would hardly be consistent with the special emergency situation normally governing the use of the secretary's contingency reserves, he said.

Finally, the matter of wilderness and shelter policies, agenda items common to all of the regional Council meetings, were brought up for discussion.[262] New England's view of wilderness was considerably different than that of other regions, the AMC's Thomas Deans observed, predicated as it was upon a long history of pragmatic use of natural resources. The matter of permits required for wilderness travel promised to be especially vexing for the through-hiker, Trail club representatives noted. The availability of shelters was fully compatible with the tradition of the Appalachian Trail, but inconsistent with the objectives of wilderness preservation, others pointed out. These specific problems mirrored a larger question – the inadequate level of management for the Trail as a whole.[263] This issue would have to await the outcome of congressional deliberations and the policies of the new national natural resource leadership just beginning to get established in Washington, the group concluded.

The decision to address the matter of direct federal intervention seemed to happen overnight,[264] although the case had been building for some time. The trigger was a long luncheon meeting held early in 1977 at Boston's staid Union Club, attended by David Richie, Thomas Deans, Paul Pritchard, Hank Lautz, and Charles Foster.[265] The decision to federalize the Trail seemed to be by consensus, with no party entirely comfortable with a stronger federal presence. But no other option seemed feasible if the Trail was to be protected in timely fashion throughout its length. The politics of such an approach were uncertain but intriguing.[266] Yet all parties, including the National Park Service's David Richie, were still idealistic about the role of voluntary action in preserving the Trail. To Lautz and Pritchard, though, the situation was quite straightforward. The Trail protection program was like a dead whale on the beach.[267] It had to be moved. But the AMC's Thomas Deans was the one who went directly to the point. It was a time to be bold, he said.[268]

In point of fact, the change in national administration had opened up a genuine window of opportunity. Paul Pritchard, the ATC's vigorous new executive director, had served in Jimmy Carter's previous state administration as Georgia's chief of natural resources planning and was personally acquainted with the incoming president.[269] For that reason, he was asked to take a leave of absence from the Trail Conference and serve on a transition committee to select key personnel for the Department of the Interior. Here Pritchard became acquainted with Robert L. Herbst, the former commissioner of the Minnesota Department of Natural Resources and an individual with the style and fervor of a country preacher. Herbst had been passed over for the position of secretary of the interior but was being advanced vigorously for the post of assistant secretary of interior for fish, wildlife, and parks, by the Minnesota senatorial delegation.[270] Herbst recalled meeting personally with President-elect Carter and conversing alternately about their common philosophy of conservation and their mutual interest in bass fishing. When his appointment was confirmed, Herbst asked Pritchard to leave the Appalachian Trail Conference for a key position in Interior's Bureau of Outdoor Recreation. Pritchard agreed to do so on one condition – that Herbst support an action program for the Appalachian Trail. Herbst was receptive in light of the AT's reputation as the "trail of the world." He saw an opportunity to put the federal government back into its earlier commitment to the Trail. But more than that, the different approach represented by the Appalachian Trail was a possible model of cooperative action for the country as a whole. All he needed was an agenda item to start with. "The idea of a commitment to the Trail was mine," Herbst recalled later, "but it was Paul Pritchard who nourished the seed within my head."

Thus, by the time of ANSTAC's meeting in Shepherdstown, West Virginia, on May 27, 1977,[271] the stage was effectively set for a revitalized Appalachian Trail program. A formal Appalachian Trail Project Office was in place with a renewed commitment by the National Park Service to see the program through to completion. ANSTAC was revived and vigorous; the ATC was under enlarged and professional management. Thanks to persistent lobbying by ATC and state representatives, and the tacit approval of the new chairman, the House Interior Subcommittee staff was reportedly excited and supportive of Trail legislative amendments. As the featured speaker at the Shepherdstown Appalachian Trail Conference,[272] it was Assistant Secretary Herbst's lot to proclaim to some nine hundred assembled Trail supporters the official fanfare. In a stem-winding speech,[273] never cleared in advance with the Office of Management and Budget, but approved by Interior secretary Cecil Andrus,[274] Herbst placed the Carter administration as foursquare behind an enlarged Appalachian Trail protection program. The administration would seek $90 million for federal acquisitions—a dramatic increase from the modest $5 million authorized in the 1968 National Trails System Act. It would strengthen its working partnership with the volunteer Trail community and the states. And, Herbst declared, the Trail protection objective would be substantially complete within three years' time.

Meanwhile, at Shepherd College, West Virginia, just across the Potomac River from the headquarters of the Chesapeake and Ohio Canal National Historic Park, ANSTAC chairman Charles Foster was calling to order the May 27, 1977, meeting of the Advisory Council.[275] There was a note of irony in the proceedings, Foster observed, because just as ANSTAC had become fully constituted and had begun to function as a genuinely productive, problem-solving unit, it was embroiled in the zero-based review of all federal advisory committees decreed by the Carter administration.[276] The left hand of government did not seem to know what the right hand was doing. Nevertheless, there had been a remarkable change in attitude over the past few years, he noted. Virtually all of the states were now working in some way to protect the Trail. The AT Project Office had emerged as a full-fledged endeavor. And Foster gave particular credit to the regional Councils for fine-tuning ANSTAC's attention to the Trail. Regardless of the outcome of the Carter administration's decision on federal advisory committees, ANSTAC should proceed to conduct its regular business and elect a slate of officers for 1978, the chairman stated.

Turning to the main agenda, roles and responsibilities for Trail protection, the well-intentioned program of preacquisition planning had reportedly run into some difficulties. Each state seemed to have its own procedures and requirements, AT project manager David Richie observed. Unfortunately, the National Park Service (NPS) was unable to give money directly to the states for preacquisition purposes.[277] There was the further problem of defining corridor widths—determining what level of information to provide in a given state. The long and short of the situation was that the Park Service had not been able to provide some states with the survey information required to enable state acquisitions.

Pennsylvania's William Eichbaum argued for a policy statement by ANSTAC favoring the widest possible corridor, a move that would counteract the federal agencies' tendency to negotiate for the maximum two-hundred-foot corridor mentioned in the 1968 Act. The ATC's Ruth Blackburn countered with a suggestion for a variable-width standard to accommodate changing terrain and land ownership patterns. Reporting later as chairman of the preacquisition working committee, Massachusetts' George Wislocki secured ANSTAC's support for a one-thousand-foot corridor—"so far as desirable and practical"—but in any event, a corridor sufficient to safeguard the Trail users' experience.[278]

With respect to acquisition strategy, ANSTAC made no bones of the fact that the grace period for state acquisitions was now over. The secretary of the interior, ANSTAC resolved, should "immediately undertake vigorous and sufficient action to insure the protection of the Appalachian Trail." The framer of the resolution was a state representative, William Eichbaum.[279]

Trail use problems next occupied ANSTAC's attention. A uniform overnight use policy was desirable, most members agreed, but the matter of permits for hikers received a varied response. Trail club representatives argued generally for minimal regimentation. Agency officials pointed to the beneficial contacts between park managers and park users ensured by a permit system. Although it was not yet timely to consider a coordinated, Trail-wide, permit system, the ATC's James Botts observed, there should at least be a concerted effort to identify backcountry water sources.

Trail management, the AMC's Thomas Deans commented, continued to be a difficult issue to resolve. But, without it, he said, "We will not know what we will have once we have protected the Trail."[280] Perhaps the individual Trail-maintaining clubs should enter into long-term management agreements with the states. Alternatively, there might be a single set of agreements for the Trail as a whole to which all interests would be party. Trail club representatives were genuinely concerned about a lessened role for the volunteer under too formal a management agreement. More work on the details was needed, all agreed, but the general concept of the cooperative agreement appeared to be sound. Deans suggested four criteria that should be common to all such agreements: (1) clearly identified terms; (2) clearly identified responsibilities; (3) a monetary value attached to such services; and (4) a review process to regularly evaluate all cooperative agreements. AT project manager David Richie promised to initiate a state-by-state review of existing agreements. Although the NPS was prepared to act as acquisition agent for the Trail, he hoped to be able to delegate management responsibility to others. With the management item behind it for the time being, ANSTAC then turned to the business of its three regional Councils.

Reporting for the southern region Council, Chairman Stanley Murray noted the large number of landowners in attendance at the Asheville (North Carolina) meeting on January 22, 1977.[281] Private stewardship appeared to be alive and well in the South. In formal resolutions confirmed by ANSTAC itself, the southern Council urged West Virginia to adopt state trails legislation and encouraged public agencies throughout the region to incorporate, in agency land-management planning procedures, the concept of the broad, protected corridor contained in the earlier Appalachian Trailway agreements.

The ATC's Ruth Blackburn, as chairman of the mid-Atlantic region Council, reported concurrence with the need for heightened activity in West Virginia. Her group also felt that Interior's current urban recreation study should emphasize the need for additional hiking trails in the densely populated East. And at the Council's meeting in Ringwood, New Jersey, on February 4, 1977,[282] she said, a delegation from Dutchess County (New York) had reminded the group of the value of local residents working to resolve location issues and to win support for supplemental protection measures.

The New England region Council had met in Boston on March 4, 1977,[283] Chairman Francis Belcher reported. Land ownership problems in Vermont and New Hampshire had occupied much of the Council's attention, but the new tax code provisions for conservation easements had also attracted considerable interest.[284] But foremost in mind was the possibility of additional contingency reserves to encourage state acquisitions. The $1 million provided by former Interior secretary Thomas Kleppe had been oversubscribed, and the account was now empty. Under general consideration by the new administration, the Nature Conservancy's Patrick Noonan advised, was a contingency reserve package expanded from $12 million to $18 million. The ANSTAC chairman should explore a second contingency reserve allocation without delay, the full Council agreed.[285]

Reporting for a special working committee on the future of ANSTAC, Vice-Chairman Ben Bolen spoke of the essential role played by the Council as a representative forum for the large number of interest groups involved in the

Appalachian Trail. The chairman should adopt a positive tone in encouraging a continuation of ANSTAC, he felt. Regardless of the fate of the parent Advisory Council, at least the regional Councils should be continued under the sponsorship of the AT Project Office and/or the Appalachian Trail Conference.[286] And if all else failed, special legislation should be sought to reestablish ANSTAC by congressional action. In the interim, new officers should be selected for 1978, Bolen advised. William Eichbaum of Pennsylvania was persuaded to serve as chairman-elect, a place from which he could more readily play the game.[287] The AMC's Thomas Deans consented to become the new vice-chairman. The three regional Council chairmen (Murray, Blackburn, and Belcher) were renominated by acclamation.

Following the close of the ANSTAC meeting, the campaign for the legislative amendments went into high gear. Henry (Hank) Lautz, the ATC's new executive director, elevated to the post following Paul Pritchard's acceptance of a position in Interior, spearheaded the drive.[288] Born and raised in Kansas, educated in mathematics and history, and fresh from jobs in banking and construction, Lautz was about as improbable a Trail advocate as the project for which he was responsible. The Appalachian Trail appealed to his romantic nature, Lautz later admitted, and working in the outdoors seemed like one continuous vacation. Besides, having traveled twenty thousand to thirty thousand miles a year visiting Trail clubs in their home territories as the ATC's director of education, he had a good working knowledge of the terrain and the key players.

Lautz the conservative Republican and Pritchard the liberal Democrat had developed an amicable synergy at the ATC, which continued as their roles and responsibilities changed. For example, Pritchard provided a firm foothold in the bureaucracy, which was cemented by Lautz's growing rapport with Kathy Fletcher, the key Carter natural resources adviser on the White House Domestic Council staff, whom he had persuaded to hike the Shenandoah River portion of the Trail in Harpers Ferry one fortuitous day. On his part, Lautz made a point of becoming acquainted with Cleveland Pinnix, the Park Service–trained House National Parks and Recreation Subcommittee staff professional, whom Lautz described later as the real unsung hero of the Trail; he began talking strategy over Szechuan lunches with Laura Beaty, a key member of the Senate Energy and Natural Resources Committee staff; and he was introduced, in turn, to congressional staffers with a special interest in hiking and the outdoors.[289] He found the situation, in Paul Pritchard's terms, much like the classic high school science project.[290] If the private organizations, government agencies, and ANSTAC could generate a sufficient charge, it would, more than likely, arc to and electrify Capitol Hill.

There were important differences in the way the two legislative branches operated at that time. In the House, the subcommittees did most of the substantive work on legislation; in the Senate, the subcommittees merely held the hearings. Full committee action prompted by member interest was the key to passage in the Senate.[291] In contrast, staff and subcommittee support was crucial on the House side. The House was traditionally the branch concerned with implementation once the measure had been passed. Parks and recreation were major areas of interest to members of the House Committee on Interior and Insular Affairs, whereas, after 1970, the energy side of the Senate Committee on Energy and Natural Resources commanded the most attention. This turned out to work to the Trail supporters' advantage, because the Senate committee staff enjoyed remarkable freedom to operate on the bill's behalf. Fortunately, the professional staff on both sides of the aisle were convinced of the merits of the Appalachian Trail amendments and worked agreeably to that end.[292]

A deliberate strategy began to emerge—not only the formation of a bipartisan coalition, but one that included ideological support from the conservative wing of Congress, an unusual feature for environmental legislation.[293] Fortunately, the issue of funds was not a negative one politically, for, despite the reluctance of the executive branch, Congress generally favored full use of the Land and Water Conservation Fund.[294] Although there was never any real opposition to the amendments, Lautz recalled, the legislation was always, in his words, one day from dying. "Almost any player could have stopped it at any time by simply saying no."[295] The biggest problem was the looming Panama Canal Treaty issue, which threatened to bog down the Senate side in time-consuming and divisive debate. Astonishingly, Lautz the Kansan and Beaty the Arizonan, who had admittedly never set foot on the Appalachian Trail,[296] combined forces to put through legislation for an eastern national scenic trail once the House action had taken place. Lautz made my life simple, Beaty said later, because he was instantly likable and totally assured everyone of the urgency of the bill. She described the legislation as readily flushing through the system. While the ATC representatives were not always the most effective lobbyists, no one could doubt their sincerity.[297] When New Hampshire senator John Durkin, then scrambling for reelection, was persuaded by the AMC's Thomas Deans to cash in a chip with committee chairman Henry Jackson to bring the Appalachian Trail amendments before the full committee, the prospects of Senate passage became even more promising.[298] In a largely pro forma session, language was added strengthening the role of volunteers and introducing the concept of carrying capacity to the Trail's management, amendments suggested by Durkin's Vermont colleague, Sen. Robert Stafford, in a letter to the committee chairman.

By November of 1977,[299] AT project manager David Richie could report a substantial measure of progress on virtually all fronts. The new administration had decided to retain ANSTAC, he told members, and the amendments working their way through Congress would ensure the Council's reestablishment legislatively. The legislation itself was also doing well, Richie advised, having passed the House on October 25 by the lopsided margin of 409–12, thanks in part to Assistant secretary Herbst's active "brokering" of the bill with House National Parks Subcommittee chairman Phillip Burton.[300] The prospects on the Senate side were good too. Still uncertain about the extent of support from the Park Service, Richie had handled the legislative representations for his agency personally.[301] Provisions important to the Trail were the revised one-thousand-foot corridor target, comprehensive plan requirements, and the promised increase in authorizations to the $90 million level. In addition, Richie reported, planning for the Trail right-of-way was nearing completion thanks to the cooperative assistance provided by the ATC. The first meeting to discuss management principles had gone well earlier in the month at Great Smoky Mountains National Park.[302] The Project Office itself was suffering growing pains, Richie admitted, midway as it was in moving from Boston to Harpers Ferry, West Virginia. Nevertheless, there had been time for him to visit a number of the states, accompanied by high officials of the Interior Department. These meetings had served to reinforce a priority status for Appalachian Trail protection at both state and federal levels, Richie said.

In an earlier report to Trail interests distributed on April 25, 1977,[303] Richie and his staff had attempted to lay out the likely dimensions of the forthcoming acquisition effort. The federal program should focus on a corridor of unprotected and undeveloped private ownerships averaging roughly one thousand feet in width, the memorandum stated. Early estimates had identified three hundred miles of Trail in this category and had placed the probable costs at $40 million. However, special problems were likely to arise in the case of lands in corporate (timber) or farm ownership and in areas where the Trail itself was in government hands but the right-of-way was too restricted. Selective acquisitions would be needed to prevent development of adjacent tracts. At this point, Richie advised ANSTAC, the role of the states, local governments, and nonprofit organizations could become crucial. The needs could not be defined accurately at this time since much of the activity would have to occur on a case-by-case basis. But no matter how the program was organized, it promised to be an immensely complex and challenging undertaking, Richie concluded.

THE PROTECTION YEARS

1978

By late 1977, passage of the amendments to the National Trails System Act appeared so imminent that a special meeting of ANSTAC in Washington could be given serious consideration.[304] Envisioned was an abbreviated official session to be followed by attendance at a formal White House bill-signing ceremony. This would be a fitting postscript to the early chapter of the Trail's history and an auspicious beginning to what all were sure would be the ultimate protection program. But the congressional signals, though strong and favorable, were lacking definitive direction. Consequently, AT project manager Richie and ANSTAC chairman Foster decided to go ahead anyway with a Washington meeting and to schedule a session at the Department of the Interior for March 10, 1978.[305] Assistant Secretary Robert Herbst and National Park Service director William Whalen lent special credence to the occasion by attending personally.[306] Herbst spoke of going out on a limb a year ago on behalf of the Trail and characterized the pending Trail legislation as one of the major conservation accomplishments of the Carter administration to date. Whalen hoped that Congress would follow up its authorizations promptly with appropriations. If so, he pledged to expand the Lands Office of the National Park Service so that the acquisition program could be completed within the specified deadlines.

AT project manager Richie then proceeded to brief the nearly forty members and guests present on the provisions of the new legislation, which was reportedly on its way to the president for signature. According to the terms of the bill, ANSTAC was to be rechartered within sixty days of enactment, but the old Council would be continued until its expiration at the end of 1978. Membership would be modified to provide more balanced representation, and the two-year rather than five-year terms for members would remove the present inconsistency with the chartering requirements of the Federal Advisory Committee Act. Among major changes, Congress had raised the maximum condemnation authority for unwilling sellers fivefold to an average of 125 acres per mile, a provision that would permit a protection corridor of at least one thousand feet surrounding the Trail. But the language of the act made it clear that condemnation should be a last resort only. The new legislation called for authorized ceilings for federal acquisition of $30 million in fiscal 1979, $30 million in fiscal 1980, and $30 million in fiscal 1981. Unappropriated authorizations could be carried forward an additional year. The amounts would extend rather than supplant the balances remaining in the earlier $5 million authorization and the allocations available to the states under the Land and Water Conservation Fund program. To be certain that the Department of the Interior was not laggard again in fulfilling its responsibilities, Congress had inserted a requirement for an annual progress report. Committee staff had been responsible for the insertion of the three-year timetable for protection, and a new section called for the submission of a comprehensive plan for management, acquisition, development, and use within two years of the date of enactment. Congress had provided deadlines to prevent slippage but not to force the agency to be overly aggressive.[307] By a quirk of transmission between the House and Senate, the final acquisition language had emerged as generic to any national scenic trail, not specific to the Appalachian Trail.

To clarify provisions of the new legislation, Chairman Foster introduced Laura Beaty, the key staff member and draftsman of the Senate Committee on Energy and Natural Resources bill. Beaty reminded the group that despite the enlarged acquisition provisions, Congress intended that less-than-fee acquisition approaches be considered before any use of condemnation. In fact, accommodating landowner concerns was so central to the legislation that she felt Congress would not object to delays in completing the protection program for such reasons. Similar sentiments governed the matter of corridor width, Beaty reported. Flexibility should be utilized to fit the Trail to the land and comply with landowner concerns. As for acquisition priorities, Congress intended those sections of the Trail most threatened by conflicting uses to receive attention first.

ANSTAC members then recessed for lunch to continue the program discussions in smaller working groups. They reassembled later to express a number of views. Early definition of the corridor and the tracts to be acquired was essential, all agreed, but the one-thousand-foot corridor should be a rule of thumb rather than a fixed objective. Acquisition deadlines should always be subject to good judgment on a case-by-case basis. Negotiations with landowners should occur before any final acquisition decisions are made, preferably with a minimized federal presence and the maximum use of state personnel and Trail club volunteers familiar with local circumstances. Federal oversight of state programs should be held to a minimum.

Charles Rinaldi, the National Park Service's chief of land acquisition, approved of the concept of flexibility in principle but warned that lack of specificity could confuse landowners, increase costs, and needlessly delay the acquisition program. In order for the surveys, appraisals, and negotiations to begin, he had to know what lands to buy.

Hank Lautz, the executive director of the Appalachian Trail Conference, raised another point. His organization, he said, was interested in continuing to play a central role in the management of any lands acquired.[308] Thus, management and acquisition needed to be considered simultaneously. If the acquisition process unnecessarily antagonized landowners, it would be impossible to manage the Trail satisfactorily.

With all of these sensitivities, Chairman Foster observed, it was essential for ANSTAC to track carefully the program's implementation. In final action, ANSTAC was persuaded to authorize a special steering committee consisting of the chairman and vice-chairman of the Council, the chairmen of the three regional Councils, a state representative from each region, and a representative of the National Park Service and the Forest Service.[309] The full

ANSTAC would be convened again in the fall to review progress. In the meantime, the National Park Service was urged to seek the full appropriation of $30 million for the first year of the program, despite the current uncertainty as to the actual tracts to be acquired.

David N. Startzell, the ATC's capable director of education, reflected many of these sensitivities in a memorandum he sent to Richie after the meeting.[310] While recognizing the need to move promptly on land acquisition, he warned that arbitrary deadlines could place undue burdens on volunteers and subvert creativity and effective human relations.

In the meantime, the three regional Councils continued to keep a close eye on local Trail matters. On February 4, 1978,[311] Regional Chairman Stanley Murray welcomed twelve Council members and/or representatives and thirty-eight observers to a meeting of the southern regional Council held at the Patrick Henry Hotel in Roanoke, Virginia. AT project manager David Richie reported a busy and productive year under way. Along with the expected favorable action by the Senate Committee on Energy and Natural Resources, he said, the president's budget for fiscal 1979 included $14.6 million for Appalachian Trail acquisitions, an amount likely to increase even more if the legislative amendments pass. He further advised that Larry Henson, a career professional with the Forest Service, would join the project on a two-year special assignment,[312] an event that would strengthen its staff management capabilities and ensure continued close cooperation between the two principal federal agencies. Even more significantly, a decision had been made to relocate the Project Office to Harpers Ferry, West Virginia, a location that would facilitate effective working relationships with the Appalachian Trail Conference and remove the project from any apparent undue influence New England's Appalachian Mountain Club might seem to exert at a Boston location.[313] In addition, Richie reported, there would be meetings held regionally with the states to lay out the details of a coordinated acquisition program. The National Park Service, the Heritage Conservation and Recreation Service (formerly the Bureau of Outdoor Recreation), and the Appalachian Trail Conference were cooperating in this endeavor.

State representatives from Tennessee and Georgia spoke approvingly of the high-level meetings arranged earlier by the Park Service in their respective states.[314] They had served to raise the level of awareness of trails programs in general, and the Appalachian Trail in particular, with the governors and ranking state officials. A number of potential highway projects were reviewed in detail, and special resolutions were adopted with respect to threats to the Nantahala Gorge in North Carolina and Sam's Gap on the Tennessee–North Carolina line. Private action was encouraged to protect Roan Mountain in Tennessee, a project to which Chairman Stanley Murray was deeply committed through his work with the Southern Appalachian

Highlands Conservancy.[315] The matter of free-roaming European wild boar in the Great Smoky Mountains National Park also merited a share of the Council's attention. Trail club representatives urged consideration of a long, loop trail that would connect Georgia's Springer Mountain with the national park through an alternate route, thus permitting hikers a week's travel through incomparable natural terrain without the necessity of doubling back on the Appalachian Trail. There was talk of naming it the Benton MacKaye Trail.[316]

Serious discussions then ensued about the management of the Trail itself once the acquisitions had been completed. A suggested memorandum of agreement between the ATC and the states, prepared by Pennsylvania's William Eichbaum, was in hand.[317] A draft set of management principles prepared by the Project Office, and a resolution suggesting a central role for the Appalachian Trail Conference in management, triggered the deliberations. There was general agreement with the concept of a single Trail embracing many different environments as expressed in the draft management principles.[318] But government representatives observed that public agencies could not give away their mandated responsibilities for the lands they manage.[319] Nevertheless, the southern regional Council urged, there should be continued efforts by the volunteer community, particularly the Appalachian Trail Conference, to expand its traditional maintenance role to that of actual management.

On April 13, 1978,[320] the mid-Atlantic regional Council convened at Boiling Springs, Pennsylvania, under Chairman Ruth Blackburn's leadership. Predictably, events in that embattled state commanded much attention. Caren Glotfelty of the Pennsylvania Department of Environmental Resources reported a turn for the better.[321] She said that Pennsylvania had already spent or committed $250,000 for Trail-related acquisitions, much of it derived from a special allocation of oil and gas lease revenues. Her department, with the full support of private sector organizations, was locked in combat with developers at Eagle's View on the Appalachian Trail. And, at long last, the Pennsylvania legislature had enacted a state trails bill, shorn, however, of its special $500,000 funding authorization.

In New York and New Jersey, Trail matters were picking up too. The emphasis was on relocations away from roads. There were significant threats to the Trail at Sterling Forest and Nuclear Lake that were being addressed. In New Jersey, $1.5 million had been allocated from the state's Green Acres bond issue for surveys, appraisals, and the initial acquisitions.

Maryland was still planning to go it alone at South Mountain, it was reported, with a corridor width averaging at least six hundred feet. Ten more miles of protected Trail was the target for the next three years. Interest in Trail protection had also awakened in West Virginia with the portion of the Trail near Harpers Ferry slated for early acquisition. And Virginia could report slow but steady progress in the sensitive northern portion of the state. Donations of land and relocations were expected to begin relieving the current gridlock.

Overall, Chairman Blackburn could sense that a revitalized federal presence had not prompted the much-feared slowdown in activities by the states. A good working partnership was developing and a common understanding emerging of the respective roles of each party. This was confirmed in AT project manager David Richie's update to the thirty members and observers present at the meeting. The amendments to the National Trails System Act were now embodied firmly in law as P.L. 95-248, Richie reported. A program for identifying the first properties to be acquired was under way and should be completed by August. Still undecided was the matter of fee versus easement acquisitions during the first phase of the protection program. The comprehensive plan mandated by the new Trail act would be a coordinated report covering all involved parties, not the standard federal planning document, members were advised.

In general comments following Richie's report, Council members stressed their concern that good will, not just good economics, should govern the acquisition program. They worried about interruptions in the flow of congressional appropriations. There was agreement that fee acquisition was generally preferable to the purchase of easements, and a suggestion that a purchase/lease-back arrangement might be better where less-than-fee approaches were to be utilized. And where time was of the essence, the states agreed to act as the federal government's agent in making a key acquisition.

In final action, the mid-Atlantic regional Council deliberated on the framework management principles drafted by the Project Office for ultimate review by the full Council. Matters of liability and the details of formal management agreements were among the items warranting careful attention, the regional Council agreed. It was suggested that the draft document be circulated widely to Trail clubs within the region before the next meeting of ANSTAC.

On May 22, 1978,[322] the redefined New England regional Council met in Hanover, New Hampshire, under the guidance of chairman C. Francis Belcher. Thirty-eight members and observers were present. AT project manager David Richie began the session by speaking positively of the steps under way to implement the new protection program. A system of state coordinators had been developed under contract with the Appalachian Trail Conference; new regional offices for land acquisition had been authorized for Martinsburg, West Virginia; Allentown, Pennsylvania; and Lebanon, New Hampshire; and a new protection instrument, the reserve interest deed, promised to successfully bridge the gap between fee and easement types of acquisition.[323] Baseline surveys of the Appalachian Trail had been completed in several of the states. Despite all of these developments, Richie warned, a delay of up to a year should be expected between the completion of the corridor design and the onset of detailed negotiations with landowners.

At the state level, reports of progress were decidedly mixed. In Maine, negotiations between the Maine Appalachian Trail Club and the twelve principal landowners, all forest products companies, were continuing. In the meantime, the state had been able to block in almost forty miles of Trail through exchange of its public land lots. Pending Indian land claims were a complicating factor, however. But the state program in New Hampshire was reportedly paralyzed by Gov. Meldrim Thomson's unremitting opposition and his budgetary vetoes. In Vermont, the situation had not changed appreciably. It continued to be the state's position that the Trail was a federal not a state responsibility.

Farther south, Massachusetts was entering the tenth year of a program to protect the Trail through cooperation with private landowners. However, the state's objective was a mere two-hundred-foot corridor, much less than the one thousand feet provided for in the new federal act. In Connecticut, discussions were reportedly continuing over the best route for the Trail through its western region. Problems of fire, litter, reluctant landowners, and a vacillating local press were complicating the situation, however. Connecticut's limited bonding authority was another problem. It was unlikely that there would be state-initiated acquisitions in the near future.

Turning to management considerations, regional Council members were told that the National Park Service would rely to the extent possible on the volunteer community for the management of any lands acquired. Former Ozark National Forest supervisor Larry Henson, on special assignment to the Project Office, was taking the lead in defining such policy positions.[324] A system of interlocking cooperative agreements was the most likely instrument for implementing the management program. The statement of management principles, circulated by the Project Office and redrafted to reflect the comments made at earlier regional Council meetings, was found to be generally satisfactory.

In final action, the New England regional Council reviewed a suggested research program to gather information for the required comprehensive plan. The Project Office was urged to utilize the existing club structure where possible, rather than initiating its own research approach, so as to use data already collected and available. There was considerable reluctance to the Trail becoming just another laboratory for the research community.

Already head over heels in corridor design and preacquisition activity, AT project manager David Richie found himself confronted with still another sensitive matter. The provisions of the National Trails System Act, as interpreted by the Office of the Solicitor in Interior, would require a termination of the administrative charter, and all current membership appointments, before the new ANSTAC could take effect. Further, there was to be less representation for the volunteer Trail community in the new organization. On July 27, 1978,[325] Richie wrote ANSTAC members advising them of these circumstances and asked them to remain available ex officio until the new membership could be determined and processed. Edwin J. Seiferle of Georgia, a longtime supporter of the Trail and a member of ANSTAC since 1975, reflected the volunteer community's concerns in a letter addressed to the House and Senate committee chairmen on July 10, 1978. "I am concerned about the present plans of the National Park Service," Seiferle wrote, "to downgrade the Council's effectiveness by upgrading its membership from working level-type individuals to more prestige types."[326] Seiferle objected especially to loss of continuity of membership, the reduced representation of local Trail-maintaining clubs, the emphasis upon commissioner-level, state agency appointees, and the rumored return to an Interior ANSTAC chairman. He conjectured that the National Park Service wanted to be able to manage the Trail program without interference from ANSTAC, and he saw in the changes an effort to downgrade the volunteer contribution and bureaucratize the management of the Trail. Not so argued Charles L. Pugh, prospective chairman of the Appalachian Trail Conference and a member of its Board of Managers.[327] Although the Appalachian Trail stands at its most critical crossroad since it was nothing more than an idea in the mind of Benton MacKaye, Pugh told the twenty-second meeting of the Appalachian Trail Conference, the ATC has the opportunity to be a prime participant in an experiment that could have a tremendous impact on our nation far beyond the boundaries of the Trail. "As incoming chairman of the Appalachian Trail Conference, I am totally committed to the establishment of a strong, viable, public-private partnership which will ensure the attainment of this important goal."[328]

1979

On August 10, 1979,[329] it was finally possible to convene a meeting of ANSTAC as reconstituted under the 1978 Appalachian Trail Act amendments. The session was scheduled to overlap with the biennial Appalachian Trail Conference held at the Mount Sugarloaf ski area in Carrabassett, Maine. Interior assistant secretary Robert Herbst, who had decided to chair ANSTAC personally to resurrect his agency's commitment to the Trail and to get something going,[330] presided over the session. In fact, the seed of Herbst's chairmanship seems to have been planted by David Richie and Hank Lautz on the train trip home from a meeting with the governor of New Jersey.[331] Herbst reminded the group that ANSTAC was special because of the diverse partnership of government agencies and private organizations reflected in its membership. All thirty-five official members were present or represented. Another thirty-two observers were on hand to witness the lively discussions. Changes in the membership had included representation from three additional federal agencies: the Tennessee Valley Authority, the Smithsonian Institution, and the Appalachian Regional Commission. Three national conservation organizations had been awarded places at the ANSTAC table: the National Parks and Conservation Association, the National Wildlife Federation, and the Nature Conservancy. With the appointments of Arthur W. Brownell of the International Paper Company and Jacob Myers, a conservation-minded county commissioner from the Cumberland Valley in Pennsylvania, a deliberate effort had been made to provide a measure of landowner representation. Although its numbers had been thereby reduced, the volunteer Trail community was not without a substantial presence. Ten of the thirty-five ANSTAC members were still drawn from the ATC's own officers or those of its affiliated organizations. In initial procedural action, ANSTAC elected a slate of officers for the coming year, including chairmen and vice-chairmen for each of the three regional Councils. These officers, plus the chairman and executive director of the ATC, and the representative of the secretary of agriculture, would constitute an executive committee to meet and act for ANSTAC between meetings of the full Council, it was decided.

The first item of business was a thorough review of the Trail protection program. It was going well, Chief of Lands Charles Rinaldi reported. Seventy-five tracts had already been acquired, all from willing sellers, and only one owner had elected the easement option. The Trail at this point had so little going that controversy was not a problem.[332] Virtually all of the tracts had been purchased at or near appraised value. If the full authorization of $30 million was to be appropriated for fiscal year 1981, Rinaldi advised, the amounts available for fiscal year 1980 would prove to be sufficient. The prospects for continued support were excellent because President Carter, in his environmental message to the nation and the Congress, had reaffirmed his commitment to the Appalachian Trail. As ATC chairman Charles Pugh advised his membership, "The elephant is finally moving."[333] But the program was not without its problems.

Cumberland County (Pennsylvania) commissioner Myers reported that the route in his area still remained unresolved. However, the area townships had formed a Cumberland Valley Trail Location Committee, a constructive approach that might warrant replication in troublesome sections of the Trail elsewhere, ANSTAC members observed. The matter of road locations to avoid landowner conflicts drew prolonged discussion too. Although the needs of landowners should be respected, it was ANSTAC's view that the highest-quality route for the Trail should take precedence wherever possible. The machinery of ANSTAC was to be available for consultation and dispute resolution in such matters, but formal decision making must remain an Interior responsibility if the protection deadlines were to be met, it was agreed.

But protection was more than just the acquisition of land. It could also be encouraged by achieving the active cooperation of other agencies, ANSTAC observed. Section 4(f) of the Federal Highway Act was one such opportunity. Road-building agencies were specifically constrained against damaging the environment. The OMB-sponsored Circular A-95 process was another. All federally assisted projects now had to be submitted to a central state clearinghouse for review by other parties. There was also a potential role for public service commissions where prospective utility projects or corridors could damage the Trail and its environs. By formal action, ANSTAC directed that the whole matter of supplemental protection become a common agenda item for discussion at the forthcoming regional Council meetings.

With the statutory deadline of September 1, 1981, for the comprehensive plan not far in the future, ANSTAC turned its attention to elements of coordination in planning. In recognition of the essential linkage between the State Comprehensive Outdoor Recreation Plans (SCORPs) and the use of Land and Water Conservation funds, ANSTAC requested the Heritage Conservation and Recreation Service to review all such documents for the fourteen Trail states with an eye to the inclusion of the Appalachian Trail in such plans and the involvement of the volunteer Trail community in their preparation. It also urged the AT Project Office to take the initiative with state and local agencies to see that Trail needs were reflected in individual area management plans. And to further encourage cooperative local planning, it recommended that the National Park Service prepare a special booklet for local governmental units showing how ongoing planning and zoning could be used to benefit the Trail.

The matter of Trail management also returned to ANSTAC's official agenda. The Council remained wholly supportive of a substantive role for the volunteer community. By formal resolution, the Appalachian Trail Conference was recognized as the appropriate organization to coordinate operations and maintenance activities. In keeping with the spirit of the new amendments, the costs of all essential and routine programs should be borne to the extent possible by the private sector, it was decided.

As Assistant Secretary Herbst later advised Secretary Cecil Andrus,[334] the Carrabassett meeting had proven to be exceptionally productive. It provided "current testimony to the vision and vitality reflected in the Appalachian Trail project," Herbst wrote. AT project manager David Richie was more specific. In a follow-up memorandum to ANSTAC members on September 24, 1979,[335] he spelled out the actions to be taken by his office on the fourteen resolutions adopted at the meeting, complete with target dates for each of the areas of concern. The all-important matter of full appropriations for fiscal year 1981 would have to rest with the administration and the Congress, he said, but Richie reported "an exceptionally good case" in hand and a sense that the ANSTAC resolutions would add to a priority consideration. By mid-1980, Richie's optimism seemed well founded. The Carter budget had recommended $27 million for acquisitions in fiscal year 1981, and the House had already taken steps to ensure that at least $15 million more would be available in the coming year.

David Sherman, on special assignment to Herbst's office from the National Park Service for the better part of a year, recalled the Trail as a project Herbst was fully comfortable with, although he observed that a different assistant secretary might have reacted differently.[336] Sherman, whose father had placed him on the Appalachian Trail at Newfound Gap in the Great Smokies at the tender age of six, remembers being inspired by Herbst's Shepherdstown commitment speech. Until then, nobody in the department had been riding a white horse for the Trail at the policy level. Sherman's involvement with the Trail was multidimensional. A south Georgia native, exposed to the mountains through summers spent there and in the highlands of North Carolina, he was an active member of the Georgia Appalachian Trail Club. A former director of planning and research for the Georgia Department of Natural Resources, he had also served as the state's representative on ANSTAC at the historic Boone meeting. Sherman's oversight responsibilities for the Trail in Secretary Herbst's office were a culmination of years of interest in, and commitment to, the protection program.[337]

As the new year turned, AT project manager David Richie wrote ANSTAC members forewarning them of the 1980 schedule of regional meetings[338] The advisory memorandum gave him a chance to update his group on events subsequent to the Carrabassett meeting. The president's fiscal year 1981 budget item, he said, was an encouraging sum but one still projected to be some $18 million short of the three-year program requirements. These deficiencies were certain to be brought to the attention of the appropriations committees of Congress by the ATC and others. In the meantime, current acquisition funds continued to be spent at a satisfactory pace. Richie estimated that the amounts available would be fully committed well before the end of fiscal year 1980. This had translated into forty additional miles of Trail now under protection. The first declaration of taking would be filed shortly—a development parcel barely three miles from the heartbeat of the Project Office and ATC headquarters in Harpers Ferry, West Virginia. Inevitably, though, controversy had flared up in several locations along the Trail.

Cumberland Valley in Pennsylvania remained a primary problem area overall. In another section of the state, a particular property, that owned by Rev. and Mrs. Charles Evans of Honey Brook, Pennsylvania,[339] promised to become the test case for an opposition group called CANT (Citizens Against the "New" Trail) and its newest ally, the National Park Inholders' Association. Richie speculated that three factors were responsible for most of the questions being raised.[340] The first was the necessity of a Trail corridor averaging one thousand feet in width. Questions also tended to be raised when relocations were proposed away from available public land onto private ownerships in order to upgrade the quality of the Trail experience. The final point at issue was often the adequacy of plans for management after acquisition, particularly if the responsibility was to be exercised by a local Trail club.

In addition to local opposition groups, Richie reported, an Appalachian Trail Landowners Interstate Coalition was in the process of formation to press home landowner concerns before the public and the Congress.[341] These efforts had been fueled by a national television exposé of National Park Service acquisition policies, carried by "Prime Time Sunday" on December 16, 1979, entitled "For All People for All Time."[342] Although the Cuyahoga Valley in Ohio was the focus of the program, many of Richie's critics felt that the scene could just as well have been the Cumberland Valley in Pennsylvania. To help counter this negative publicity, the Appalachian Trail Conference was reportedly planning to sponsor a coordinated public "walk-through" of the whole Appalachian Trail on a weekend in May of 1980.[343]

The main focus of organized opposition was a new national organization called the National Park Inholders' Association, the brainchild of a former Los Angeles–area insurance executive, Charles S. Cushman, now of Sonoma, California.[344] Incensed by persistent reports of high-handedness by the National Park Service and other federal officials, especially in his native Yosemite Valley, Cushman traveled the country by motor home in 1977 to determine whether there was a definite pattern of discrimination nationally against inholders. Convinced that there was, Cushman set about establishing a counterlobby, building a base of more than one hundred thousand dues-paying members by the ingenious device of demanding, under provisions of the Freedom of Information Act, the names and addresses of every national park inholder. Brought up in a Park Service family, Cushman claimed not to be antipark or antienvironment, but his actions at times seemed otherwise. "I'm a political guerilla fighter," Cushman would admit. "I hit the Park Service where I can and magnify the situation to make my point."[345] The point was that the federal land-owning and land-managing agencies were hurting local people in their attempts to eliminate all inholdings. The Appalachian Trail was a case in point. The early Trail, in Cushman's view, represented conservation and cooperation the way it should be. It worked because people had to cooperate and could not be forced to agree. When the National Park Service entered the picture, the sense of kinship among landowners disappeared. Cushman was accusing AT project manager David Richie and chief of land acquisition Charles Rinaldi of using intimidation and threats of condemnation to acquire private ownerships along many sections of the Trail. He had even visited Arthur Brownell, a member and future ANSTAC chairman, to try to enlist him in the crusade.[346]

1980

Another potential problem area in western Connecticut, at the Trail's portal into New York State, prompted Richie to try his hand at a prototype cooperative management agreement and to share his thoughts with ANSTAC members by special memorandum on February 1, 1980.[347] The entire Trail should be divided into management units, Richie suggested, and overall management responsibility should be spelled out in a master agreement between the National Park Service and the Appalachian Trail Conference. Subsidiary agreements should then be developed by the ATC with local Trail clubs, and state and federal agencies. Limited funding support would be available from the National Park Service and channeled to the management partners through the ATC master agreement, but the bulk of the contributions would still remain private and/or voluntary. The prototype agreement was based on the assumption that protection and management of the Trail should be a partnership endeavor—a concept easy to endorse, Richie observed, until one of the partners is asked to pick up the check.

The management prototype lost little time in appearing on the discussion agendas of the regional Council sessions. The southern regional Council, meeting twenty-eight strong in Johnson City, Tennessee, on February 15–16, 1980,[348] endorsed a system of decentralized management in principle and especially favored a strengthened role for the states in its implementation. This was prompted in part by the continuing contradiction of the Appalachian Regional Commission's areawide highway and development program which was proceeding apparently oblivious to the state-supported goals of a fully protected Appalachian Trail. In the meantime, both the National Park Service and the Forest Service were moving in the direction of private management of the Trail within their respective jurisdictions. Robert Jacobsen, for example, the superintendent of Shenandoah National Park in Virginia, reported a recent agreement with the Potomac Appalachian Trail Club for total maintenance of the Trail within his park. And in the course of preparing formal land management plans under the provisions of the National Forest Management Act of 1976, Charles Hinson advised, the Forest Service was giving careful consideration to the new systems of cooperative management being recommended during the public participation process, an arrangement formalized in a pathbreaking cooperative agreement with the ATC signed by Chief R. Max Peterson on May 18, 1980.[349] The comprehensive plan for the Trail called for in the 1978 amendments to the National Trails System would also contain a specific section on management, the AT Project Office's chief planner Christopher Brown reported.

At the Kent School in Kent, Connecticut, on March 29, 1980,[350] the New England regional Council continued the discussion of the Trail management issue. Eleven members of ANSTAC took part in the meeting, and attendance overall swelled past the fifty mark because of the heightened interest in the Trail throughout New England. Chairman Charles Foster called for comments state by state to provide a basis for discussion. In Connecticut, state, local, and Trail club leaders had formed a Connecticut Management Committee in February of 1979 to discuss needs and resolve policies and problems. The committee was being staffed by an ATC professional assigned to the area under the ATC's master contract with the National Park Service. In Massachusetts, state government involvement in the Trail was nothing new, Commissioner of Environmental Management Richard Kendall reported. A representative committee had been meeting on a monthly basis for over a year to hammer out agreement on the placement and management of the Trail in Massachusetts.

The New Hampshire and Vermont spokesmen were less sanguine about management efforts in their respective states. Penny-pinching was the term used to describe New Hampshire's past and present involvement in Trail protection and management.[351] Because of political problems, and the federal neurosis displayed by some landowners,[352] the state was following a hands-off policy with respect to the Trail relocation issue in Hanover. In Vermont, a new steering committee with landowner participation, encouraged by the Ottauquechee Regional Planning Commission, was helping to elevate the Trail to a position of priority in the state's conservation program. Maine continued to be active in negotiations with industry landowners (especially the International Paper Company thanks to new ANSTAC member Arthur W. Brownell), but problems of spruce budworm control had arisen to complicate the picture. But the leadership being exercised by the Maine Appalachian Trail Club appeared to be a fine example of the cooperative management prototype suggested by AT project manager David Richie for the Trail as a whole.

In the mid-Atlantic region, the sentiment for cooperation also remained strong. Meeting at Camp Swatara in Bethel, Pennsylvania, on May 9, 1980,[353] the thirty-seven members and guests present confirmed the sense that protection and management of the Trail should go hand in hand. As an example, the New York–New Jersey Trail Conference reported the establishment of a committee to begin the process of local management planning for its section of the Trail. These efforts were prompted, in part, by the questions raised by Philipstown (New York) officials and a local "Nail the Trail" committee concerning the club's Trail-managing capabilities. The adequacy of law enforcement services was a particular point at issue. Acting Chairman Donald Graham of New Jersey asked for a roundup of issues and events generally from each of the states represented.

The program in New York's Dutchess County was going surprisingly well, Ivan Vamos reported—so much so that efforts had been started in Putnam County as well. Acquisition of the Nuclear Lake tract by the National Park Service had given a genuine lift to Trail spirits, he said. A three-way agreement between the state of New Jersey, the ATC, and the New York–New Jersey Trail Conference was in the works, it was reported, which will result in the development of an annual work program and a review procedure for Trail maintenance and management. Commenting on the Pennsylvania situation, Trail club member Boyd Sponaugle characterized the NPS's efforts as receiving generally favorable marks for the fair, honest, and professional manner in which negotiations were being carried out. But tensions continued in the Cumberland Valley, Sponaugle reported, an illustration of how important it is to involve affected landowners and local public officials at the earliest possible stages of a protection program. In Maryland, the policy of acquisition from willing sellers only was reaching its natural end, and the prospect of federal involvement was being reconsidered for the remaining parcels. However, a letter of intent to protect had been negotiated with the Hagerstown Water Company, the owner of 15 percent of the entire South Mountain tract, the regional Council was told. With only one mile of Trail remaining to be protected in West Virginia, and over forty miles of Trail in northern Virginia already in the final acquisition stages, the situation was looking promising in this key part of the region.

In other matters, the mid-Atlantic regional Council was advised that the appropriations for fiscal year 1981 were still up in the air. However, the AT Project was benefiting measurably from the unremitting lobbying efforts of the administration, the Appalachian Trail Conference, and its cross-organizational allies such as the Wilderness Society and the National Parks and Conservation Association.[354] So far, the cost reductions projected through reliance on easements were not proving out in practice, chief of land acquisition Charles Rinaldi reported, because only five landowners to date had elected to sell a less-than-fee interest. They understandably preferred to avoid paying taxes on land they did not control completely.

By July 10, 1980,[355] AT project manager David Richie could alert ANSTAC by memorandum to its forthcoming annual meeting in Mountain Lake, Virginia, scheduled for August 22–23, 1980.[356] After the opening gavel was struck by Chairman Robert Herbst, Richie told the fifty-one members and guests assembled that the year had proven to be a mixture of challenges, frustrations, and achievements. On the good side, all of the planning and baseline surveys would be completed by the end of fiscal year 1981, he said. In the meantime, acquisition had been proceeding steadily, with key tracts in Pennsylvania and New York among the genuine accomplishments. On the down side, the appropriations situation was still largely unresolved. There had been debate over the administration's proposed recisions for fiscal year 1980, including $6.5 million for the Appalachian Trail. Looming overall was a current appropriations backlog of $3.2 billion for authorized National Park Service projects systemwide. A continuing grass roots campaign by Trail clubs was needed if the prospect of congressional support was to be kept alive. Nevertheless, chief of land acquisition Charles Rinaldi reported, the delays in funding had at least permitted the National Park Service to extend its participatory negotiation process with landowners and others, thereby reducing the necessity of acquisition by condemnation in order to meet arbitrary deadlines. Yet, there were still "smoking guns" in the Cumberland Valley of Pennsylvania and in western Connecticut, where the Appalachian Trail had been characterized as the fourth most controversial issue of the decade.[357]

In key reports from the states, ANSTAC learned that formal proposals for a corridor designed by the Maine Appalachian Trail Club had been presented to all major landowners in the state by Club president David Field during the first four months of 1980. The state had agreed to cooperate in these negotiations and to accept donated lands. The first priority was a six-mile corridor to be donated by the International Paper Company, to be followed by the remaining nineteen miles of its ownership by the end of 1981. In Massachusetts, the seven-hundred-acre Upper Goose Pond tract adjoining the Trail was in the final stages of acquisition by the National Park Service,[358] with state personnel reportedly hard at work on other key parcels. In New Jersey, all seventeen unprotected miles remaining were targeted for acquisition by June 30, 1981, using matching state and federal LAWCON funds. And in Pennsylvania, hard-line negotiations by state and federal officials had led to the purchase of the proposed Eagle View subdivision adjacent to the scenic Wolf Rocks section of the Trail.

ANSTAC then directed its attention to the comprehensive plan being prepared under provisions of the 1978 amendments to the National Trails System Act. Two general meetings had been held, NPS planner Christopher Brown reported, to settle on the process to be used and the topics to be addressed.[359] Among the main sections of the plan would be a statement of governing principles, a proposed cooperative management system, a description of the process to be used to identify and resolve issues, and a set of reference materials indexed to the elements specified. Beyond the plan itself, several other key documents would be provided. A formal land acquisition plan would be included, also a stewardship manual for subsequent management and maintenance activities. Local management plans would be incorporated for specified sections of the Trail and would be drawn up, for the most part, by the volunteer clubs that would be exercising the management responsibility. Cooperative agreements and memoranda of understanding, plus the related plans of associated state and federal units, would complete the supplemental comprehensive plan material. Finally, the AT Project Office hoped to have a public information brochure that would summarize all this information for the benefit of landowners and concerned citizens. Brown clearly had his work cut out for him.

The formal business of the first day concluded with a review of the regional Council discussions relating to cooperative management, led by Maine park director Herbert Hartman. There was clear consensus on the desirability of decentralized management of the Trail, but some disagreement on how this might be achieved. The states needed to be encouraged to take part, ANSTAC agreed, because they had access to crucial powers, such as law enforcement. But the details of each cooperative agreement could not be provided from the top; they had to be hammered out through three-way negotiations in particular states between the NPS, the volunteer Trail community, and state officials. The agreements should be expected to vary on a case-by-case basis.

In the resolution portion of ANSTAC's meeting the following morning, the states were formally invited into the cooperative management system, and a timetable for adoption of the statutory comprehensive plan was agreed upon by the membership. By February of 1981, a draft plan was to be available for public review; by June of 1981, the plan was to be presented to the biennial Appalachian Trail Conference and the associated ANSTAC meeting for formal ratification. In further action, ANSTAC addressed itself to the sensitive appropriations issue. It urged a reversal of the Office of Management and Budget (OMB) position to permit the Forest Service to reprogram LAWCON funds for some seventeen miles of Trail corridor already optioned for purchase. It recommended that the Congress make available some $25 million in acquisition funds for fiscal year 1981, and another $20 million for fiscal year 1982, so that the protection of the Appalachian Trail could be carried out expeditiously to ensure its continuity as the Congress intended by the passage of the National Trails System Act.

1981

Before any of these objectives could be realized, however, an event of some magnitude occurred. In national elections held before the turn of the year, the liberal Carter administration was ousted from office. An early target of the incoming Reagan administration became the land acquisition programs of the Department of the Interior. Secretary James G. Watt, a skillful and knowledgeable Washington hand, and a former head of the Bureau of Outdoor Recreation, the federal agency most directly concerned with land acquisition nationwide, called for an immediate moratorium on all such projects, including those affecting the Appalachian Trail. There would be no new acquisitions for the remainder of the year, and only selected acquisitions in fiscal year 1982. Moreover, Interior policy officials had been replaced in depth. Appearing at a meeting of Interior employees held in the departmental auditorium, Watt had minced no words. Every political appointee would be expected to clear his desk and be out of office by the close of business that very same day.[360]

With major change in the offing—as some said, "asking Dracula to guard the blood bank"[361]—Appalachian Trail proponents needed to move swiftly to preserve their program. The first need was ANSTAC itself, whose chairman, Interior assistant secretary Robert Herbst, would most certainly be out of office at the turn of the new year. Consensus was unanimous on the selection of the Appalachian Mountain Club's personable executive director Thomas S. Deans as Herbst's successor.[362] Deans, a history/geology graduate of the University of Maine, had been with the AMC virtually all of his professional career, rising from summer hutsman in the White Mountains to become director of the organization's entire North Country program and eventually the AMC itself.[363] Already a vice-chairman of ANSTAC, Deans was intimately familiar with its program and, in fact, had been a member of its "shadow cabinet" since the Council's revitalization in 1975.

Once appointed, Deans lost little time in developing both a strategy and an action plan to cope with the likely policy changes.[364] A meeting with James Watt would be highly desirable, he felt, because the Appalachian Trail seemed to meet the secretary's standards of a cost-effective, participatory, environmental program. Effective working relationships must also be developed with the new assistant secretary, former California fish and game director G. Ray Arnett, and the recently constituted Land Planning Group within Interior. Even more important, Deans felt, was the need to keep lines of communication open with National Park Service director Russell E. Dickenson,[365] one of the few career administrators left, and his associate director for operations Stanley T. Albright, the man to whom the AT Project Office reported. Since Herbst's resignation, Albright had become the official representative of Interior on ANSTAC.[366] Protecting the project's flank within the new bureaucracy could become crucial, Deans had concluded. This would require a list of people who could be called upon to help—and perhaps a few who could hurt too.[367]

But the most urgent need of all—how to protect the 1981 appropriations and the 1982 budget recommendations—brought Deans to Washington on February 24, 1981, to testify before the Interior appropriations subcommittee. The Appalachian Trail is not your usual federal project, Deans observed. It is viewed around the world as a model of private and public partnership. But the project is based on all participants in this unique effort holding up their end of the bargain, Deans declared. "If the federal government fails to meet its obligations, then all the other parties will suffer." The subcommittee would hear a great deal from the Reagan administration about new directions for federal land management, Deans predicted, such as an enlarged role for the states and private organizations, better cooperation and coordination among governmental agencies, and low-cost recreation opportunities where people work and live. "The Appalachian Trail has been all of these and much more for many years," Deans asserted.[368] Meeting privately with NPS director Russell Dickenson the following day, he was advised that the response from legislators on the Hill would be generally cordial toward completion of the Appalachian Trail program as authorized and scheduled.[369]

The next ANSTAC meeting would come at a crucial time, the Trail strategists agreed. Accordingly, Chairman Deans wrote the membership on February 26, 1981,[370] adding several action items to the formal agenda for the meeting scheduled for March 6–7, 1981,[371] in Harpers Ferry, West Virginia. One was the encouragement of local land trust involvement in Trail protection projects. The other was immediate action to shift the responsibility for management to the private Appalachian Trail Conference. Both of these initiatives, Deans felt, would be responsive to the concerns of the new administration for sensitivity and cost-consciousness in public park programs. National Park Service director Russell Dickenson, the man in the eye of the hurricane of the new policies, would be the best weathervane, many felt. It was to him that ANSTAC now turned for advice and counsel.[372]

Appearing first on the Harpers Ferry program, Dickenson spoke of the present as a new era—one where the federal government would no longer be required to do it all. He viewed the moratorium as just that—a short-term, budgetary phenomenon, necessary to attack inflation, but not a full-scale, program termination—"a pause, not a menopause," one AT observer remarked.[373] The National Park Service still intended to see worthwhile projects through, Dickenson said. In the meantime, ANSTAC was advised to search for tools other than fee acquisition to prevent irrevocable damage to resources. In that regard, the Appalachian Trail seemed to be the kind of cooperative initiative the Reagan administration was most anxious to promote. Nevertheless, "it was a scary time," ANSTAC's new chairman Thomas Deans recalled.[374] The mood in Harpers Ferry was far from optimistic.

After the usual round of reports by ANSTAC members, many genuinely concerned about the interruption in program activity midstream, Deans put his fifty-member group to work in three subcommittees. The first was led by Richard Carbin of Vermont's Ottauquechee Land Trust and dealt with alternative protection strategies. Protection of the Trail by private sector land trusts was not only feasible in principle, but workable in practice, ANSTAC was told. One or more demonstration Trail projects should be undertaken during the year, it was agreed. Moreover, the chairman of ANSTAC should be empowered to appoint a development committee to formulate a strategy for raising substantial private funds and enlisting the help of existing land trust organizations to serve as conduits. The National Park Service was also asked to formulate a technical assistance program to educate and help organizations use alternative protection techniques wherever possible.

New York's deputy commissioner of parks Ivan Vamos took responsibility for the working group on cooperative agreements. These could be all-important in the Reagan era, ANSTAC agreed, particularly where no Park Service or Forest Service management capacity existed. A strong, collective, back-up, governmental presence should be ensured through the details of such agreements, but there must also be an underlying, mutual trust to provide a measure of flexibility. With realistic standards of maintenance and safety, and professional staff to provide backstopping, the voluntary sector could be expected to bear a large part of the management burden of the Trail, it was felt.

With a first-draft copy of the comprehensive plan in hand, a third subcommittee probed its provisions in the light of the recent changes in administration policy. It was felt that the congressional mandate to ultimately protect the Trail should not be compromised and should remain embodied in the plan's general objectives and broad strategies. The discretion needed should be incorporated in the supplemental land acquisition plan. Mindful that their two-year terms would expire in June of 1981, ANSTAC members asked the Project Office to set a target deadline of mid-May for the distribution of a final, annotated, draft comprehensive plan. They wanted the opportunity to endorse the final product before leaving office.

Returning to the main business of the Trail program, ANSTAC reaffirmed its support of full appropriations for fiscal years 1981 and 1982 to ensure continuing progress toward the completion of the project. As Connecticut's Joseph Hickey observed, the federal government had a moral responsibility to complete negotiations with those landowners where they have begun. ANSTAC also voted to remind the new secretary that the Council itself could be a useful adviser to him during this new era, acting as a forum to facilitate communications and agreement, monitor program activity, and stimulate the search for cost-effective, protection strategies in the state and private sectors.

With the ink scarcely dry on the official proceedings, Deans moved to implement ANSTAC's resolutions and recommendations. He conveyed them formally to secretary Watt on March 18, 1981,[375] using the occasion to request an opportunity to brief the secretary personally on the Appalachian Trail project. Vermont was agreed upon as the site of the first experimental land trust project, with Connecticut's Housatonic Valley as a strong runner-up.[376] In an internal memorandum to his staff,[377] AT project manager David Richie encouraged serious consideration of the private land trust route as a contingency if the regular acquisition program were held up by the administration and the Congress. After conferring with the ATC's new executive director Laurence Van Meter, the former executive director of Vermont's Green Mountain Club, Deans also constituted a group to pursue the idea of private funding,[378] suggested by former ANSTAC chairman Charles Foster, now engaged in active fund-raising for the Yale School of Forestry and Environmental Studies. The approach might work, Van Meter advised, if it does not compromise several delicate situations—the efforts of Trail clubs to raise their own foundation monies, the continuing need for federal appropriations, and the current sensitivities within the National Park Service to any form of land acquisition.[379] The latter was especially important, AT project manager David Richie later discovered. He was advised privately by NPS associate director Stanley Albright that any initiative the new administration did not like, directly traceable to an NPS employee, would cause deep trouble.[380] Nevertheless, Richie did attend a session Foster arranged with National Park Foundation president John L. Bryant, Jr., on April 22, 1981. In later correspondence,[381] Bryant made it plain that his foundation would not consider any land acquisition project except upon recommendation of the director of the National Park Service, with the concurrence of the secretary of the interior, the chairman of the Foundation's board. Albright's view that a private fund-raising initiative might be looked upon as a subterfuge appeared to be correct.

Unsuccessful though the Trail community would be with the philanthropic sector, the idea of a private fund-raising effort did earn one important dividend. It encouraged the Appalachian Trail Conference to establish a private Trust for Appalachian Trail Lands with its own administrative committee and professional staff.[382] The Trust would subsequently play a key role in partnership with the project's land acquisition office, securing pivotal tracts such as the Wintergreen corridor in Virginia adjacent to a major ski facility and banking the proceeds from these transactions to serve as a "ready fund" for other Trail-related acquisitions.

Meanwhile, AT project manager David Richie continued to have his hands full within the Department of the Interior. The new management team had been successful in routing out the hundreds of former environmental-group activists appointed by the Carter administration. Secretary Watt's "government in the sunshine" policy, and his intimate, personal knowledge of the workings of the Interior bureaucracy, had begun to break up the system of individual fiefdoms that former secretary Cecil Andrus had described as a centipede, "each little pair of feet scuffling off in its own direction".[383] Even career employees were caught up in the widespread process of performance evaluation. Two of Secretary Watt's declared program objectives were to be the cornerstone of a new land protection policy for Interior: a balanced perspective between economic use and preservation, and a good neighbor policy with the states.[384]

The first move of the administration had been to halt all current acquisition projects, replacing the lower-level administrative discretion with a required sign-off in the office of the assistant secretary. A second development was the creation of a special policy group "to develop a clear and positive national policy outlining the proper federal role in open space conservation."[385] The third initiative was to embark upon significantly different Park Service projects within which the new directions might be tested.[386] The Appalachian Trail was among the eight chosen for case-study analysis.

In May of 1981, assistant secretary Ray Arnett ordered a survey of troublesome NPS acquisitions in the Santa Monica Mountains (California), the Cuyahoga Valley (Ohio), the Indiana Dunes (Indiana), and Fire Island (New York).[387] Chairing the Interior Land Policy Group as special assistant to Arnett was Ric Davidge, a former staff member for Sen. Ted Stevens (Alaska), but also an individual who had headed the National Park Inholders' Association for six months in 1980.[388] Davidge's appointment assured Park Service critics ready access to the new Interior policymakers on land acquisition matters. ANSTAC strategists were clearly anxious about the appointment, fearing that Davidge's preconceptions about the Trail, based upon the information he had been given by Charles Cushman on the Rev. Evans case, might lead to a reversal of the policy decisions on Trail location and corridor widths.[389]

By July of 1981, word of the prospective new policies had begun to leak to the Appalachian Trail community. "There are not many surprises," the AMC's Thomas Deans advised his staff.[390] "Creative conservation" was the administration's term for the new land protection policies.[391] This translated into reducing the amount of fee acquisition, developing more cost-effective strategies, keeping land in productive, private ownership and on the local tax rolls, and improving relations between federal land managers and local communities. A major objective of the Reagan administration would be to divert Land and Water Conservation funds away from land acquisition and facility development into parks operations and maintenance, a move more than justified by the current neglected state of the parks but one that augured poorly for projects like the Appalachian Trail that were in midstream.

By September of 1981,[392] a case-study team had been assembled under the leadership of Robert McIntosh, former northeast regional director of the terminated Heritage, Conservation and Recreation Service, now assigned to the regional office of the National Park Service in Philadelphia. Messrs. Richie, Rinaldi, and Golden of the AT Project Office, plus regional planner Glen Eugster of the Mid-Atlantic Regional Office, rounded out the team. Survey information was to be gathered first from managers along the course of the Trail, and meetings would be held with ANSTAC and ATC principals to obtain the views of outsiders concerning the Trail program.[393] Looming over the relatively dispassionate appraisal of policies and programs was the celebrated case of Rev. and Mrs. Charles Evans in Pennsylvania, an acquisition project in which Chairman Ric Davidge of Interior's Land Policy Group was reported to have a personal interest.[394] Yet, at the case-study report session, held at the NPS's Denver Service Center, December 9–11, 1981,[395] David Richie recalled, the issue of Trail corridor width illustrated by the Evans case did not become the target of hostile questioning. Davidge, who attended personally, observed only that volunteers engaged in negotiation could confuse landowners and get the NPS off on the wrong foot, an oblique reference to the early experience of the ATC representatives in the Cumberland Valley. Davidge also managed to hearten the federal land managers present by predicting that funding for land acquisition would resume as national economic recovery occurred. He remained supportive of the use of condemnation in cases where the need for it was carefully demonstrated. By the turn of the year, the Mid-Atlantic Regional Office had come to several conclusions about the Appalachian Trail case experience,[396] which reflected the now-positive feelings of the Park Service toward the project. The project had already made extensive use of alternative protection techniques, it was discovered, and should be empowered to do more through new policy legislation. Its proposed cooperative management system should be put firmly into place through intergovernmental/interorganizational agreements and funds. Finally, a federal acquisition program to protect the Trail corridor could be a significant incentive to help make alternative strategies work, the planners concluded. But the policymakers within Interior were the ones who had really become convinced of the merits of the Trail. The program had survived because quality people were involved and doing exactly what the administration had been talking about.[397]

Throughout 1981, the Appalachian Trail Conference coordinated a strong campaign to ensure that the federal government sustained its financial commitment to protect the Trail. Guided by David Startzell, the ATC's able associate director, a legislative alert system was put into place using clubs and influential individuals along the course of the Trail.[398] This helped win immediate restoration of funds for the fiscal year 1981 Land and Water Conservation Fund program, and promised to be instrumental in the fiscal year 1982 and 1983 appropriations battles where the administration was still advocating not only zero funds for the Appalachian Trail, but a four-year moratorium on land acquisition in general. A "dear colleague" letter signed by virtually the entire Appalachian Trail senatorial delegation testified to the growing skill and influence of the Trail community and its conservation allies in legislative affairs.[399]

ANSTAC's "shadow cabinet" continued to meet periodically to confer on strategy, but it would have to do so largely without portfolio after June of 1981 when all ANSTAC appointments were scheduled to expire. The administration's view was that ANSTAC was little more than a tool of the ATC.[400] Accordingly, a meeting was held with NPS director Russell Dickenson on June 1, 1981,[401] to gain top-level administration support for a continuation of ANSTAC and the Trail program. Dickenson's response was generally encouraging. The moratorium had been imposed for fiscal rather than philosophical reasons, he said. If a project is on the books, it will be completed. The existing cooperative management system would not be disrupted, Dickenson advised, and the NPS would be willing to provide technical support for private protection initiatives. While he could not speak directly to the appropriations situation, it was his impression that the OMB target figures for fiscal year 1983 would be well above the modest $45 million systemwide proposed for the NPS acquisition program in fiscal year 1982.

Dickenson would also support a continuation of ANSTAC in its present configuration, the group was told.[402] By October of 1981, the prospective new appointments had reached his desk.[403] Nominations had been received from all but one of the fourteen governors. Thirteen ATC representatives had been selected to speak for each of the Trail's principal regions as the law required. Four landowners/land users had been designated for the secretary's discretionary appointments. And AT project manager David Richie was recommending a return to the previous practice of a nongovernmental chairman.[404] He and Thomas Deans had concurred that the best candidate would be Arthur W. Brownell,[405] currently a lobbyist for the International Paper Company in Washington but also a former commissioner of environmental management for the commonwealth of Massachusetts. As a businessman and lifelong Republican, Brownell seemed to fit the current administration mold nicely. He would also command the loyalty and respect of ANSTAC members as an experienced natural resources professional with years of direct experience in Appalachian Trail matters. Brownell's prior acquaintance with James Watt, when both were involved in outdoor recreation, would do no harm either, strategists like the AMC's Thomas Deans believed.[406] Indeed, in a later meeting with Watt,[407] Brownell gained some useful intelligence. The secretary had nothing against the Trail and, in fact, felt that its emphasis on voluntary and often less-than-fee land protection approaches was fully consistent with the administration's new policies.

1982

On May 14, 1982,[408] the reconstituted ANSTAC assembled at Harpers Ferry, West Virginia, forty-five individuals strong. Only the state of North Carolina was not represented. The new chairman, Arthur Brownell, opened the session and asked AT project manager David Richie for a status report on the program. Richie began by reviewing the draft findings of the resource protection case study, which had generally confirmed the effectiveness of the AT project. He credited for this accomplishment the careful corridor design; the complex planning process involving landowners, representatives of state and local governments, the Appalachian Trail Conference and member clubs, and other federal agencies; but especially the skillful work of Charles Rinaldi, the project's chief of land acquisition. Of the nearly seven hundred parcels acquired to date, only fifteen had gone to condemnation. One in five transactions had been satisfied by Trail easements, rather than fee acquisition, for an average savings of 25 percent of the estimated purchase price. Another seven hundred parcels remained to be acquired at a projected cost of $28 million (about 70 percent of the original estimate), Richie and Rinaldi informed ANSTAC, but the administration's budget request for the entire national park system for fiscal year 1983 was only $4.2 million.

In the absence of regional Council meetings held during the year, ANSTAC devoted a portion of its regular meeting to regional sessions to discuss issues of mutual concern. The New England regional meeting,[409] chaired by Maine's Herbert Hartman, was predictably preoccupied with the problem of federal funding, both for the Trail itself and for companion state efforts via the Land and Water Conservation Fund. The 1982 level should be the minimum provided for fiscal year 1983, it was felt. In the meantime, state agencies and Trail clubs should be encouraged to complete the local management plans for their areas and to take on direct management responsibility via cooperative agreements.

The mid-Atlantic regional meeting,[410] with New York's Ivan Vamos in the chair, reviewed progress throughout its portion of the Trail. There was much to commend. For example, New Jersey's program was now virtually complete—so much so that assistant environmental protection commissioner Helen Fenske was beginning to plan a major celebration for the fall.[411] Only a few key parcels were left to be acquired in New York. Major relocations were under way in northern Virginia, it was reported, and the Maryland commitment to the Trail still seemed to be firm. Although the route through the Cumberland Valley was still a thorn in Pennsylvania's side, the sum of $150,000 was available for key Trail purchases thanks to a commitment from the governor's discretionary fund. But as protection moved toward completion, management, liability, and law enforcement questions were assuming added prominence.

In the South,[412] Virginia's Ben Bolen reported that the Forest Service was down to just a few miles of unprotected Trail. Half of the tracts needed in southern Virginia had already been purchased, he said, and a bargain sale of a corridor from the Wintergreen Corporation was a distinct possibility. Pending legislation in the Congress (H.R. 861) promised to clear up uncertainties, provide new authorities, and generally streamline the protection effort.[413] Sen. Malcolm Wallop (Montana) had taken a personal interest in the legislation. This and federal acquisition funding were legislative musts for the coming year, ANSTAC members agreed. But two special issues continued to plague the southern region. Off-road vehicles were a recurring problem everywhere. And the reservation of mineral rights was a particularly common practice among landowners in the South and could complicate Trail management in the future.

ANSTAC chairman Brownell then proceeded to establish special committees to recommend formal resolutions arising from the regional sessions. By unanimous action, ANSTAC later endorsed the coordination activities of the Appalachian Trail Conference, urging all parties to get on with the task of working together. It recommended speedy passage of H.R. 861, and "sufficient" appropriations and administrative support funds to substantially fulfill the mandate of P.L. 95-248 as amended. It also bestowed its blessings on the April 1982 resource protection case-study report for the Appalachian National Scenic Trail issued by the new administration.[414]

In concluding business, ANSTAC confirmed Chairman Brownell's choice of New Hampshire's George Hamilton, New Jersey's Helen Fenske, and Georgia's Margaret Drummond as regional vice-chairmen for the coming year. Fenske and Hamilton were veterans of previous ANSTACs, Hamilton's reappointment occurring only after an unsuccessful run at the secretary's National Advisory Board.[415] Now a regional bank president in New Hampshire, Hamilton felt that he might warrant a different secretarial-level appointment from the new administration and thus be in a better position to help the Trail community. Returning to ANSTAC was like meeting yourself again, Hamilton commented later, because so many of the issues had not changed in ten years' time. The possibility of reviving the earlier regional Council meetings as interim ANSTAC activities was discussed, but AT project manager Richie preferred to try a series of special events and field trips in each of the three regions to provide an opportunity for ANSTAC members to learn more about the specifics of particular sections of the Trail.[416]

The first such session occurred at Roan Mountain, Tennessee, late in June, 1982. ANSTAC members and guests were treated to misty views, blankets of yellow hawkweed, and blooming rhododendron. For AT project manager David Richie, having just completed the last leg of a 175-mile hike from Springer Mountain, Georgia, to the Great Smoky Mountains National Park, the occasion was especially memorable. "Overall, my respect for the recreational resource with which so many of us are affiliated was considerably enhanced," he wrote ANSTAC members.[417] In subsequent weeks Trail openings were scheduled at Hanover, New Hampshire; Tyringham, Massachusetts; and Wingdale, New York/Kent, Connecticut, where hundreds of supporters took part in ribbon cuttings and abbreviated Trail hikes. Good feelings and positive publicity ran rampant, a sentiment not lost on the congressional delegation hard at work on legislative and appropriations matters. As fall approached, additional events were held in Vermont, at Fontana Dam in North Carolina, and at Sugar Camp Farm in West Virginia.

But the premier occasion of all occurred at High Point State Park, New Jersey, on October 2, 1982,[418] where a representative group of Trail adherents listened first to brief welcoming remarks from New Jersey governor Thomas H. Kean and then put their commemorative walking sticks to good use hiking a four-mile stretch of New Jersey's relocated Appalachian Trail. In a year-end memorandum to ANSTAC members,[419] AT project manager David Richie could properly characterize 1982 as an extraordinarily good year for the Appalachian Trail, for in addition to the landmark occasions along its route, Congress had approved an Interior appropriations bill containing $10 million for Trail-related acquisitions by the National Park Service and another $1.36 million for the Forest Service. The protection program was back on track once again.

THE MANAGEMENT YEARS

By the end of 1982, the matter of who should manage the Appalachian Trail lands had become a central focus for the Trail community. Opinions were varied. AT project manager David Richie, mindful of the immense value of the volunteer tradition and the importance of flexibility in meeting varying needs, remained supportive of a substantial role for the Appalachian Trail Conference and its member clubs. But, conditioned to the order of a government bureaucracy, he knew that a way had to be found to make the new approach acceptable within the National Park Service itself. Fortunately, his relationship with the Trail community in general, and ATC executive director Laurence Van Meter in particular, was such that these sensitive matters could be discussed openly and thoughtfully.

A prime mover throughout the management delegation discussions turned out to be Laurence Van Meter, the ATC's energetic young executive director.[420] Born in south Jersey, and the son of a successful obstetrician who liked to hike the New England section of the Appalachian Trail, Van Meter came to the ATC by way of Vermont's Green Mountain Club, where he rose from seasonal caretaker at Camel's Hump to executive director of the sixty-year-old hiking organization. Joining the ATC in 1969, Van Meter was singularly unimpressed by the Conference's old guard membership. Reflecting the parochialism and biocentrism of his Vermont colleagues, he was less than convinced of the need for an expanded federal presence ("Who needs those guys!").[421] Nevertheless, Van Meter was persuaded to attend the 1976 ANSTAC meeting at Bear Mountain as an observer, grudgingly agreed to represent the Green Mountain Club on the ATC's Board of Managers, and joined the corridor planning group at the urging of David Richie as much to protect his club's interests as to advance the Trail project as a whole. Recruited by the ATC as its executive director in 1981, Van Meter found the Conference to be a "happy though wary environment." He brought two needed qualities to the organization: direct experience in managing a trail system, and the consensus-building predilections of his Quaker education.

In a series of memoranda and handwritten notes titled simply "thoughts," Van Meter and Richie exchanged ideas. Richie began by visualizing the Trail as analogous to an educational institution[422] – a remarkable outdoors classroom served by a dedicated "faculty" and "custodial staff" and used by a large and diverse "student body." Who owns the classroom, Richie suggested, does not matter so much when the principal focus is providing an educational (or recreational) experience. The "educator" for the Trail could and should be the Appalachian Trail Conference, he observed, under a broad delegation of management responsibility from the National Park Service. Yet the details of that arrangement, as spelled out in a long line of draft cooperative agreements, were making some of the ATC professionals uneasy–"a renewed befuddlement over the gordian knot of our relationships," one staff member observed.[423] In conflict were two management themes: the traditional public/private arrangement where authority was channeled from a government agency to a private partner, and a visionary effort to enlarge a historic, traditional form of stewardship through grants of government authority in a way that would make the private partner fully accountable. The bottom line, Van Meter responded, was to be sure that the verbiage of the cooperative agreement "does not interrupt the naturally-constructive inclinations of all managing partners."

The spirit of cooperative management, fortunately, was expressed forthrightly in the language of the National Trails System Act and reinforced in the comprehensive plan submitted to the Congress in 1981. The central question remaining was how much direction should be applied by the National Park Service to its managing partners. In discussions with his own staff,[424] Richie continued to favor local initiative over centralism. On its part, the ATC's Board of Managers was of several minds about an enlarged management responsibility. Most favored the idea as being consistent with the long tradition of volunteer involvement. But could a relatively weak and heavily decentralized organization fulfill such responsibilities, some asked.[425] Still others were concerned about inviting the National Park Service "fox" into their own "henhouse".[426] The AMC's president Andrew Nichols, representing the ATC's member club with the most cooperative management experience through its work with the Forest Service in the White Mountains, expressed his sense of the situation in a letter to Richie on March 5, 1981.[427] If you can keep the relationships flexible and foresee more or less perpetual negotiations among the parties, then the cooperative management system will work, Nichols wrote.

By early 1981, the ATC had reached out to enlist the help of its members with legal training for this and other technical matters.[428] It was fortunate to have a Virginia practicing attorney, Charles W. Sloan, with the time and interest to supply leadership for such an effort.[429] In 1971, Sloan had built a small cabin near Harpers Ferry and had begun hiking the Appalachian Trail. Captivated by his exposure to the volunteer Trail effort, Sloan had responded to the call for counsel put out by ATC executive director Paul Pritchard in 1975 and had served as an officer ever since. He was known to be more of an iconoclast than any of the other members of the Board of Managers.[430] On his part, AT project manager David Richie knew that he must confront the thicket of procedures and regulations within the Department of the Interior before any such agreement could be exercised. He turned for help to Charles Peter Raynor, the specialist for parks and recreation within the Office of the Solicitor, but also an individual with unusual creativity and insights.[431] But working independently on the management issue could compound the problem, all parties agreed. The solution seemed to be a small working group, acting much like an executive committee, containing representatives of the likely management partners, a concept that seemed fully consistent with the cooperative spirit of the comprehensive plan.[432] ANSTAC would be ideal as the sponsoring agency, but its charter was due to expire in June. It was, therefore, agreed that the ATC's Board of Managers would establish what came to be called the "partnership committee,"[433] a term reflective of the business philosophy of the committee's chairman-to-be, Charles Sloan. The first meeting of the new committee took place on May 5, 1981,[434] and it convened virtually monthly in open session from then on. Veteran ATC members such as Thurston Griggs, the veritable conscience of the Board of Managers,[435] were willing to give the concept a try, but they were concerned that a committee including state and federal governmental members might begin to supplant the policy capabilities of the ATC itself.[436]

Within weeks of the formation of the partnership committee, the first of many drafts of a cooperative management agreement began emerging from Sloan's skilled hands, so much so that the ATC's executive director Laurence Van Meter expressed concern at the many radically different ideas proceeding at such a dizzying pace.[437] We didn't know where we were going at times," Sloan later admitted. "We were like Alice in Wonderland."[438] The situation was compounded by the National Park Service's announced intentions of making the Appalachian Trail fully subject to the Service's systemwide regulations.[439] To many in the Trail community, this was a prospective threat to the tradition of volunteer involvement, and a direct contradiction of the consultation provision contained in the language of P.L. 95-248 as amended. The regulations issue had one beneficial effect, however, and that was to motivate the ATC to look harder at the potential usefulness of accepting a more extensive delegation of management responsibility from the National Park Service.

1983

Acting assistant solicitor Peter Raynor, in a long and thoughtful legal opinion addressed to the AT Project Office on March 17, 1983,[440] found clear authority for the NPS to delegate management of the Trail to the Appalachian Trail Conference, including provisions for liability protection, limited financial assistance, and even the operation of federal facilities. The redelegation of that authority to member clubs presented no problem either in his opinion. Any residual uncertainties were likely to be removed by the provisions of pending legislation which he had helped draft. Even more significant, Raynor found that the earlier (1970) NPS/ATC cooperative agreement included language that could be interpreted as a broad delegation of management responsibility. The implications of this finding were considerable, for the arrangement under review would thus constitute implementation of an earlier agreement, not the creation of a precedent.

Raynor's involvement yielded one other important dividend to the Trail program. It sparked another round of perfecting legislative amendments which were added on to a related hiking bill.[441] The range of new authorizations made the Appalachian Trail an even more extraordinary experiment. For example, there was authority to assign land to the Forest Service for management outside of national forest boundaries. Tax credits were permitted for donated easements. Liability and trespass protection provisions were spelled out to cover both volunteer managers and involved landowners. And the cooperative agreement authorities were expanded.

But there were still problems on other fronts. ANSTAC had taken action at its March 7, 1981,[442] meeting that appeared to reject the concept of a broad delegation of management responsibility to the ATC. At that time, state representatives were fearful of being shut out of the management system. Member Trail clubs had also expressed some uneasiness, as illustrated by Steven Clark's concerns on behalf of the Maine Appalachian Trail Club that a central ATC role might jeopardize ongoing relationships between local clubs and state agencies.[443]

But by far the largest potential problem was the reluctance of traditional federal land managers to embrace the concept of private management of public lands. These attitudes flared up at two special sessions arranged by

AT project manager David Richie. A meeting was held at Pipestem State Park, West Virginia, September 24–25, 1982,[444] to discuss the relationship of the NPS-acquired Appalachian Trail lands to Forest Service ownerships in southern Virginia and West Virginia. After a candid dialogue between the parties, it was agreed that the Forest Service and the Virginia Division of Parks would use their organizations to "backstop" the ATC in its management functions, an understanding that led Virginia's Ben Bolen to remark: "we know what we need to do; let's get at it."[445]

A second session held at Waynesboro, Virginia, July 21–22, 1983,[446] involved key Park Service superintendents, including former National Park Service director Gary Everhardt, now superintendent of the Blue Ridge Parkway. Everhardt and Robert Jacobsen, superintendent of Shenandoah National Park, engaged in some searching questioning of the cooperative management system, particularly the concept of a federal agency performing only a secondary role in the management of federal lands. They were frankly offended by having to take a back seat to volunteers. Nevertheless, after what was later characterized as "an initial mating dance,"[447] a constructive assessment of the concept and its implementation ensued.

The upper-level bureaucracy within Interior was still a potential problem, and the partnership committee was never entirely sure that its NPS representative, David Richie, was able to reach the top rung of the ladder.[448] Nevertheless, Richie set about convincing associate director for operations Stanley Albright of the merits of management delegation. Albright, a Park Service career professional, had risen through the ranks to become associate director, a position at this point that embraced both acquisition and management responsibilities. Fortunately for the Trail, he had grown up in the mountains of California. Two questions nagged at Albright, however: was the Trail really a unit of the National Park System, and how would the lands acquired be managed? To Albright, the Appalachian Trail was a beautiful concept but a "bear managerially."[449] In an internal memorandum dated December 23, 1982,[450] Richie spelled out the likely configuration of the delegation issue, observing that he was optimistic that the ATC could build a highly competent staff of Appalachian Trail management specialists capable of assuming virtually all the management responsibilities the NPS had for the Trail outside existing NPS units. Once the delegation had taken place, Richie observed, his own position as manager would become superfluous.

On May 20, 1983,[451] Albright advised Chairman Ruth Blackburn that the National Park Service agreed in principle with the concept of a broad delegation of responsibility to the ATC for management of lands the National Park Service was acquiring for the Appalachian Trail. This was confirmed by a memorandum from secretary James Watt to NPS director Russell Dickenson on June 7, 1983. "I trust you will find the delegation proposal to be consistent with National Park System policies and that it will be possible to enter into an appropriate agreement with the Appalachian Trail Conference in the near future," Watt wrote.[452] Even former critic Ric Davidge was now on board. Management delegation "truely [sic] was and is an unprecedented step," he advised the ATC's Laurence Van Meter. "I think the future for conservation is groups like the ATC."[453] It was now time to move swiftly to confirm the growing degree of consensus.

On February 5, 1983,[454] a special meeting of ATC officers and others was held at the Potomac Appalachian Trail Club headquarters in Washington to go over the delegation issue. A question-and-answer sheet had been prepared by ATC executive director Laurence Van Meter setting forth the options ATC faced.[455] Further discussion took place within ATC's executive committee two weeks later.[456] Updating his Board of Managers after these meetings,[457] Van Meter could report widespread consensus within the Trail community that to allow the National Park Service to accumulate control would be undesirable. It was his view that the ATC should seize the initiative and tailor the Trail management program through acceptance of a delegated management responsibility.

On the eve of the Board of Managers meeting in Shepherdstown, West Virginia, March 19–20, 1983, the partnership committee met to formally recommend such action.[458] And on March 19, 1983, the Board confirmed its views, voting without dissent "to anticipate a broad delegation of management responsibility from the National Park Service for National Park Service–acquired lands."[459] The Board authorized the creation of an ad hoc committee to explore the relationship between the ATC and member clubs if delegation occurred, and it instructed the partnership committee to define the particulars of the new delegation responsibility, including potential financial impacts, and to report its findings to the next meeting of the Board of Managers. Round one of implementation was underway. The next move would be up to ANSTAC.

On February 9, 1983,[460] AT project manager David Richie advised ANSTAC members of a number of current developments. A draft Land Protection Plan had been prepared to satisfy the administration's insistence on new directions in Interior's land acquisition programs.[461] NPS director Russell Dickenson and Interior assistant secretary Ray Arnett would be briefed on the plan personally two weeks hence, Richie reported. With any luck, the plan would supplant the present requirement for tract-by-tract purchase approval. As for the delegation of management responsibility issue, it had reached the stage of serious exploration, Richie advised. The proposal would be considered at regional meetings of state and local club officials sponsored by the ATC, and by the Board of Managers itself. If these gauntlets were run successfully, ANSTAC could expect the matter to be on its April meeting agenda. In a supplemental memorandum a month later,[462] Richie could advise Council members of other encouraging developments. Interior officials had agreed to pick up an ATC-negotiated option for a twenty-eight-hundred-acre tract at the Wintergreen ski area in Virginia bordering the Trail and the Blue Ridge Parkway, a section with unparalleled vistas and superb natural terrain. And further amendments to the National Trails System Act,[463] reinforcing the role of volunteers and providing new tools for protecting land along the Trail, were on their way to the President for signature.

Taking no chances with the pending regional and ANSTAC meetings, Richie and ATC executive director Laurence Van Meter urged the state representative on the partnership committee, Pennsylvania's Theodore Kelly, to prepare a special advisory for ANSTAC's state representatives.[464] On April 11, 1983,[465] a letter went out under Pennsylvania state forester Richard R. Thorpe's signature expressing the view that adequate Trail management is most likely to come from organized volunteers, not from the states or the federal government. Thorpe's advisory came on the heels of generally encouraging signals from the Trail regions. On April 7, 1983, for example, delegates to the strong New York–New Jersey Trail Conference had expressed their support of the delegation concept. Even in prickly New England, the concept of delegated management appeared to pass muster.[466]

On April 22, 1983,[467] ANSTAC assembled at the Park Service conference center in Harpers Ferry, West Virginia, for its annual meeting. Twenty-two members and fifteen observers were present. Among the missing, for reasons of illness, were ANSTAC chairman Arthur Brownell and AT project manager David Richie. New Hampshire's George Hamilton presided as acting chairman. Chief of Land Acquisition Charles Rinaldi reported that acquisitions had slowed to a trickle but, on a positive note, estimated that the Appalachian Trail project could now be completed for some $25 million less than the $95 million authorized. An extensive use of less-than-fee approaches promised to make the difference. State acquisition programs appeared to be faring no better, several ANSTAC members observed, with little real progress discernible in states such as Maryland and Maine. Rinaldi promised that the Project Office would meet with the key states individually and was prepared to fulfill the protection responsibility directly should any state be unable to complete its program. But Interior's special assistant for land policy, Ric Davidge, attending his first ANSTAC meeting in a setting later described as pregnant with problems,[468] relieved the tension by confirming the federal government's commitment to the Trail, including the use of condemnation where legitimate and necessary. He estimated that the formal land protection plan for the Trail would be cleared and ready for public review by May. Once adopted by Interior, land acquisition could then proceed on a program basis. In response to questions, Davidge assured ANSTAC of his personal support for the concept of management primarily by the private sector and by the states.

In the two regional discussion sessions to follow, the problems and opportunities along the Trail received detailed scrutiny. The New York and New Jersey sections were reported as virtually complete and, even in New England, problems were beginning to be resolved.[469] In 1982, for example, more acres of Trail had been protected in Vermont than in any other New England state. Yet, it was clear that the project was now down to the most difficult of cases. A stronger NPS presence would be required to complete the program and ensure Trail continuity, but this should happen only after the level of commitment of the states had been determined, the New England group felt.

The mid-Atlantic and southern contingents of ANSTAC reported few remaining problems but similarly difficult local situations.[470] For example, in the Virginia, North Carolina, and Tennessee sections, it was taking longer than expected to work out agreements with landowners. In the troublesome Cumberland Valley, Interior's Ric Davidge reported, recent exchanges of opinion between local leaders, the congressional delegation, and the National Park Service had left him guardedly optimistic. The group echoed the sentiments of ANSTAC members to the north by favoring a delegation of overall management responsibility from the NPS to the ATC. However, it felt that state-by-state cooperative agreements were an essential adjunct to the new management system.

With the Massachusetts representative the only dissenting voice,[471] ANSTAC adopted an official resolution of support for the proposed ATC/NPS agreement. It pressed for a restoration of appropriations and a return of acquisition authority directly to the Project Office. It also encouraged and commended the ATC for its new Trust for Appalachian Trail Lands. And in unmistakable language, it urged the National Park Service to step up its efforts in Maine, Massachusetts, and Maryland—the states where 90 percent of the remaining unprotected acreage lay.

On May 18, 1983, AT project manager David Richie wrote ANSTAC that the resolutions adopted were all being pursued vigorously. Interior assistant secretary Ray Arnett had approved several land transactions and, as Richie observed, "it is a relief to see progress toward complete protection of the Trail once again."[472] He further advised ANSTAC that the matter of acceptance of delegated management authority would be on the agenda of the ATC's Board of Managers meeting in New Paltz, New York, within the week. If approved, the next move would be a specific proposal for all parties to consider.

To prepare for both eventualities, and to size up the current situation, Charles Sloan convened a meeting of the partnership committee on May 17, 1983.[473] The ATC's ad hoc committee on the delegation of management responsibility, under the chairmanship of Earl Jette of the Dartmouth Outing Club, had met in Washington on April 30, 1983,[474] executive director Laurence Van Meter reported, and the matter of ATC–Trail club relations had been explored in depth. The proposed system would be workable if the ATC professional staff did not try to set policy or encroach upon local club responsibilities, the ad hoc committee had concluded. However, the ATC rather than the clubs would have to carry the additional financial burdens. In reviewing these developments and the generally favorable reception accorded the concept of management delegation by the Trail clubs, the states, and other federal agencies, the partnership committee voted to recommend acceptance to the Board of Managers.[475] A sample delegation agreement was forwarded which suggested that dependence on federal funding for management should be held to a minimum to preserve ATC's own independence. The partnership committee also urged that the Forest Service become party to this or a companion agreement.

On May 27, 1983,[476] the ATC's Board of Managers met in New Paltz, New York, to consider the delegation of management responsibility and other matters. Chairman Ruth Blackburn presided. The Board was advised by executive director Laurence Van Meter that formal votes of support had been received from the New York/New Jersey Trail Conference, the southern Virginia clubs, ANSTAC, the ad hoc management delegation committee, and the partnership committee. Official National Park Service encouragement had been offered by Associate Director Stanley Albright, and Ric Davidge claimed to have secured the advance consent of assistant secretary Ray Arnett and secretary James Watt within Interior. At the state level, only Massachusetts was reported to have been reluctant to see the volunteer community assume a primary role in Trail management. It was now time for speedy action on the Board's part, Van Meter concluded. Speaking for the ad hoc committee, Earl Jette confirmed Van Meter's assessment of the situation. "Experience shows that we should not fear a government takeover as we did several years ago," Jette observed.[477] After much discussion by Board of Managers members, the matter was brought to a vote. With one abstention,[478] the ATC was authorized to enter into a cooperative agreement with the NPS which delegated to the ATC the responsibility to "operate, maintain, develop, and manage the Appalachian Trail."

By July of 1983,[479] the ATC's Laurence Van Meter had developed a draft statement of policy to be incorporated in a formal agreement. It referred specifically to the thirty-five thousand acres of NPS-acquired lands in eight different states, but allowed for an aggregate acreage nearly double that amount once the protection program had been completed. The rationale behind the proposed agreement was the appropriateness of such action from the standpoints of the long tradition of volunteer involvement and the current national priority of a heightened role for volunteers in the management of national parks and forests. Under the proposed cooperative agreement, the NPS would delegate responsibility for certain management functions only; it would retain overall authority for the properties it had acquired along the Trail. But the ATC and its member clubs would deal not only with what happened on the Trail, but with what happened within the Trail corridor as well. Since land management would take time to learn, and local clubs could be expected to ebb and flow in degrees of participation and leadership, the ATC would obligate itself to even out the fluctuations and serve as a guarantor of adequate management to the National Park Service. Local management plans would constitute the basic building blocks of the Trail-wide system, with provisions of the comprehensive plan governing management in general. Oversight would be supplied by the ATC through its regional management committees, units representative of all the managing partners and staffed by an ATC professional. Matters lacking regional consensus would be settled ultimately by the ATC's Board of Managers. Monitoring of the Trail corridor to guard against encroachments and other forms of quality deterioration would be a new responsibility exercised by the ATC and its member clubs. The matter of special use permits raised both technical and policy implications. The ATC was prepared to assume these added responsibilities, but any fees involved would be sent directly to the NPS to avoid even the appearance of a conflict of interest. In matters of search and rescue, fire suppression, and law enforcement, the ATC would continue to depend upon local authorities for direct action. The ATC's role would be limited to education and prevention. The provisions of the new Trail act amendments had now authorized the extension of liability protection to both the Trail clubs and individual volunteers. Through a system of back-up government services, and extensive use of private fund sources and volunteers, the costs of management of the Appalachian Trail to the taxpayer would be much reduced, Van Meter concluded.

At the October 4, 1983,[480] partnership committee meeting, the status of the delegation agreement came up for detailed discussion. The draft developed by the ATC's Charles Sloan with input from Interior assistant solicitor Peter Raynor had been modified substantially by AT project manager David Richie to give more weight to Van Meter's concept paper. Richie preferred "to have ATC tell NPS what it proposes to do rather than to have NPS tell ATC what it cannot do."[481]

By the Board of Managers' meeting on November 19, 1983,[482] the differences in approach had been bridged and draft agreement language was ready to be approved. Rather than a separate document, it was constructed as an amendment to the existing memorandum of agreement between the NPS and the ATC dated May 13, 1970.[483] The basic authority stemmed from the amendments to the National Trails System Act, enacted on March 28, 1983, which stated in part: "it is further the purpose of this Act to encourage and assist volunteer, citizen involvement in the planning, development, maintenance, and management, where appropriate, of trails."[484] The initial agreement was to be valid for a five-year period but subject to renewal indefinitely for additional terms. Either signator was entitled to request revisions or even terminate by written notice at the end of each agreement period. The agreement itself was a mere three pages long, but included in it as Attachment A was Van Meter's concept document, *Management of Residual NPS-Acquired A.T. Lands*, describing the manner in which the Appalachian Trail Conference intended to meet its responsibilities. Without dissent, the Board of Managers endorsed the draft for submission to the National Park Service.[485] The long cooperative management journey was now ready for its final step.

1984

On the afternoon of January 26, 1984, some ninety Trail supporters met in Washington to witness the signing of Amendment No. 8 to National Park Service Cooperative Agreement No. 0631-81-01. The audience was a mixture of current and former ATC board members and chairmen, representatives of public agencies, congressional offices, conservation organizations, and the news media.[486] The setting was the handsome headquarters of the American Institute of Architects, a haunting reminder of Benton MacKaye's seminal article in the October 1921 AIA *Journal* which had provided the initial stimulus for more than six decades of activity on behalf of the Appalachian Trail. The new Interior secretary William P. Clark attended personally. He was accompanied by assistant secretary G. Ray Arnett and director Russell E. Dickenson, who executed the document on behalf of the National Park Service. Arthur W. Brownell, chairman of ANSTAC, witnessed the ceremonies; ATC chairman Raymond E. Hunt signed the historic agreement for the Appalachian Trail Conference.[487]

Secretary Clark termed the Appalachian Trail "a model of cooperation and good will. Yours is an exciting adventure," he declared.[488] For the ATC's Raymond Hunt, the agreement was "the most important document that I ever hope to sign. We have rounded another significant corner into a new era for the AT and the ATC, and we intend to accomplish what is expected of us."[489] As the National Park Service's own newsletter reported later, the agreement was a landmark occasion with implications extending far beyond the Appalachian Trail itself. For as director Russell Dickenson had said at the conclusion of the signing ceremonies, "our signatures on this agreement evidence faith on the part of Government and private partners alike that extensive public lands can safely be entrusted to a private organization."[490]

Retrospect

THE APPALACHIAN TRAIL CONFERENCE

Prominent among the institutions responsible for the Appalachian Trail has been the Appalachian Trail Conference, formally constituted in 1925 but with antecedents reaching back to the early part of the twentieth century. At the outset, the Conference consisted of a loose and casual confederation of local trail clubs, largely from the Northeast, groups of individuals who cared enough about trails to take responsibility locally and develop systems within easy reach of people.[491] These early projects furnished opportunities for use, generated a need for workers to expand and maintain the trails, and thereby attracted others to the cause. The times were generally favorable for such initiatives.

The early part of the post–World War I era generated a feeling of general well-being.[492] Wealth and leisure were on the upswing; intellect and culture were respected attributes. For the elite, the cities had become places for innovation and beckoned as sites for social experimentation. European romanticism had entered America with a vengeance in the early part of the century. One manifestation had been the rediscovery of Henry David Thoreau. Thus, together with an emerging social consciousness, there was a parallel interest in the natural environment. For activists such as Lewis Mumford, the interrelationship between people, resources, and environment was only logical. This naturally awakened new interest in design, planning, parks, and open spaces and sparked concerns for proper urban growth and development. A veritable renaissance of regionalism took place, predicated upon the obvious artificiality of human political boundaries. A man for the times was Benton MacKaye, an individual who was professionally trained, practically experienced, and intellectually and conceptually able. The Appalachian Trail he espoused was as much a cultural construct of the times as a physical reality.[493] His vision of a regional project for the Appalachians, using a wilderness footpath to interlink the various cultures and environments, fell on fertile ground. Although MacKaye's initial concept of the Trail was quite different from the one that emerged later on, he served as a source of inspiration for the Appalachian Trail community throughout his lifetime, conveying views by letter and even by film when he became too frail to attend the biennial Trail Conferences.[494]

But the Appalachian Trail had other active proponents as well. Maj. William A. Welch, the general manager of the Palisades Interstate Park Commission, encouraged the formation of the New York–New Jersey Trail Conference.[495] In New England, C. Francis Belcher, son of a China missionary,[496] was overseeing the development of trails and other activities as executive director of the Appalachian Mountain Club, a private organization headquartered in Boston but with chapters throughout the north-Atlantic region. And a state-of-Mainer named Myron H. Avery would first come to know the Trail as a Connecticut resident, and then move to Washington, D.C., where he would help found not only the Potomac Appalachian Trail Club and the Maine Appalachian Trail Club, but the Appalachian Trail Conference itself.[497] Avery was destined to dedicate virtually his entire volunteer life to placing securely on the ground MacKaye's conceptual Appalachian Trail.

On March 2, 1925,[498] in Washington, D.C., a number of the separate strands would be woven firmly together. Major Welch would serve as the presiding officer and first chairman of what the organizers came to call the Appalachian Trail Conference. Mumford's Regional Planning Association of America, acting through the Federated Societies on Planning and Parks, would facilitate the session, observing through spokesman Clarence Stein that the Appalachian hinterland to be protected by the Trail would help offset the vast eastern urban complex it termed "Atlantis." National Park Service director Stephen T. Mather would speak positively of trails as elements of expanded eastern and western park systems. But the star performer was to be Benton MacKaye himself, who outlined the Appalachian Trail project for the assembled group, terming it a kind of "trailway" to open up the country "as an escape from civilization."[499] In his view, a federation of trails interests was the best way to accomplish an Appalachian Trail. The effort should be divided into five regions, he said: New England, New York–New Jersey, Pennsylvania, the central Appalachians, and the southern Appalachians. The new Conference, MacKaye challenged, should complete the initial portions of the Trail in time for the nation's 150th birthday celebration on July 4, 1926.

The early Trail leadership had characteristics in common that have endured to present times.[500] Most were generally active in the professions and, thus, free to pursue interests with independent means. Their occupations also gave them important connections to sources of influence and power. Importantly, the leadership was dispersed geographically and, thus, was strategically well placed. For the most part, the interest in trails was merely a subset of a larger concern for conservation and the outdoors. And theirs was a long-term commitment. Once involved in the Trail effort, they never left it.

The decision to aggregate into a larger Conference reflected certain realities. Trails themselves provided the first imperative. Since they had to go somewhere, designing a connective system was a must. Also, if MacKaye's concept of exposure to varying environmental and cultural conditions was to prevail, there would need to be some central, unifying presence. Further, the sheer enormity of marking, clearing, and maintaining a two-thousand-mile footpath with largely volunteer assistance demanded at least a central, coordinative capacity. And there were other advantages to confederation. Uniform standards could be established. An army of volunteers could be enlisted. A sense of the whole would not only encourage each disparate element in its own activities, but also create a genuine critical mass for the Trail. Looking down the road, some could see the emergence of an eastern seaboard constituency for the conservation of the entire Appalachian region, a concept put to the test successfully once before with the passage of the Weeks Act in 1911 authorizing a new system of national forests for the eastern half of the United States.[501]

The fledgling Appalachian Trail Conference, representing the amorphous mass of the Trail community, operated much like another trail club.[502] In fact, for much of its early life, it was housed in Washington under the wing of the Potomac Appalachian Trail Club.[503] Until 1964, it met officially only at the then-triennial Trail Conferences.[504] Dominated by a few individuals, the Conference had no real character of its own. Many of the clubs were quite ancient and lacked a young nerve.[505] Like an extended family, there was a lot of posturing and too many heads to be effective.[506] The meetings were often stupefyingly unsubstantive.[507] Volunteers ran the organization, generally from their own homes. New Englanders were not prominent in the later ATC leadership despite the preponderance of members from the Northeast and the distinct spark for preservation in this section of the country.[508] Organizations like the Appalachian Mountain Club deliberately maintained an arms'length relationship, because their focus was much broader than the Trail. Their goal was to be full management partners, not just "weekend warriors."[509] In return, the AMC's professionalism was looked at askance by the volunteer purists. In the spirit of volunteerism, professional staff was to be utilized only as a last resort. The result was a measure of constructive tension between the two Trail organizations. But as the Trail program began to grow, so inevitably did the Conference itself, doubling in membership during the single three-year period 1966–69.[510] Functional needs began to emerge—a newsletter to facilitate the flow of information among member clubs and keep the central Trail spirit alive, a secretary to cope with correspondence and to process memberships,[511] and eventually the measure of professionalism the ATC would need to warrant its management contract from the National Park Service.[512]

Stanley T. Murray, along with Benton MacKaye and Myron Avery, one of the three most important individuals in the history of the Appalachian Trail Conference, has provided personal recollections of these early days.[513]

Murray's love for the mountains was engendered during a childhood spent on the rocky coastline of Penobscot Bay, Maine. A chemical engineer in the Manhattan Project during World War II, he came to know and appreciate first the southern Appalachians and later the Great Smokies through army special training assignments, finally moving in 1949 to a permanent base in Kingsport, Tennessee. Exposed to his first triennial conference at Skyland, Virginia, in 1952, he was promptly adopted by the ATC's corresponding secretary, Jean Stephenson, and, in the informal style of the times, served successively as committee chairman, vice-chairman, and, in 1961, as the duly elected chairman of the Conference, a post he held for fourteen years. Murray was called upon to preside over the ATC's initial transition from an all-volunteer to a staffed organization. He provided much of the leadership for the campaign for federal legislation. One day, driving to work in Kingsport, he came up with the term *greenway* to describe the broader environmental corridor that many felt should surround the Appalachian Trail,[514] and the concept became an odyssey for him as well as a campaign for his organization. Always knowledgeable, invariably thorough, and tactfully persistent, Murray typified the dedication of the Trail volunteer and the unusual capacity the program has had throughout time to capture, harness, and hold the best of human talents.

By September of 1969, a decision had been made to engage an executive secretary for the Conference on a part-time basis. Among other factors, the struggle for federal legislation had made it plain that the ATC had outstripped its strictly volunteer capacities and could not operate the way it had much longer. Col. Lester L. Holmes, the former NATO military liaison to the Turkish general staff, longtime Boy Scout activist, and one-time disciple of naturalist Ernest Thompson Seton, consented to serve in such a capacity. A big "teddy bear" of a man, who appeared to know everyone and was much beloved by the Trail community, Holmes kept the machinery of the Conference working.[515] Peter Dunning, a skilled writer and editor, took over the editorship of *Appalachian Trailway News*.[516] A sense of organization, structure, and professional management slowly began to emerge. Prodded by Chairman Stanley Murray, its real agent of change,[517] the ATC took on new concepts and ideas. A major rethinking of the purpose of the Appalachian Trail began to take place. In the spirit of Benton MacKaye, it was to become more than a trail. As MacKaye himself observed, "the physical trail is no end in itself; it is a means of sojourning in the primeval or wilderness environment."[518] Fresh faces on the Board of Managers, such as New York business executive George Zoebelein, were supportive.[519]

Steeped in the Bavarian tradition of walks in the countryside every Sunday, Zoebelein had encountered the New York–New Jersey Trail Conference during the course of his accounting preparation at Manhattan College, and had risen rapidly in the organization to become its president and chief delegate to the Appalachian Trail Conference. Fortunately, Zoebelein was much more than a green-eyeshade man. He had an abiding interest in the larger mosaic of recreational pursuits, such as the ATC's greenway project, which he visualized as a broad swathe of the East Coast, with the Appalachian Trail as its centerpiece. Yet, unlike his predecessor, Stanley Murray, Zoebelein had an arms' length, managerial view of the chairman's responsibilities. They should be restricted to matters relating to housekeeping and financial discipline.[520] Encouraged by Zoebelein and others, modifications in the constitution relegated the Board to more of a policy-making role.[521] Inevitably, tensions arose: tensions between an increasingly independent professional staff and its volunteer Board, but also tensions between an increasingly independent central Conference and its member clubs. Slowly but surely, corporate management was beginning to replace the earlier model of simple confederation.

With the stress of change visiting the Trail Conference again,[522] a major decision threshold was reached in 1975. A full-time executive director would be engaged and the dues structure for members revamped to provide the resources necessary for a fully staffed Conference.[523] A separate headquarters facility in Harpers Ferry, West Virginia, would replace the sequence of borrowed and leased spaces that had characterized the early period.[524] For the first time, the Conference would have distinct institutional recognition.[525] With a bigger and more active central organization, it would have the energy and visibility to get something done for the Trail.[526] Coincident with these internal changes came a curious choice of the new executive director. Breaking with tradition, he would be not a Trail activist but an individual with governmental credentials. Paul C. Pritchard, former Georgia state natural resources planner and Pacific Coast regional coordinator for NOAA's coastal zone program, who had impressed the search committee with his fresh vision and extensive networking skills, accepted the position at the 1975 Trail Conference session held in Boone, North Carolina.[527]

Growing tired of government service and, admittedly, captivated by the Harpers Ferry environment, Pritchard responded enthusiastically to the challenge of the ATC assignment.[528] He had his hands full, however, finding clichotomy in the staff, inadequate financial and tax reporting, no membership or fund-raising efforts, and generally poor relations with the National Park Service. The state of internal disarray within the Conference extended even to its governance, for the legality of Pritchard's proposed appointment was promptly challenged from the floor at the Boone meeting.[529] Nevertheless, backed by the supportive new chairman George Zoebelein, Pritchard began to make changes. He started by focusing on the identity of the organization. He elevated Education Director Hank Lautz to the position of associate director with responsibiity for regular liaison with the National Park Service. And he assigned to David Startzell, planner, amateur ornithologist, and, reputedly, the most consummate technician on the staff,[530] the sensitive role of liaison with member clubs, an assignment that later ripened into expanded lobbying activities on behalf of Trail legislation and appropriations.

Thus, by a stroke of sheer coincidence, revitalization of the Trail program occurred on several fronts simultaneously. Just as the national effort was taking on form and substance with the reactivation of ANSTAC and a pledge of renewed commitment by the National Park Service, so also was the Trail to receive a revitalized private working partner, the Appalachian Trail Conference, an organization now fully capable of pragmatic action. The days of marking time appeared to be about over. As events unfolded, the alliance promised to become crucial. The driving force was to be a leadership role for the federal government in protecting the Trail.

Myron Avery, the archdruid of the volunteer movement since its infancy, was among the earliest to recognize the need. In the January 1946 issue of *Trailway News*, Avery had written: "Any Trail which is to survive must be in public ownership."[531] His observations accompanied the early and abortive attempt by Pennsylvania congressman D. K. Hoch to obtain federal legislation, later replaced by the more sophisticated lobbying efforts of the Potomac Appalachian Trail Club and the Appalachian Trail Conference to win passage of the 1968 National Trails System Act. Distressed at the lack of progress by the National Park Service to protect the Trail, the Conference's only recourse was to try again. This time there was real hope—a new Park Service professional, David A. Richie, charged with responsibility for the Trail, a revitalized Advisory Council, and new staff capabilities at ATC. Not every Conference member was pleased with these developments, however. To many, government was still the court of last resort.[532] The volunteer tradition still rang loud and clear in the hearts and minds of many Trail club members, particularly those from the New England region. While reasonably preconditioned to a role for public agencies by the AMC experience with the Forest Service in the White Mountains, the cordial linkages with the states forged during the CCC era, and the early precedent at Harriman Park, veteran members could not forget that it was volunteers who really put the Trail on the ground and kept it maintained. The specter of a heightened public presence, particularly a federal one, could threaten their state working part-ners and choke off the burgeoning citizen movement.

The Potomac Appalachian Trail Club and southern club leaderships, long conditioned to a proximate federal presence, offered reassurances to the contrary. Their views prevailed, and the ATC set about utilizing its far-flung support structure to persuade the administration, the Congress, and the states of the merits of an accelerated, public, Trail protection program. Here again, a stroke of good fortune intervened. The incoming Carter administration became convinced that the Appalachian Trail would serve as a valuable capstone to its national program for the environment. And so the Trail protectionists won still another ally—a convert in charge of the governmental bureaucracy.

True to its word, the Carter administration set about righting the deficiencies of nearly a decade of unfulfilled promises. It confirmed the separate Appalachian Trail Project Office and streamlined reporting arrangements right to the top of the National Park Service and the Department of the Interior. An acquisition staff of some fifty lands professionals was engaged and, again, set apart from the normal Park Service bureaucracy. The states were facilitated in their own acquisition efforts by a special allotment of LAWCON funds. While these developments were genuinely welcome, they created additional pressures on the Conference itself. If the volunteer tradition was not to be engulfed by the new bureaucracies, it would have to assert its rightful place in the Trail protection effort. And so the emphasis within ATC began to move away from lobbying and support to more of a direct role in planning, preacquisition, coordination, and even management. Aided by grants from a sympathetic project administration, the Conference's own bureaucracy began to grow too. On-the-Trail-education expanded, staff professionals and volunteers began to play central roles in the definition of the Trail corridor, and a set of new regional representatives was created with the help of Park Service contract funds to ensure coordination at state and regional levels. Inevitably, the federal contribution to the Conference's operating budget crept up over the 30 percent mark.[533] Despite the reality that federal contracting, the "easy money,"[534] had contributed greatly to the growth of the Conference, the Board of Managers was clearly worried.[535] Would the Conference become just another appendage of the federal government? Would it still be able to express differences of opinion—even litigate against its federal partner if necessary?[536] And if it did not play a direct role in the authorized National Scenic Trail, how could the volunteer tradition of the Appalachian Trail be sustained? Just who would bear responsibility for managing the federal lands acquired to protect the Trail seemed to be the threshold question. If the ATC did not step forward, it was likely that bureaucracy would begin to close in.[537]

Thus began a remarkable inquiry. Sparked by an able and committed Trail club volunteer, Charles Sloan, and a supportive project manager, David Richie, what came to be called a "partnership committee" was created under the auspices of the Conference. Virtually an executive committee for the Trail, including representation from the Trail community, the federal government, and the states, the committee plunged into a host of issues, especially the uncharted terrain of private management of public lands. When federal managers questioned a possible loss of authority, the federal project manager argued on behalf of a new kind of management partnership. When Trail club leaders spoke of volunteers becoming simply agents of the federal government, the Conference representative stepped forward with reassurances to the contrary. And when states bristled at a possible loss of autonomy to both the federal government and the private Trail community, the state member of the partnership committee circulated an unqualified letter of support to his agency compatriots. The capstone of this unusual effort was, appropriately, a partnership agreement, signed in January of 1984, wherein the National Park Service delegated to the Appalachian Trail Conference the day-to-day responsibility for managing lands outside the boundaries of established federal areas. Thus was born still another "epoch in Appalachian Trail history,"[538] to paraphrase Conference chairman Myron Avery's words forty years earlier— a landmark, psychological commitment by the Park Service in recognition of the management capabilities of the ATC. In a sense, though, the Conference had come full circle to where it was when the Trail idea was first born.

Viewed in retrospect, the Conference has displayed many of the growth characteristics of the classic conservation organization. Put succinctly, it has been successively the player, the coach and, more recently, the player-coach of the Appalachian Trail effort.[539] Like others of its kind, it has owed much to the dedication and energies of a handful of central figures[540] Benton, MacKaye, Myron Avery, and Stanley Murray—each active in the Trail's three principal regions, New England, the mid-Atlantic, and the South. Arising first to provide essentially social opportunities for those interested in trails, the clubs were forced to form a confederation to share talents and apply their collective energies to prosecuting a larger Trail program. The new Conference attracted a sizable constituency and, with it, a concomitant need to organize and strengthen the central institution. Once the goal of a marked and identified Trail had been accomplished, the Conference became conservative and even complacent, dedicated to caring for what it had put in place. With the 1968 National Trails System Act securely on the statute books, it could rest on its laurels, convinced that the protection of the Trail was in safe hands. But, as events developed, that was not to be the case. The shortcomings of the federal protection effort, coupled with growing evidence of encroachment throughout much of the Trail's course, reinvigorated the Conference. Provident and compelling voices were heard, and opportunities for new leadership arose. The Conference responded by professionalizing, occupying a central place in the planning and protection programs, and ultimately assuming a direct role in management, one that it could not have won without having such professional credentials.

Like many such organizations, the specific and central mission—securing a protected, interconnected footpath for the entire length of the

Appalachians—had broadened over the years to become one of general conservation. This was manifest in the growing interest in an Appalachian greenway, an accompanying belt of controlled and cared-for lands not just for the hiker, but for the regions generally through which the Trail passed. A new mission had materialized which promised to capture the attention of the Conference for many years to come. There would be hazards associated with this new program effort, among them the risk that the simple and compelling objective of the footpath itself would become diffused by a larger environmental effort. If so, the Conference could lose its hard-core and dedicated constituency and its sense of institutional definition.

Yet, fate had intervened once again to make that event unlikely in the foreseeable future. A new national inquiry had been launched under the auspices of the President's Commission on Americans Outdoors.[541] Lands adjacent to established parks and new forms of working agreements between federal, state, and private partners were high on the list of topics to be explored.[542] The Appalachian Trail and its private Conference represented exactly such an experiment. It was likely that the Commission would come to share Benton MacKaye's views, conveyed to the nineteenth Trail Conference meeting in Plymouth, New Hampshire, in June of 1972: "Thus far you have wrought well; you have turned dream into fact—a program on paper into an institution on its feet."[543] A decade and a half later, that assessment was still an accurate one.

THE APPALACHIAN NATIONAL SCENIC TRAIL ADVISORY COUNCIL

A second participant warranting attention and analysis is the Appalachian National Scenic Trail Advisory Council (ANSTAC), created by section 5(a)(3) of the National Trails System Act of 1968 (P.L. 90-543). Composed of thirty-five representatives drawn from federal and state agencies and Trail club interests, and appointed by the secretary of the interior for fixed, five-year terms, the early ANSTAC was a classic federal advisory committee, destined to be seen and not heard.[544] Its titular parent, the Department of the Interior, was largely indifferent to its existence. The receiving agency for its advice, the National Park Service, had never been keen about institutions of this sort.[545] At times, Washington appeared not to know what to do with the new Advisory Council.[546] To the state members, nominated by their governors after prodding from the outside, the institution was hardly earthshaking.[547] ANSTAC seemed to be dominated by private Trail club interests; it had no real role or function; and it could do little to help the states meet their burgeoning outdoor recreation responsibilities. Consequently, the states' was a watchful kind of participation. It paid to keep an eye on the federal presence to ensure that what had traditionally been a state and private responsibility did not blossom into a full-fledged federal venture.[548] How ANSTAC emerged as an institution initially is worth considering for a moment.

The early Hoch legislation contained no such body. The Trail Conference itself was deemed to be the one to provide the outside advice. It was Sen. Gaylord Nelson's legislative assistant, Fred Madison, architect of the principal Appalachian Trail bill, who seems to have seized upon the idea of a formal advisory body. The Advisory Council, he told the Potomac Appalachian Trail Club, should be more than an auxiliary arm of the Park Service and must play a role in the development of the National Scenic Trail far beyond what is described in the legislation. To its members will fall much of the responsibility for mobilizing local support for Trail maintenance and development. "The Advisory Council," he said, "can, if it wants, set the tone for the program."[549] True to his convictions, Madison saw to it that a formal advisory mechanism was contained in the Johnson administration's National Trails System Act. There was no difficulty because, by this time, public participation was in vogue nationally.

During the transition years, the Advisory Council fell far short of Madison's standards. The meetings were poorly attended and largely superficial events.[550] With Trail maintenance in the safe hands of its member clubs, the ATC could have played more of a direct role in ANSTAC but did not do so.[551] Constituted as a token and largely ignored, the Council disappeared without a trace in 1973 in the wake of the controversy over the role of federal advisory committees in general. Interior's seeming indifference to ANSTAC and the Trail led to indignation on the part of the Trail community. Even the states were stirred to protest. Lack of action to protect the Trail but, more important, lack of nonfederal representation in that effort, fueled a growing demand for a congressional overview. The oversight hearings in 1976 finally caught the attention of Interior administrators, and by 1978 the Trail program and its Advisory Council were back on track.

Burned twice by an administrative reluctance to constitute such an advisory body, the Trail community saw to it that the Advisory Council was reauthorized by statutory action in the 1978 amendments to the National Trails System Act. The net result was that ANSTAC was revived, and a more definitive role was charted for it. A revitalized ANSTAC, in turn, helped bring the Trail protection program to the forefront of Interior priorities and elevated the significance of the Trail in the eyes of the National Park Service.[552] Yet the revival came at a price. Although the amendments to the National Trails System Act settled the permanence of the Advisory Council, they also brought about reforms in the composition of ANSTAC. Representatives of other interests were added, and Trail club representatives would no longer be the dominant voices on the Advisory Council.

During the postamendment years, ANSTAC became a genuine force for the Trail program. It served as a representative forum for Trail interests;[553] it forged an alliance among the states;[554] it became a constructive sounding-board for Park Service and Trail Conference program initiatives;[555] and it ultimately validated all such decisions.[556] Lacking direct power to control or to intervene, the Council had an open license to inquire. And so it did—at its annual meetings and, increasingly, at the regional Council sessions. No participant was exempt from review. At times, ANSTAC was as critical of the states as it was of the federal or private Trail efforts. Without the staff or authority to follow through, ANSTAC posed no real threat to anyone. Yet, because of the representation it enjoyed, neither could it quite be ignored. Cumbersome and time consuming though the Council's involvement might be, there was always the hope that its support would be helpful, and the corresponding view that to overlook it could become fatal.[557] Sensing that degree of ambivalence, AT project manager David Richie was not averse to using ANSTAC upon occasion to prevent the Park Service from becoming too involved bureaucratically in the Trail.[558]

The result was that ANSTAC literally blossomed. Fresh faces appeared. New leadership emerged in the wake of the decision to move to a nongovernmental chairman. ANSTAC was clearly not just an auxiliary arm of the National Park Service.[559] A heady period of virtual independence ensued, nurtured by a sympathetic project manager and a time of heightened opportunities. One such opportunity was the need to develop state constituencies for the Trail program. State concurrence would be necessary if there was to be an orderly transition to an enlarged federal effort. The move to obtain additional resources for those states willing to take action, through a special contingency fund allocation for Trail protection purposes, helped the Advisory Council develop a state membership that was strong and committed. But leadership from ANSTAC was also needed to obtain the political base necessary for a heightened federal commitment to the trail.[560] The full gamut of legislative and budgetary changes required gave ANSTAC a full agenda to work from during the postamendment years. The business at hand was always fresh and challenging.

Still another set of opportunities emerged from what was beginning to happen along key sections of the Trail. Private ownerships were changing, and development pressures threatened to reverse literally decades of painstaking efforts to secure a continuous Trail corridor. ANSTAC was thus forced into serving as a policy forum for a number of pressing Trail issues: physical encroachments, corridor definition and planning, conflicts in Trail management and usage, and the general philosophy of managing the Trail and its associated environments.

As if the above were not enough, ANSTAC had to play an active role in the ambitious acquisition program authorized by the 1978 amendments. In addition to general oversight, it helped sort out federal and state acquisition priorities and the organizational mechanisms necessary to ensure federal-state and public-private cooperation of the first order. It was called upon to mediate differences among the principal actors, ventilating corridor location and acquisition disputes and lending its support to the most promising approaches. Through a regular reporting system, it also kept a weather eye on the ambitious timetable for action. And in close conjunction with the Appalachian Trail Conference and its allies on Capitol Hill, ANSTAC lent its official presence to the lobbying effort to ensure that funds were available to accomplish the program authorized by Congress.

In later years, it was time to consider how the Trail would be managed once it had been protected.[561] ANSTAC was a good forum for these discussions, too, since it represented all of the principal actors. The philosophy and principles of management, not just the mechanisms, needed to be thought through carefully. Management for whom, by whom, to what degree, and to what end occupied ANSTAC's attention at numerous regional and national sessions. Monitoring current issues, problems, and accomplishments made it certain that the management discussions would have a ring of reality to them. The actual devices for management, such as partnerships and cooperative agreements, were potentially legion. A persistent issue was the extent to which the National Park Service's systemwide regulations, such as prohibitions against hunting and timber harvesting, should be applied and enforced within this special unit of the national parks.[562] Throughout it all, ANSTAC expressed a general sense of the need for innovation and experimentation in dealing with the Trail, a sentiment that was reinforced by the legislative record of the National Trails System Act. Consensus on management came slowly and often incrementally, the end product of many agenda discussions on many individual management issues. And so when ANSTAC was finally called upon to affirm the delegation of management responsibility to the Appalachian Trail Conference, there was virtually no opposition.

Like all such organizations, ANSTAC's activities were, at times, contrived. With the help of a nongovernmental chairman, and the blessings of a supportive federal officer from the Department of the Interior, a "shadow cabinet" began to take shape composed of key individuals from the Project Office, the Trail Conference, and the states, the forerunner of what later came to be called the partnership committee, and it was this group that was largely responsible for shaping ANSTAC's activities and representations. There was much to be done to remedy nearly a decade of indifference and neglect. For example, there was the need to develop state constituencies for the Trail and to negotiate the delicate transition from state to federal responsibility. The price would be one final carrot to the states, it was decided—a special allocation of LAWCON funds to help those states that were willing to play a direct role in the protection of the Trail. There was also a need to secure a heightened federal commitment to the Trail. While the administrative and Congressional winds of change seemed soft and favorable, they needed to be translated into concrete evidence of support—appropriations, staff, and program expenditures.

There were also emerging policy problems warranting ANSTAC's careful attention—substantive matters that could affect the vitality of the Trail program for many years to come. Threats to the Trail in such places as western New England, the mid-Atlantic region, and northern Virginia were likely to produce permanent discontinuities unless remedied promptly. This issue raised the question of which objective should take precedence—good relations with adjacent landowners or the long-term needs of the Trail. Where and how large the protected corridor should be was a subset of that problem.[563] The question had to be answered before lands could be acquired. Trail maintenance and management standards were equally thorny matters warranting concerted attention. If excessive, they could exceed the capacities of the clubs and destroy the traditional fabric of Trail-maintaining organizations. But the overriding issue was a philosophical one, the proper division of roles and responsibilities among public and private participants. For all of these matters, the democratic structure of ANSTAC could be employed successfully. The setting for the discussions was almost inspirational at times.[564] Trail-wide topics were identified, assigned to working groups, reviewed first at regional Council meetings, and later brought to ANSTAC for final resolution. The process ensured careful attention to complex issues; it also provided a precedent for a true partnership of interests that would result in the 1984 management delegation agreement.

Perhaps the wisest decision made early on by ANSTAC was to recognize the reality that the Appalachian Trail, though a single footpath, traversed many different regions. The concept of subregionalization was hardly foreign to the participants, because the Appalachian Trail Conference was itself organized into six districts (later three regions). The Trail could and should never be homogenized, all agreed. The geographic and environmental diversity displayed and the mix of managing entities already in place dictated otherwise. As examples, the South's heavy reliance on large federal ownerships, such as the national forests and national parks, contrasted sharply with the predominantly private nature of the Trail in portions of the mid-Atlantic and New England regions. The subsequent creation of regional Councils for the southern, mid-Atlantic, and New England sections ensured that ANSTAC's policies would be fine-tuned to the problems of a given region.

It also kept the annual ANSTAC agenda from becoming unduly cluttered with local issues. But the reverse was also true. The regional Councils furnished a common framework to look at problems systemwide, such as relocations and maintenance standards. The three regional Council sessions held annually had the effect of enlarging ANSTAC's meeting schedule to a quarterly basis, thereby enhancing the sense of meaningful participation. In so doing, they provided an antidote to the more cumbersome group meetings of the full ANSTAC, enabling its members to meet at least once in small working sessions and providing a sense of intimacy and relevance to the discussions. This was particularly useful when land acquisition was the primary concern of the Trail community.[565]

In later years, the formal regional Council meetings were abandoned, victims primarily of budgetary exigencies but also of the growing time demands on a small project staff. Nevertheless, to this very day, ANSTAC still follows the practice of allocating a portion of its regular meetings to concurrent regional sessions. It has also encouraged its working partner, the Appalachian Trail Conference, to incorporate the spirit of regionalization into its own management approach to the Trail.[566] The three regional management committees established by ATC have tended to mirror the ANSTAC experience and are generally regarded as constructive developments. The substitution of ATC's regional management committees for the Councils has reduced the sense of competition with ANSTAC. It has also made the ATC less parochial about involving others in the Trail program.[567]

As an institution, ANSTAC has certainly contributed to a successful Appalachian Trail program. It provided ready access to the higher echelons of state government and, thereby, ensured a higher level of state involvement.[568] It brought structure to a very complex constituency and provided a process for getting ideas out and implemented.[569] With its geographic representation, and its mix of individuals and backgrounds, ANSTAC has become a fitting forum to debate problems, issues, and policies, at the same time maintaining a sense of equilibrium among partners. Over the years, it became skillful at building dialogue and understanding, serving as the principal conduit for problem solving along the Trail.[570] Interest and attendance have remained high. This has been particularly true of the states, for, unlike the Trail club representatives, who had their own Trail Conference to fall back on, the states had no vehicle other than ANSTAC to utilize for policy discussions.[571] Traveling to the geographically dispersed annual and regional Council meetings, state representatives found a ready way to meet and talk to each other, and they came to genuinely welcome the interchange and to respect the institution. The meetings contributed important building blocks of experience.[572] They also began to learn more about trails from the hiking community, for, in truth, few of the state officials had experienced trails personally. Friendships began to develop between the state representatives and Trail club members. The result was a heightened spirit of camaraderie, a renewal of contacts for the Trail community, and a less parochial and increasingly united voice for the Trail, which could be put to work politically.[573] With almost a third of the congressional membership from Appalachian Trail states, an ANSTAC view could be advanced readily, as was the case with annual appropriations requests.

ANSTAC's relationship with the ATC has also been a generally positive one over the years. In the early period, the dominance of ATC members was such that a sense of virtual ownership prevailed.[574] They were anxious to exercise their traditional sphere of influence, but lacked the clout to bring in state members directly. ANSTAC thereupon became the ATC's primary instrument to reach the Park Service policymakers and the states. But Interior's dominance of the early Council proved to be a blessing in disguise. Although the first ANSTAC was significantly flawed, it forced the Trail clubs and the states to work together. When ANSTAC subsequently failed, so did the ATC's and the states' leading channel of influence. ANSTAC's revival in 1975 received substantial impetus from individual members of the ATC but, at times, posed a sense of competition, assuaged by David Richie's assiduous reassurances to the contrary. The real test came in 1981 when the number of ATC appointments to the Advisory Council was much reduced. At the time, there was serious talk about a lawsuit to ensure the "sufficient representation" guaranteed the Conference by statute.[575] To their credit, the state representatives provided a steady anchor until the Trail club balance could be restored.[576] At this stage, ANSTAC emerged as an institution in its own right. Nevertheless, the synergism between ATC and ANSTAC continued to be largely positive. Out of the sense of rivalry was spun a new enthusiasm.[577] By elevating the interest and attention to the Trail generally, ANSTAC was able to create a climate of concern in which the ATC could operate successfully.

Among other attributes, ANSTAC enjoyed a license to inquire and explore, unfettered by specific operating responsibilities. It could, thus, serve as a force for change. Yet, the nature of the institution was sufficiently cumbersome, and the procedures it employed often so involved, that it constituted only the most conservative of change instruments,[578] even during the expansive Carter years. At times, it performed a valuable service by actually keeping the program from moving too fast. ANSTAC's most important contribution was to assure a measure of program continuity. At no time was this need more urgent than during the rapid changes in national policy taking place from the Carter to the Reagan administrations.

But other values aside, the real strength of ANSTAC was its utility as a validating mechanism.[579] Once agreement had been reached, a confirming resolution of the Advisory Council could provide a tangible manifestation of accord. With its broad representation, an ANSTAC decision had a convincing ring of reality to it. It could apply substantial moral suasion to any involved party.[580]

Nevertheless, the Advisory Council was not without its share of difficulties. Thirty-five members strong, it was, at best, a cumbersome institution. "It was like the United Nations at times," the Forest Service's Raymond Housley recalled. "I was never sure I would be able to get air time. But you always had a chance to hear what was on people's minds directly."[581] Beyond sheer numbers, the range of viewpoints represented was bound to be as troublesome as it was constructive. With the Appalachian Trail now firmly sanctified in legislative form, perhaps ANSTAC no longer needed to be so large, nor so dutifully representative.[582] And over the years, much of the Council's leadership energy seemingly had to be directed toward securing each new charter and a full complement of secretarial appointments. Subject to administrative whim every two years, ANSTAC was essentially a fragile instrument, ripe to be snuffed out by any indifferent administration. Here, the benefits of a broad oversight mandate worked to its disadvantage, for, without a clear mission to perform, the Council could always be termed superfluous to the Trail protection program. However, without a Council, there would be no way to focus all of the myriad interests on the Trail as a whole.[583]

Like all such organizations, ANSTAC seemed to rest on its laurels once the acquisition program had been launched. It had a tendency to rubber-stamp the actions of the Project Office and the ATC.[584] Unlike the earlier days, when ANSTAC was talking about the serious issues,[585] Council members now came together agreeably to review progress and to enact supportive resolutions. Status enhancement, rather than serious consultation, was the order of the day. At least momentarily, the primary cutting edge seemed to be gone. To be sure, flurries of issues would arise upon occasion, such as the wholesale turnout of the previous nongovernmental members when the Reagan administration came into office. There was not as much change as everyone had feared. The new breed of political appointee, rather than threatening the program, actually invigorated it.[586] And the periodic experimentation with a federal and a nonfederal chairman seemed to come down firmly on the side of the desirability of independent leadership for the Advisory Council.

But for a complex project like the Appalachian Trail, it would only be a matter of time before ANSTAC's deliberative capacities would be needed again. A number of straws were in the wind. The ATC's Laurence Van Meter was preparing to move on to another assignment. Project manager David Richie, after a decade of shepherding the Trail program, was close to retirement.[587]

The choice of his successor, the nature of the next assignment, and the style of operation could be crucial. A more authoritarian, chain-of-command presence could materially affect the open and democratic process of decision making enjoyed to date.[588] And in the age of management, there was growing interest by ANSTAC in what should be done at the margins of the official Trail corridor[589]—an inquiry not unlike the earlier greenway concept. Indeed, the whole matter of the control of adjacent land usage had become a priority topic for discussion nationally by the new President's Commission on Americans Outdoors, a development that presaged a time ripe for new ideas.

For ANSTAC too, it might be an occasion for fresh faces and fresh ideas.[590] At the least, its capacities would continue to be needed to mediate the split over where and how large the Trail corridor should be. With new agenda items to contend with, ANSTAC's composition might have to change too. Individuals with land management, not policy expertise, would be needed.[591] They would likely be lower-level governmental representatives, not agency administrators. A higher level of consistency in appointments would also be necessary.

In summary, ANSTAC had proved to be no better an institution than its membership, no more accomplished than the caliber of its leadership, and no more useful than the context of the times.[592] If put to work, it could perform constructive—even vital—service. If ignored, it could become a burden and even an impediment. It was both the symbol and the mechanism of the working partnership that had come to distinguish the Appalachian Trail.[593] Overall, the Trail had become a better project for ANSTAC's input, most observers agreed. It had given professionals the sense that, collectively, they could get some things done.[594] The clear consensus was that the Advisory Council was a valued part of the Trail program, was getting better as time went on by virtue of the improved diversity and caliber of members, and should be continued.[595]

THE APPALACHIAN TRAIL PROJECT OFFICE

Throughout much of the Trail protection effort, the institution of central importance has been the National Park Service's Project Office for the Appalachian Trail. But in the early days, responsibility for the Trail was lodged in a purely volunteer organization, the Appalachian Trail Conference, or in individual jurisdictions (e.g., state or national forests and parks) through which the Trail passed. Before examining the Project Office in some detail, its predecessors are deserving of a measure of comment and review.

During the first four decades of Trail activity, largely under state and private auspices, it was only logical that institutional arrangements would be largely ad hoc in character. The primary thrust was to locate, mark, and establish the Trail on the ground, tasks that required decentralization to local participants. The net result was an interconnected Trail, but one with varying standards. Recognizing the need for some degree of uniformity, the Appalachian Trail Conference established the volunteer position of Trails Coordinator, who regularly reported on the condition of the Trail, especially sections where relocations had occurred, in issues of the *Trailway News*[596] The ATC also served as the central mechanism for awarding Trail maintenance segments among its member clubs. A reward of sorts was provided, for these Class A maintaining clubs received voting privileges in return—one voting member for every ten miles of Trail maintained. The vexing matter of varying standards was approached through still another volunteer channel, the creation of a special committee on trail standards.[597]

Following passage of the National Trails System Act in 1968, the National Park Service won the assignment in the East for what would be a new system of national scenic trails. In the case of the Appalachian Trail, the Park Service also inherited an ongoing network of management participants, both private and public. Reading into the act largely oversight and court-of-last-resort responsibilities, it chose to concentrate on the tangible mandate to lay out and survey an official Appalachian Trail route. These tasks could be performed under contract or through inside agency staff; they did not seem to require a formal management institution.[598]

Further, although the *Trails for America* report was titularly a product of the Department of Interior, the real authorship belonged to a different Interior agency, the Bureau of Outdoor Recreation, which was championing its provisions.[599] Many of the traditional Park Service professionals were troubled by the BOR-promoted emphasis on trails, fearing a siphoning of support away from the classic natural national parks, the heartbeat of the national park system.[600] These new kinds of parks threatened to blur the conventional management structure—a clearly bounded area under the full control of a superintendent. Though never overtly opposed by the Park Service hierarchy, they just did not seem to fit. In the case of the Appalachian Trail, two thousand miles long and barely two hundred feet wide, the management implications were not only unfamiliar but potentially horrendous.[601] The National Park Service, on the whole, was grateful to play a reduced role in the Trail's prosecution and to lean as heavily as possible on the established presence of state and Trail club interests.

A diminished institutional presence for the Trail was further mandated by the tenor of the times. Ever since the passage of the milestone Cape Cod National Seashore legislation in 1961,[602] which created the precedent for national park units bought and paid for with federal funds, the National Park Service had been swept up in a heady period of parks expansion and recreation development. The agency was hard-pressed as never before to keep pace with the demands for new parks and expanded facilities. A complex and potentially cumbersome project such as the Appalachian Trail just was not a priority for the nation's premier park agency.

Nevertheless, the Park Service had been given a job to do by Congress which could not be ignored. The task of shepherding the first official actions fell to Richard L. Stanton,[603] a career professional operating under the general oversight of Robert Moore, associate director for operations, under whose official aegis the land acquisition effort and the chairmanship of ANSTAC fell. Elmer V. Buschman, the Park Service's jack-of-all-trades in legal and procedural matters, was enlisted in the effort to sort out the steps required to formally establish the Trail. But it was Stanton, a former navy land acquisition specialist with the requisite engineering skills for the job, who really took charge. There were three jobs to be done: delineate the Trail, develop guidelines, and activate ANSTAC.

Blunt, forthright and, at all times politically savvy, the new project officer operated out of the Park Service's land acquisition office in Philadelphia. His aerial survey of the Trail, using ground control markers placed on the Trail by volunteers, was an imaginative and cost-effective approach to the difficult task of defining the route. Guidelines for the Trail emerged at the eleventh hour, largely the labor of Stanley Murray, one of Stanton's secret weapons.[604] They provided a regulatory framework, for the first time, with a degree of articulateness and integrity, but one lacking much public involvement or interest outside of the immediate Trail community.

In the course of the assignment, Stanton developed an abiding affection for the Trail.[605] This was nurtured by his own predilection for what he called "the special sense of adventure" of trails, rivers, and canals and his longstanding relationship with the leadership of the Potomac Appalachian Trail Club. To the extent he could, Stanton tried to keep ANSTAC's spirits alive, serving a term himself as ANSTAC chairman until reassignment to the National Capital Region of the Park Service. Even there, he managed to keep his hand in on Trail matters whenever possible. Stanton's handpicked successor, surveyor Edgar Gray, seemed ideal for the job because of the massive relocations that lay ahead for the trail.[606] A managerial chairman could come later. Lulled by a sense of false security that the job had been done, Stanton felt free to move on to other Park Service assignments.

Following completion of the establishment and regulatory phases mandated by the 1968 act, the Appalachian Trail program, however, fell into disarray. For a while, nobody noticed.[607] A strict reading of the act, fortified by the Park Service's decision to give the states a wide berth to accomplish protection on their own, meant that the immediate federal role would be diminished. It was only logical that the federal presence would be minimal too.

Transfers of key personnel to other assignments compounded the problem. And when ANSTAC itself lapsed, caught up in the swirl of debate over the proper role of Federal advisory committees, the last official voice for the Trail disappeared—so much so that Interior assistant secretary Nathaniel Reed, when confronted by a questioning House oversight subcommittee,[608] was hard-pressed to find a locus of responsibility within his own bureaucracy. The Trail was at a nadir within the National Park Service.[609]

There was a rush to remedy the situation. A new professional had to be found to staff the program. The Park Service nominated David A. Richie for the assignment, an individual with full-time responsibilities already as deputy regional director of the North Atlantic Regional office. Richie was given collateral responsibility for the Trail, and a small Trail office was carved out of the former Charlestown Navy Yard in Boston by a reluctant regional director.[610] But the choice of Richie for the job proved to be a stroke of immense good fortune for the Trail. Although he had formal superintendencies to his credit, and was a product of the Park Service mold, Richie turned out to be appreciably different from the conventional Park Service professional— virtually a square peg in a round hole.[611] He was accustomed to working with public interest groups; he was always distrustful of bureaucracy; he was a consensus builder by preference; and, even more important, he was receptive to new ways of accomplishing objectives.[612] That led him to constantly explore within himself, always try to do his best and, ultimately, lean over backwards on behalf of the Trail.[613]

One can only speculate upon what prompted Richie's selection. Unlike the choice of first superintendent for the sensitive Cape Cod National Seashore, which was a conscious and deliberate effort by none other than the director of the National Park Service, the Appalachian Trail assignment seems to have come about through a casual conversation in the hall with NPS Deputy Director Russell Dickenson, Richie recalled.[614] "Dissatisfied with the Trail's moribund status, Dickenson felt that Richie's reputation for working well with community groups and taking on new ventures might be appropriate for the Trail. Richie had no other qualifications for the assignment and, in fact, had hiked the Trail only once while growing up in Pennsylvania and New Jersey. But with the congressional oversight hearings literally in the wings, Richie's prior service as a Congressional Fellow in the mid-1960s with the Senate Interior and Insular Affairs Committee must have been a factor for consideration.[615]

Richie's personal qualities—his stature, persistence, and credibility within the bureaucracy—and his growing rapport with the Trail community were put to work promptly on behalf of the moribund Trail program. As a former superintendent, he could talk persuasively to the operating professionals of the National Park Service. Trained in law, he was familiar with land acquisition and regulatory procedures. An avid runner and, increasingly, user of the Trail, his natural affinity for the Trail community grew correspondingly. Wise in the ways of Capitol Hill, his views on the Trail program and policies were listened to with respect by congressional and committee staff. But the quality that astonished and impressed everyone was Richie's capacity to serve as the touchstone for the Trail, keeping all the pieces together.[616] He was "Everyman."

Richie moved quickly to remedy a working situation he found to be almost impossible.[617] The remnants of the records were still lodged at the Park Service's Eastern Service Center in Philadelphia. They were moved to Boston. A career Park Service employee, Norman Roy, was transferred from Acadia National Park in Maine to provide a measure of temporary staff services. Richie then arranged to meet with ATC chairman Stanley Murray and help him set up a meeting with the Forest Service to discuss troublesome Trail policies in the South. Richie, in turn, was invited to the ATC Board of Managers meeting in Harpers Ferry in November of 1974 where he was put on the spot for the Park Service's lack of progress in protecting the Trail. Their high degree of interest and concern made it only natural that he would want to be responsive. It was clear that Richie's activities were to become the test of the commitment of his agency to the Trail. On his part, despite the many problems at hand and ahead, Richie remembers being filled with enthusiasm. The project appealed to all of his maverick tendencies.[618]

Richie was quick to spot one of the principal problems facing the Trail, the absence of an effective working relationship with the states. The answer appeared to be a revived and vigorous ANSTAC, nearly half of whose membership would come from the states. Richie was astute enough to fortify his own capacities with strong ANSTAC leadership drawn from the states. The prospective chairman, Charles Foster, the former Massachusetts commissioner of natural resources and its first cabinet-level secretary of environmental affairs, would provide an experienced and respected spokesman from the New England region.[619] When Foster suggested a southerner, Virginia state park director Ben Bolen, as vice-chairman, it was clear that the ANSTAC leadership would be well fitted to the delicate task of enlisting state support for a revitalized Trail protection program. The Boone ANSTAC session was a test of that strategy. It passed with flying colors. Subsequently hailed as a threshold occasion,[620] the ANSTAC meeting was where all the parties came together and focused for the first time,[621] and where Richie himself became intellectually engaged with the project once and for all.[622] In short, everything began to come together.[623]

Two other institutional reforms were also necessary to get the Appalachian Trail project firmly back on track. Establishment of a full-scale project office, reporting out of the conventional channels of the Park Service directly to the upper echelons of the NPS and the Department of the Interior, was facilitated by the oversight hearings and by the later decision of the Carter administration to highlight the Trail protection program. This unusual degree of independence was rationalized by the unique nature of the project and the accelerated effort required.[624] But Richie's immediate supervisor, Stanley Albright, the Park Service's associate director from 1981 on, also encouraged that managerial freedom. He respected Richie and found him to be "always very square." Richie, in turn, made a point of keeping Albright up to date. The associate director, plagued with management problems systemwide, was a pragmatist. "If things are going well, leave them alone" was his philosophy. Under Richie, the Trail program seemed to be on the mend. The more elevated the problems became, the harder they were to fix, he had found. Although to date the parade of Park Service directors had never opposed the Trail program directly, none had yet to take a substantial interest in the project.[625]

But separating the land acquisition program for the Trail from the systemwide Park Service lands bureaucracy was more than unusual and created genuine concern within the agency. Here again, a series of fortuitous events intervened to make these reforms possible. Assistant Secretary Robert Herbst took a personal interest in the Trail and cleared it of procedural downfalls. The NPS's associate director James Tobin, concerned about the serious embarrassment of not having specific tracts identified for acquisition, helped orchestrate the coup, with the active assistance of administrative specialist Cleo Layton in the secretary of the interior's office.[626] Herbst assigned to two members of his personal staff, David Hales and David Sherman, the task of monitoring the protection program.

But the die was really cast when the Park Service's able Charles R. Rinaldi, forced to vacate his post as chief of lands for reasons of ill health, agreed to head up the special Appalachian Trail lands office. Seasoned to the unusual from his prior experience on Cape Cod, Rinaldi was intrigued with the project. To meet the ambitious three-year deadline, the project would need what Rinaldi termed a "flow and go" capacity,[627] and he was given it. Rinaldi's stature within the Service was such that he could get away with setting up a virtually independent operation, and his credibility with Congress helped sustain the flow of perfecting legislation and appropriations.[628] But Rinaldi, personally, was another individual almost tailor-made for the Appalachian Trail venture. He combined the toughness of an accomplished professional with the visionary zeal of the most ardent Trail advocate. In the citation accompanying the honorary membership awarded him in 1983 by the Appalachian Trail Conference, his capabilities were summarized well: "a common man with uncommon qualities . . . the quality we most admire and recognize is his integrity."[629] Rinaldi's extraordinary ability to deal with people would assure him a key role throughout. Behind the veneer of pragmatism was a special fondness and caring for the Trail and a genuine appreciation for the idea of accomplishing something really tangible for all time.

With two strong-willed and accomplished professionals charged with Trail protection responsibilities, the program was in good hands. Richie and Rinaldi, both appreciably different from one another but equally idealistic, put their several qualities to work in a complementary fashion. Rinaldi was better at implementation—Richie at stimulation. Rinaldi was always forthright and direct—Richie more inclined toward consensus and compromise (some said changeability)[630] by virtue of his Quaker upbringing. But they invariably did things in a gentlemanly way. On the most sensitive of land acquisition issues, such as the Rev. Evans case in Pennsylvania, all of these qualities would be needed. Richie, in essence, called the shots on what lands to acquire, and Rinaldi took it from there. As manager of the entire Project Office, Richie was technically responsible for Rinaldi, but neither seemed to stand on ceremony.[631] Richie gave Rinaldi substantial authority to act independently, something that a traditional superintendent would have been less inclined to do. But Rinaldi also had collateral reporting responsibilities channeled through the Park Service acquisition bureaucracy. Having established many of them himself in his previous capacity as chief of lands, Rinaldi encountered few impediments.

The second institutional reform necessary was to cement working relations with the private Appalachian Trail Conference. It was critical that the principal actors in the protection effort be kept viable,[632] and the ATC was perhaps the most principal of them all. There would be unending sensitivities in the emerging federal role and a host of problems as landowners were approached for a permanent Trail corridor. While generally supportive of an enhanced federal presence, the Trail club volunteers could not help wonder what it would eventually mean for them. But the unconditional support of the Conference would be essential if Congress was to follow up its $90 million authorization with actual appropriations. And a visible and committed private constituency could be instrumental in Richie's efforts to win policy support within his own bureaucracy.

AT project manager David Richie resolved any uncertainty by moving the Project Office from Boston to Harpers Ferry in January of 1978, a calculated risk in light of the fact that the ATC, though firmly entrenched as a key actor, still did not have its act together on the ground.[633] The Park Service leased a house just around the corner from the ATC headquarters, and communication between the two institutions began to flourish, particularly when Laurence Van Meter acceded to the ATC executive directorship.[634] Proximate to the larger staff capabilities of the ATC and its far-flung network of volunteers, Richie now had ready access to an optional route in carrying out the tasks assigned to the Project Office—contracting such functions to the Appalachian Trail Conference. Though titularly the manager of the Trail protection program, Richie became, in fact, its facilitator. He used the mechanisms of cooperative agreements and contract funds deliberately to strengthen the Conference.[635] And when Rinaldi opened up his administrative office for lands in nearby Martinsburg, the institutional triumvirate became complete.

There was now a way of adjudicating readily the occasional policy differences, such as the size and location of the corridor to be acquired and the accommodations to be extended to the landowners involved. The latter was an especially sensitive issue because of the Trail community's long tradition of working cooperatively with landowners. Rinaldi, whom Richie had placed in charge of both planning and acquisition, felt that Trail club representatives exercised too much tunnel vision and had a tendency to overcompromise the Trail.[636] They were so close to the landowners that the corridor design often lacked long-term integrity. Yet, others felt differently. The Park Service, it was said, was too hard-nosed at times, especially about relocating the Trail away from roadsides, and tended to go too much for the ultimate experience.[637] It was no accident that the equally sensitive and critical debate over the future management of the Trail subsequently took place in the supportive environs of Harpers Ferry.

A good example of the innovation and teamwork was the statutory responsibility given the Park Service for preparing a comprehensive plan. Instead of selecting a conventional park planner and following the procedures spelled out in the NPS-2 planning manual, Richie turned first to a veteran forest supervisor, Lawrence Henson, and then to a young professional, Christopher Brown, a former schoolteacher freshly minted from Yale's graduate-level School of Forestry and Environmental Studies.[638] He placed Brown under contract with the Appalachian Trail Conference to reinforce the cooperative nature of the assignment. Out the window went the conventional environmental impact assessment and the cumbersome process of public hearings. In their place was substituted nearly a year and a half of close consultation, Trail-wide, with public and private interests in order to get a true sense of what the plan should be. Rather than statistics, fact, and proscription, Brown was advised to incorporate description, tradition, and what some called "poetry"—an effort to capture the soul of the Trail. It was six drafts later that a version of the comprehensive plan could be distributed for review. The tension between proscriptive and general language was apparently just right, for, to this day, the comprehensive plan remains a valid instrument guiding both the acquisition phases and the current cooperative management system. In later years, Brown admitted to being disappointed by the lack of substantive comment on the draft plan, but, in truth, it was evidence that he had done his job well. The plan had captured the convictions of the Trail community, and they shared a genuine sense of authorship and ownership in the finished product.[639]

And so, what might be said about the contributions of the Appalachian Trail Project Office? They have been central to the success of the protection program, most would agree, providing the means to achieve its objectives, yet also a special kind of glue to combine the disparate Trail interests into a workable whole. With the establishment of a formal Project Office, accountability for the federal side was at last fixed. A sense of direction and purpose emerged, and a central mechanism was available to bridge the gap until a cooperative management structure had been designed and determined. The years of empty promises and unfulfilled expectations were over. At last there was a place with stature, staff, influence, and funds to follow through.

Different kinds of bureaucrats would have functioned more conventionally.[640] It is a measure of both Richie's and Rinaldi's personal qualities that they chose the more difficult and uncertain course to follow, accepting the mixed contributions of volunteers, stressing the importance of partnerships, fanning the flame of experimentation, and validating the sense of history and tradition associated with the Trail. In consequence, their program turned out to be remarkably free of the flavor of government.[641] While their institution made it possible to carry out the initiatives in practice, it was the individuals themselves who really made it happen. As one observer put it,[642] Richie and Rinaldi had an unusual capacity to leave behind their federal baggage and address issues in terms of the people expressing the problem.

THE FOREST SERVICE

Much has been made of the historic competition between Interior and Agriculture agencies over the management of the federal public lands. Indeed, the rivalry between the National Park Service and the Forest Service has become part of the folk tradition of Washington.[643] Conflict is alleged to be rooted in the early placement of the forest reserves within the Department of Agriculture, not the Department of the Interior, and in the fact that many of the first national parks and monuments were carved out of lands administered by the Forest Service. The rivalry achieved particular force and color during the celebrated conflict between Secretary of the Interior Harold Ickes and Forest Service champion Gifford Pinchot over the proper placement of land management functions within the federal bureaucracy.[644] It subsided during the Kennedy and Johnson administrations when Secretaries Orville

Freeman and Stewart Udall of the Departments of Agriculture and Interior, respectively, forged what was described as the "Peace of the Potomac,"[645] an agreement honored more in the letter than in the breach, however.[646] Differences in philosophy and approach practiced by the two agencies have continued into recent times. Outdoor recreation is one such example.

As early as 1902, Gifford Pinchot's "Use Book" for the National Forest Reserves,[647] the precursor of the present day Forest Service Manual, observed that the value of the national forests as "playgrounds for people" was "well worth considering". The Forest Service has done just that since its first recreation appropriation was received in 1915 (an authorization that, in fact, predated the Park Service's own 1916 organic act).[648] For the fifty years of their history, the National Park Service and the Forest Service engaged in a lively competition for the federal recreation responsibility. The Forest Service's interest stemmed, in part, from the growing national interest in the recreational use of the national forests, which generally brought plaudits and thanks from the public, but also a pragmatic need to stem the tide of administrative and legislative transfers of Forest Service lands to the National Park Service. On its part, the rivalry with the Forest Service spurred the Park Service to protect itself by forging alliances with private sector organizations, framing a distinct mission, and developing a wide base of support drawn from the commercial and intellectual elite.[649] It did so by claiming that the Forest Service was so committed to commodity interests that it could not perform the recreation mission evenhandedly. Passage of the Parks, Parkway, and Recreation Act of 1936, which assigned to the National Park Service the preeminent responsibility for recreation planning on all federal lands, seemed to settle the jurisdictional dispute once and for all. But it was not to be.

Swept up in a preoccupation with the upgrading of its own system through Mission 66, the Park Service largely neglected its external responsibilities for recreation. The report of the Outdoor Recreation Resources Review Commission, published in 1962,[650] made note of that oversight, relegating to the Park Service only a modest role in the nation's future outdoor recreation program. Further dissatisfaction with the Park Service's limited view of recreation led Secretary of the Interior Stewart Udall to favor the creation of a special Interior agency, the Bureau of Outdoor Recreation, to take responsibility for the new national recreation effort authorized by the Outdoor Recreation Program Act (1963) and the Land and Water Conservation Fund Act (1964).[651]

Although deliberately exempted from actual land management functions, the BOR entered the bureaucratic arena as a potential rival to both the National Park Service and the Forest Service. The primary weapon at its disposal was its central role in overseeing distributions from the Land and Water Conservation Fund, the lifeblood of state and federal acquisition projects. Its subsidiary weapon was its influence with the states in administering their share of the LAWCON apportionments, and the political leverage that function represented. With the appointment of Edward Crafts, a career Forest Service professional, as the first director of the BOR, the age-old rivalry between the Forest Service and the Park Service threatened to erupt again.[652]

But the environmental concerns of the late 1960s and early 1970s intervened, forcing both agencies to concentrate on their own responses to a larger set of questions. While the Park Service was struggling with an accommodation of its traditional mission to the new public concerns for the urban environment and for ecosystem management, the Forest Service was moving more readily to adapt its multiple-use management philosophy to the new imperatives. What was described as a classic pas de deux between the two agencies subsided into a wary respect for the ability of the other to stir up mischief.[653] Caught up in the expansionist era of the executive branch agencies, each was too busy with its own problems to engage in overt rivalry.

But the Appalachian Trail was a place where interagency conflict could well break out again. The Trail crossed the boundaries of four national parks and eight national forests, each with its own administrative system, operating procedures, and regulations. As an example, although the National Trails System Act assigned to the Department of the Interior the primary responsibility for overseeing the entire Appalachian Trail program, the Trail was already embedded deeply within the functional management plans developed for each national forest. The supervisors had priorities for their forests other than trails. They were concerned about the operational conflicts of a superimposed national scenic trail and felt threatened by the prospect.[654] But rather than becoming rivals, the federal agencies joined forces in a remarkable display of accord. The BOR released funds regularly to the Forest Service for the acquisition of priority inholdings and, in later years, accorded Forest Service and Park Service funding requests a consistently high priority in budgetary recommendations under the Land and Water Conservation Fund program. And, during the uncertain years up to the 1978 amendments, it was the Forest Service that really sustained most of the activity in protecting the Trail. In fact, at a particular moment of desperation in dealing with his own bureaucracy, AT project manager David Richie gave serious consideration to having the responsibility for Trail-wide acquisition reassigned to the Forest Service.[655] Whereas the Park Service could never visualize the Trail as a continuous whole, and was reluctant throughout, the Forest Service seemed to understand that a project of this sort might work, particularly through a cooperative management system.[656]

Along the way, there were many opportunities for the agencies to reassert their historic rivalries. Although the Forest Service received generally high marks from the Trail community for its acquisition efforts, it was in trouble on other fronts. In the South, for example, the management plans for certain forests (such as Tract 22 in the Nantahala National Forest) seemed to threaten the Trail environment with extensive tree cutting and road building.[657] In New England, a reverse problem had erupted—the proposed assignment of the Bristol Cliffs area of the Green Mountain National Forest to pristine status as a wilderness, which might exclude trail use.[658] Among systemwide issues, there was concern that the Forest Service was preparing to back away from its earlier commitment to the broad Trail corridor incorporated in the 1938 Appalachian Trailway Agreement.[659] And central to Trail groups throughout its length was the question of whether the Trail system would be overbuilt in the interest of accommodating the widest possible range of users, the Forest Service's opinion of its responsibilities under the law.[660]

Viewed in retrospect, the generally cordial relations that developed among federal agencies were the result of a number of factors. Under the terms of the National Trails System Act, the responsibility for long trails was divided evenly—the Forest Service in the West (the Pacific Crest Trail), and the National Park Service in the East (the Appalachian Trail). Further, both agencies were fundamentally composed of professional land managers.[661] Delegation of responsibility to decentralized field administrations was the accepted practice for each. Even the Bureau of Outdoor Recreation was privy to that tradition, for many of its senior administrators were former Park Service or Forest Service professionals. Beyond these factors, the parallel relationships existing with individual states and Trail clubs complicated head-on rivalries and made it unlikely that there would ever be a full-scale confrontation. However, occasions such as the 1975 Boone Appalachian Trail Conference,[662] when the ATC passed resolutions praising the Forest Service and condemning the Park Service, were used to put the slumbering rivalry to constructive use. Interior officials were awakened to the need for concerned attention to the Trail's problems. As perceived by others, what they had done until then just was not good enough.[663]

But by far the most important ingredients were the personal relationships that emerged between key federal officials involved in the Trail. Even if they did not participate directly in Appalachian Trail affairs, the body language of these policy administrators encouraged their subordinates to be constructive.[664] For example, there was Raymond F. Housley, the deputy chief of the Forest Service for the national forests, who had previously headed its nationwide recreation program and had developed a personal affinity for the Trail program. Brought up in New Mexico, and strongly influenced by Colorado State University's J. V. K. Wagar, a modern Aldo Leopold, Housley had an unusual degree of respect for the noncommodity uses of the forest. When the Forest Service reassigned the Trail away from engineering to recreation, it brought in a cast of characters who were genuinely interested and committed. Maurice ("Red") Arnold, the regional director of the Bureau of

Outdoor Recreation for the Northeast, was another seasoned bureaucrat who worked well with both Park Service and Forest Service professionals. Arnold became intrigued with and committed to the Trail too.[665]

More than any other individual, however, AT project manager David Richie made the alliance an effective one. A good listener, he had a quiet, understated way of working with people.[666] Exposed to Forest Service programs from his Mount Rainier National Park experience in the West, Richie carried with him none of the usual interagency baggage.[667] Neither hidebound nor tradition-bound, he became not the Park Service's, but everyone's man for the Trail, one participant recalled.[668] In Richie's view, the cooperation of the Forest Service was a vital and essential part of the Appalachian Trail effort. Richie put these convictions to the test in a remarkable move. He invited the Forest Service to assign a senior management professional to the Project Office to head up the management planning for the Trail. In this fashion, Lawrence W. Henson, the forest supervisor of the Ozark National Forest, who knew generally about the Trail but had never been on it, joined the staff on a two-year special assignment.[669] There were some risks involved, Associate Chief Raymond Housley recalled, but as a career professional, the Forest Service was certain that Henson would not give away the farm.[670]

"It happened, I believe, absolutely coincidentally," Henson remarked later on.[671] In 1977, he was finishing up a seven-year term as forest supervisor and ready for a fresh challenge. With eight separate national forests crossed by some eight hundred miles of the Appalachian Trail, the Forest Service was understandably anxious to have the agency represented in the Trail program. But it was AT project manager David Richie who ended up asking for the assignment of a top Forest Service professional. "He thought he could get more done with a guy with green underwear," an observer later remarked.[672]

Henson's assignment, ostensibly, was the preparation of the comprehensive plan specified by Congress. But he became an ace troubleshooter for the Trail, advising the Project Office on landowner timber-cutting reservations, helping negotiate with the Solicitor's Office in both Agriculture and Interior, and pacifying his fellow Forest Service supervisors and other professionals. "It was pure motherhood and the American flag – all good stuff," Henson recalled. "They were a great crew to work with."[673] He found the Park Service materially different than the Forest Service – top professionals, too, but less hierarchically disciplined than the Forest Service where decisions seemed to emerge rather than be made.[674] He was constantly amazed by David Richie's knack of never offending people and staying in constant touch with key individuals. "The project could have been blasted out of the saddle from any number of quarters at any time," Henson observed.[675] Richie was equally appreciative of Henson's many talents – a wiser head who pulled him back from the brink upon occasion.[676]

When he left the Project a year and a half later, Henson bestowed upon his successor, Christopher Brown, an important legacy—the comprehensive plan premise that the Trail should be managed in harmony with the lands through which it passes.[677] This meant that the Trail was to be an integral part of surrounding land uses, not superimposed upon them. There could, thus, be many management systems, not just a single, uniform, bureaucratized approach. The policy was the first step toward the type of decentralized, cooperative management that emerged later on. But, more than that, it guaranteed a living Trail—one that would interlink different human environments and cultures—and not just provide a footpath for the recreational user. When he was through, Henson's labors had earned one other important dividend for the Trail. The agency's respect for David Richie had enabled him to move the Forest Service without appearing to superimpose Interior's views on it.[678] While this may have caused the Forest Service to abdicate more management responsibility than it should have, Raymond Housley observed later, it had also produced one of the brighter episodes in the relationship of the Forest Service with the Park Service.[679]

THE STATES

The role of the states in Appalachian Trail matters is deserving of close scrutiny. Though it was not to be, theirs could well have become a pivotal contribution. The official route crossed the boundaries of fourteen states. In many of them, trail programs had become an integral part of state governmental outdoor recreation responsibilities. Local Trail clubs and state officials had developed cordial working relationships over the years which augured well for the future of the Appalachian Trail. And nowhere in federal-state relations were the cooperative programs with federal agencies more fully developed than in outdoor recreation, the aftermath of the careful delineation of governmental responsibilities by the 1962 Outdoor Recreation Resources Review Commission report and the passage of the Land and Water Conservation Fund Act in 1964.

In truth, the states had already made significant contributions to the establishment and protection of the Appalachian Trail even before the National Trails System Act became law in 1968. In New York, for example, the first six miles of Trail were cut and marked as early as 1922. Maj. William A. Welch, general manager of the Palisades Interstate Park, was an early leader in the entire Trail movement, presiding over the first Appalachian Trail Conference held in 1925.[680] In Massachusetts, a general trails act was on the statute books as early as 1922, but the isolation of western Massachusetts, where the primary trails were located, meant that little program activity developed.[681] And in Maine, the active cooperation of the Civilian Conservation Corps during the 1930s and 1940s contributed state work crews to cut trails and build shelters and other facilities.[682]

In other portions of the route, state conservation lands represented important building blocks for a systemwide Appalachian Trail. In Vermont, for example, a mosaic of state and federal lands traversed by the Long Trail gave instant status to some one hundred miles of the prospective Appalachian Trail.[683] State forests and reservations in Massachusetts and Connecticut already safeguarded much of the crestline the Trail would follow. The "skylands" of New Jersey, the State Game Commission holdings in Pennsylvania (a place where, regrettably, hunters and hikers did not mix well),[684] and the legislatively protected natural environment area of South Mountain in Maryland represented other significant state contributions, either prospective or already in place. And in Virginia, an enlightened state park commissioner, Ben H. Bolen, was advocating the Appalachian Trail as a major element of his state's total recreation program.[685]

States could also be expected to contribute in more subtle ways. As the central element in political federalism, state government had all the powers necessary to make the Trail a reality. It could raise funds by taxation or bonding; appropriate money; acquire and develop land; and manage, maintain, and enforce any program of use or improvements. Moreover, the power to impose land use controls through zoning and subdivision controls resided fundamentally in the states through their general police powers and could be exercised to ensure a corridor of adjacent, protected, private lands. And as the linchpin between federal and local governments, the states could reach up for technical and financial assistance, and reach down to set standards and guidelines for local action. A central role for the states in protecting the Appalachian Trail thus seemed both desirable and necessary.

The National Trails System Act of 1968 attempted to do just that. While it empowered the secretary of the interior to take responsibility for the designated national scenic trail in the East, the Appalachian Trail, the secretary was to do so only with the advice and assistance of the states and others. A specific section of the act (section 7) empowered the secretary to acquire lands to protect the Trail, but only after state and local governments had failed to do so themselves within two years after selection of the official right-of-way. Yet despite every predisposition and persuasion to the contrary, the states never lived up to the general expectation of a central role in protecting the Appalachian Trail. To be sure, they played a part in the protection program—and, at times, made significant and even crucial contributions—but the real actors were primarily private and federal. Why this was so is a complex but important part of the Appalachian Trail story.

It must be remembered that the major growth in state government took place incrementally.[686] The first agencies came into being at the turn of the century, encouraged in part by the national conservation movement, but also by growing natural resource concerns emerging regionally and locally. In New England, for example, the founding of state conservation agencies was a major objective of private organizations such as the Appalachian Mountain Club, the Society for the Protection of New Hampshire Forests, the (Massachusetts) Trustees of Public Reservations, and the Connecticut Forest and Park Association. Natural resource protection enjoyed a state of genuine urgency in the aftermath of widespread logging and forest fires, and the import of serious insect pests such as the gypsy moth from Europe. The early conservation agencies were established essentially to protect and manage resources. In places like the White Mountains of New England, land acquisition became a major objective for the new bureaucracies, particularly after the Weeks Act of 1911 authorized the establishment of a new system of national forests east of the Mississippi River.

Thus, the earliest state functions came to be tied to pragmatic objectives: the regulation of fish and game; the control of shorelines, harbors, waterways, and natural ponds; the protection of public health; and the safeguarding of forests from fire, disease, and overcutting. The inevitable proliferation of independent, functional agencies led to the first governmental reforms—what came to be called departments of conservation—loose confederations of natural resource agencies coordinated by a single commissioner. But by the late 1940s and early 1950s, bureaucracy had taken hold only too well again. Further government reforms, encouraged by the "Baby Hoover" commissions of that time, modified many of the departments of conservation into departments of natural resources, administered by a commissioner/director with genuine authority, and often insulated from politics by a citizen commission or board.[687]

By the 1960s, another wave of state government involvement in natural resources was underway. The first focus was on water resources, the aftermath of successive periods of drought and floods in the late 1950s. The second stimulus came from the outdoor recreation movement, born during the post–World War II decade. Hitherto unheard-of sums began to be appropriated and spent for the acquisition and development of park and recreation facilities, straining the capabilities of modest state park agencies and stretching them beyond their traditional sylvan settings and their classic uses for picnicking, swimming, camping, and nature study.

By the late 1960s and early 1970s, another conservation imperative had materialized—the need for a quality environment in a holistic sense. Ecology became first a concern then a crusade, spawning new environmental agencies at federal and state levels, and bringing about sweeping policy and procedural reforms. It was time for state reorganization once again. The move was toward superagencies, elevated to cabinet status, with an increasing degree of regulatory as well as management authority. And under provisions of the National Environmental Policy Act (NEPA) and its counterparts at the state level,[688] constraints on development were now not only possible but mandated by law.

Throughout it all, the state park agencies sort of tagged along. Their early holdings were largely confined to high-elevation lands, carved from the state equivalents of the forest reserves or derived from gifts of estates from wealthy individuals. Administratively, parks were most frequently components of state forestry agencies. During the 1930s, thanks to the Civilian Conservation Corps (CCC), parks were rediscovered. As late as midcentury, the bulk of the developed facilities for park and recreation usage could still be attributed to CCC construction crews. With respect to trails, relations between state park officials and trail club leaders were sufficiently cordial that the brief windows of opportunity, such as the CCC movement, could be put to work effectively. Although there was not much else they could do to help, the states lent a ready presence at trail-related events (such as the founding session of the Appalachian Trail Conference in 1925) and offered at least moral support for the programs.[689]

With the passage of the Land and Water Conservation Fund Act in 1964, and the emergence of the national outdoor recreation movement, circumstances changed for the better. New bureaucracies emerged at state and federal levels with the means and influence to advance park programs measurably. A required system of State Comprehensive Outdoor Recreation Plans (SCORPs) created the basic building blocks for state park expansion and set the stage for a systemwide approach to outdoor recreation. The reforms came none too soon, for studies had demonstrated convincingly that recreationists were indiscriminate in choice, paying little attention to political or jurisdictional boundaries in their quest for facilities and experiences. In this era, the recreation landscape was writ boldly: large tracts of land, camping and picnicking grounds for thousands, specialized state bond issues with provocative names such as Green Acres and Heritage, and multi-milliondollar expenditures at federal and state levels. The needs of urban recreationists moved to the forefront too, and the social values of parks and open space spawned a whole series of new initiatives. The more traditional nature parks were not forgotten, but they tended to take a back seat to the more active recreation components. Programs such as trails tended to be in the hinterland, out of the view of those with policy influence and political power.

Despite their reputation and experience, the state park professionals were usually not the leaders in the outdoor recreation movement. With money and authority now available, the individual SCORP officers were more frequently planners and administrators.[690] As the Trail advocates began to discover, the park professional was now at some distance from the true locus of power and influence. If enlarged state commitments were to be obtained, a new level of administration would have to be involved—often individuals without the personal knowledge and commitment to trails displayed by their predecessors.

Much of the sweep of events in the past has seemed to occur in separate channels—federal and state—but there were times when the movements came together. Pres. Theodore Roosevelt's celebrated 1908 Conference of Governors was one such event,[691] an effort to convey a sense of common cause to the burgeoning conservation movement. Professional relations improved under the state planning and technical service programs of the National Park Service in the 1930s and 1940s.[692] Communication and linkage, both between the states and among park professionals, were facilitated by a modest National Conference of State Parks and an increasingly influential National Recreation and Park Association, dominated by municipal and private sector recreation interests. A national association of SCORP officers became inevitable with the passage of the Land and Water Conservation Fund Act, but the device was used more to lobby for appropriations than to encourage cooperative activities. The new Bureau of Outdoor Recreation (BOR), Interior secretary Stewart Udall's answer to a seeming lack of leadership in recreation by the National Park Service,[693] saw the value of interstate cooperation and served occasionally as the gadfly and switchboard to get states together. But this had to be done carefully, for, despite their reliance on the federal recreation dollar, the states were still strongly assertive of their own rights and responsibilities.

But for certain recreation projects, such as the Appalachian Trail, this essentially vertical distribution of responsibility in proscribed hierarchies —federal, state, and local—just would not do. Because they went somewhere else, trails, by definition, were strongly horizontal in character. An interconnected trail system presupposed an intergovernmental network. Concerted action by fourteen separate states, in close cooperation with their federal partners, would be required to fully protect the Trail, an objective for which there was no ready precedent and which seemed to cut across the grain of the existing outdoor recreation system.

The context of history helps explain why the states have been generally unwilling or unable to act decisively to protect the Appalachian Trail. For most states, trail projects have not commanded a high priority in their overall state outdoor recreation programs. Public interest and support, mirrored in legislative enactments and passage of implementing bond issues, have tended to favor projects that would service people in numbers. Dispersed activities like hiking and nature appreciation smacked of elitism at a time when populism was in full sway. State park specialists, much like their federal counterparts, also found linear parks awkward to manage in the traditional sense. It was only natural that forested or shoreline parks, with conventional boundaries and facilities, would command the highest priority in the allocation of efforts and dollars. And the fragmented nature of the trail community meant that no collective, assertive voice would be raised in opposition to such a policy.

With respect to the Appalachian Trail itself, other circumstances contributed to the general state of benign neglect displayed by many of the states.[694] The strong tradition of volunteer involvement labeled the Trail a private, not a public venture. It was only natural that state park professionals would direct their attention to places with less developed constituencies. The federal legislation did not help either, for the National Trails System Act designated the Appalachian Trail as a national scenic trail and made a federal agency, the National Park Service, ultimately responsible for its protection. Absent an imperative to the contrary, state officials need only to wait out the statutory two-year hiatus until the federal government was required to act. In a few states, executive hesitancy was coupled with legislative indifference and outright gubernatorial hostility.[695] Only an impetuous state bureaucrat would venture to run such gauntlets.

There was a measure of distance, too, between the states and the implementing federal agency, the National Park Service. Passage of the new national outdoor recreation legislation had relegated the Park Service's role in recreation subordinate to that of the new Bureau of Outdoor Recreation, the custodian of the massive federal assistance funds now available for planning, acquisition, and development.[696] Until the mandated study *Trails for America*, the BOR was caught up in the general fervor for conventional recreational space and facilities. The *Trails for America* report, which BOR researched and wrote, captured the agency's attention but caused the rest of the federal bureaucracy to view trails as primarily a Bureau of Outdoor Recreation responsibility.[697]

One other general problem tended to impede the involvement of the states in protecting the Trail—the level of state representation engaged in the effort. Trail specialists tended to be lower-level professional employees. Their interest in the Trail was genuine; they often had personal linkages with volunteer Trail clubs; but their degree of influence was limited. With interest in outdoor recreation now widespread, policy decisions had moved up the governmental hierarchy to the level of commissioner, cabinet secretary, or even the governor. The Appalachian Trail community found itself often unable to influence the people really responsible for policy decisions at either the state or federal levels.[698]

A measure of recognition and change took place in 1975. Reorganization of the Appalachian Trail program into a formal Project Office gave the AT project manager, David A. Richie, readier access to the higher echelons of both the National Park Service and the Department of the Interior. Correspondingly, every effort was made to persuade the governors to name policy-level natural resources officials as their designees on the Appalachian National Scenic Trail Advisory Council (ANSTAC).[699] Selection of chairmen with significant state governmental connections and experience enabled ANSTAC to pay closer attention to the role of the states.[700] A distinct pulse of action became noticeable.[701] And in the crucial 1975–78 period, even though the statutory two-year grace period contained in the 1968 act had long since expired, considerable attention was, in fact, paid to the states. The series of state-by-state meetings arranged by AT project manager David Richie in 1975 is one such example, as are the high-level meetings with governors and other key state officials conducted by Park Service and Interior administrators in 1977 and 1978 at the behest of Assistant Secretary Robert Herbst.[702] In fact, starting with the Boone ANSTAC meeting in June of 1975, a threshold occasion if there ever was one, there began what one observer has described as the great moment for the states in Appalachian Trail history.[703]

Perhaps the best illustration of the degree of solicitude for the states occurred in 1976 with the allocation of $1 million from the secretary's contingency reserves for the sole purpose of expediting state Trail protection projects. The strategy was many faceted: a genuine attempt to encourage state action where the necessary funds, authority, and interest were present, but also an effort to demonstrate tangibly that few of the fourteen Trail states were prepared to move effectively on behalf of the Trail. In the absence of state action, the enlarged federal effort contained in the 1978 amendments could now be termed the best alternative available for the Trail, and the states and the private Trail community could give the approach their unqualified support in the halls of Congress.

Viewed in retrospect, the weakest link in the entire Appalachian Trail institutional system has remained the role of the states. Yet, potentially, they have had the most to offer. Although tied firmly into the present management system through specific cooperative agreements, the states still exercise no real individual or collective presence. Theirs is a series of paper handshakes. Were it not for the periodic meetings of ANSTAC, and the regional sessions arranged by the ATC, the states would have no occasion to work together. With adjacent-lands issues very much in the forefront, a more definitive role for the states would seem to be especially timely. A redefinition of ANSTAC to this end, or possibly a facilitating compact arrangement among the states for supplemental management and regulatory assistance, might furnish the Appalachian Trail the true state working partners it will certainly need in the future.

Bioregionalism Revisited

What does the Appalachian Trail experience say about bioregionalism and bioregional institutions in general? Was the Appalachian Trail merely an isolated, special case or a likely precursor of successful bioregional approaches in the future? To answer these questions, it is necessary to return to the introductory portion of this treatise and measure up the Appalachian Trail experience against the premises set forth about bioregional approaches in general.

Turning first to the Trail as a region, it is fair to say that the Appalachians display many of the qualities of a viable bioregion. They are readily defined physiographically; they have distinguishable economic characteristics; they are politically and socially distinct; and they are accepted generally in cognitive terms. One might say that the stage is well set for a successful bioregional program. Nevertheless, appearances can be deceiving, for the Appalachians are, at best, only a unifying concept. The Trail's route is really a region of regions. Were it not for the central mountain spine and the continuous footpath along much of its crest, there would be no effective linkage among its component parts. Viewed pragmatically, there are at least three Appalachian regions: New England, the mid-Atlantic, and the South. Each is distinct in terms of the criteria mentioned earlier, and each has been reflected in the day-to-day business of managing and protecting the Trail. Good examples are the regional Councils of ANSTAC, the regional management committees of the ATC, and the regional offices of the Project Office established for acquisition purposes, to name just the most obvious.

Where to draw the divisions administratively has stimulated lively discussion over the years.[704] The initial temptation has been to subregionalize in terms of trail mileage: for instance, an equal amount in each region—or by topographic distinction: for example, divisions at the Housatonic River, at the Delaware Water Gap, and at the confluence of the Potomac and Shenandoah rivers in Harpers Ferry. In later years, the segmentation has rested more on social and political reality—groups of states in their entirety (e.g., all of New England), or established aggregations of Trail clubs (e.g., the New York–New Jersey Trail Conference). The adjusted ANSTAC regional Council boundaries, as carried forward today in the ATC's regional administrative structure, represent probably the most viable regional arrangements.

Regardless of the actual boundaries, every effort should continue to be made to encourage a sense of subregional affinity, for this is the stuff from which program activity and accomplishment derive, and the most likely source of leadership in depth for the future. A sense of belonging cannot help but carry with it a concomitant sense of commitment and involvement. And, as former ATC executive director Hank Lautz has observed,[705] the essence of true confederation is the ability to have face-to-face meetings without difficulty. Subregionalization makes that possible. Creating relationship building blocks of this sort is in no way inconsistent with the concept of the Trail as a whole and, in fact, facilitates aggregation of the subregions to reflect a larger dimension.

As an institutional experiment, the Appalachian Trail is faithful to the observations made earlier. Its periods of heightened activity certainly have been coincident with moments of timely opportunity. Such was the case conceptually, for example. Benton MacKaye's proposal just happened to fall on a particularly fertile social and intellectual seedbed. The early era was also a time when the public's interest in trails was expanding and a unifying concept was most needed. The CCC period, coincidentally, lent institutional and operational strength to the commitment of volunteers, despite MacKaye's concern that it would deprive the workers of primeval environmental benefits.[706] The national interest in outdoor recreation following World War II, and the generally benevolent view of government, hastened the involvement of state and federal agencies and the passage of legislation. The post-1968 period lent itself readily to a major rethinking of the purpose of the program.[707] And an extraordinary sequence of political events brought to the White House an environmentally committed president and an administration favorably predisposed to an accelerated Appalachian Trail protection program. There was also the further coincidence of the protection movement coming to a head when the key member of Congress, Phillip Burton, was an individual with the capacity to follow through.[708] None of these developments was planned or could have been foreordained. They just happened.

In the early days, the Appalachian Trail program was both blessed and burdened by its private character. A self-selected constituency was able to move rapidly and flexibly, but it lacked widespread credibility and staying power. The designation of the Appalachian Trail as a National Scenic Trail in 1968 resolved those uncertainties, furnishing a sense of legitimacy to the venture, but it also created a gray area of just who was really responsible for the Trail. The legislation made the Department of the Interior ultimately accountable, but the Trail's state and private character was also preserved in the authorizing language of the act. The National Trails System Act and its subsequent amendments, rather than dictating the roles and responsibilities, simply enabled and encouraged, thus providing the broad authority for an extraordinary array of cooperative activities that later emerged among the public and private participants. Here the private character of the Trail movement intervened again, seizing upon the opportunity for an unprecedented delegation of management responsibility from government to the private sector.

But simple good fortune was not far behind either. The cast of characters involved in the Trail proved to be just right. A different mix of individuals might have found its multidimensional and multijurisdictional characteristics baffling and counterproductive.[709] But the Trail leadership came to use its legislative tools wisely, creatively, and fully as the needs and opportunities emerged. The Trail was found to be something not in the ordinary pattern that could be made to work.[710]

Turning to the institutions involved in the Trail's implementation, many have displayed the characteristics of the typical bioregional organization mentioned earlier. The Appalachian Trail Conference, for example, went through an almost classic organizational development cycle before it evolved into a professional conservation organization. The Appalachian National Scenic Trail Advisory Council began with a limited set of functional tasks, fell into disrepair when these were largely completed, and was later resurrected to serve as a catalyst and validating mechanism for a wide range of program initiatives. This same sequence of peaks and valleys of activity is certain to occur again. The Appalachian Trail Project Office has been the most consistent of the bioregional institutions, moving steadily forward to carry out the declared intent of Congress to establish an Appalachian National Scenic Trail. But the Project Office has deliberately facilitated rather than supplanted the functions of others; it has taken advantage of inferred as well as explicit authority;[711] it has proven willing to share power and responsibility;[712] and by remaining modest in size and carrying out its responsibilities to the extent possible through others, it has kept from becoming a threat to the existing mass of federal, state, and private agencies. By refraining from exercising federal authority, the National Park Service has given the project greater credibility and strength.[713] Overall, the institutions have clearly played a significant role in the Trail program, both in their own right and through their supportive network of cooperative agreements.

The Appalachian Trail institutions have not been immune from the periodic drift and decay of the typical organizational life cycle,[714] but, in every instance, a process of renewal and restored vigor has ensued shortly thereafter.[715] For the Appalachian Trail Conference, the pursuit of revised federal legislation and a stronger federal presence provided the antidote for its mid-life crisis. So too was ANSTAC reinvigorated at a crucial moment by the adrenalin of the push for federal legislation.[716] A preoccupation with management has been the driving force for all of the parties in recent years.

A similar concern for the fate of adjacent lands promises to spark still another round of initiatives and reforms in the future. As policy analyst Sally Fairfax has observed,[717] the time warp involved has to be recognized as a critical variable in assessing the experience of the Appalachian Trail institutions. Some have argued that there is an even greater need for institutional arrangements now that the bulk of the formal land protection is in place.[718]

With respect to operations, the Appalachian Trail has displayed many of the characteristics of a viable bioregional program. As an example, the acquisition effort is a regional, service function carried out for the benefit of both public and private Trail interests. It provides access to special funds for Trail protection purposes and contributes the special technical skills and authorities of a major federal agency. It does for the participants what they cannot do readily for themselves. Land acquisition, of course, is not uniquely a National Park Service function. It could well have led to rivalry with similar programs at state and private levels. Yet, the Project Office's direct involvement in land acquisition came about more by the default of others than by a conscious desire to federalize the Trail. The decision emerged from a painstaking process of first exhausting other options. When it became obvious that the enormity of the protection job ahead would simply overwhelm the capabilities of the private sector, and the states proved unwilling or unable to carry the acquisition burdens themselves, only then was a federal role prescribed. Even subsequently, the Project Office has been meticulous in conveying a sense that the land purchases represent consensus decisions by Federal, state, and private participants alike.[719]

The distinction drawn earlier between the use of authority and the exercise of influence is also well illustrated by the Appalachian Trail experience. Take ANSTAC, for example. Lacking any direct functions or authorities, ANSTAC has, nevertheless, been enormously influential at times. When needed, it has cast the long shadow of the fourteen eastern states that control more than a third of the votes in the Congress. It has drawn at will upon the prestige and experience of two major federal agencies, the National Park Service and the Forest Service. Its substantial block of delegates from the Trail club community has ensured a measure of independent thought and action at all times. And, in later years, the addition of nonallied members, such as corporate and landowner representatives, has given a heightened ring of reality and credibility to the institution.

ANSTAC has also managed to enlist the full sweep of the leadership of the Trail movement, formal and informal, in its affairs. The chairman and immediate past chairmen of the ATC have usually been members. The state designees have often been policy-level officials. In its most halcyon day, the assistant secretary of the interior himself served as chairman. Consequently, ANSTAC has invariably had all the right buttons to push even though, as an institution, it was accorded no direct powers or responsibilities.

For that reason, the ANSTAC agendas have been joyously unfettered. To be sure, there were certain routine functions to perform, such as receiving the report of the AT project manager, convening to deliberate as regional Councils, and taking the pulse of the Appalachian Trail protection effort as a whole. But beyond these few particulars, the absence of a fixed agenda has enabled ANSTAC to turn its attention to any issue it wished to address. The institution has become malleable enough to devise a fitted response to a given problem, independent enough to initiate an inquiry into any matter of concern, and representative enough to reflect a full spectrum of viewpoints on any given issue. Thus, ANSTAC has been able to do much right and little wrong. In that sense, it has echoed the cardinal precept of a viable bioregional institution – sufficient breadth of purpose to remain constantly relevant.

Perhaps the most successful operational element of all has been the full sense of constituency enjoyed by the Appalachian Trail program – the really great experiment of government protection on the one hand and volunteer management on the other.[720] The net benefit of this diversity has been that the people who participated all felt responsible for the project. The most prominent constituency, of course, has been the Trail club contingent – an army of volunteers more than sixty thousand strong spread over the fourteen-state region. Divided though it could be upon occasion, and uneven in its contributions, the ATC element has contributed historic and unflagging commitment to the Trail. The volunteer human component, and the delightful informality it represents, has been among the program's most compelling facets.[721] Volunteers have become the program's veritable conscience and soul, and the primary instrument for keeping its governmental partners honest. The private constituency also has enjoyed an indirect source of influence through its contacts and credibility with the legislative branches, both federal and state, and its ability to take issues to the public and the press at any time.

Yet, the Trail's governmental constituency has been important too. Government commands the resources and technical facilities the private sector lacks, and many of the regulatory tools necessary to fully protect the Trail environment and experience. The state constituency, in addition, has served upon occasion as an alternate channel of approach to the federal bureaucracy and the Congress, one not lacking in potential influence at a time of the New Federalism. Given so highly developed a sense of constituency, the authorizing legislation itself has needed few teeth. There would always be others to go for the grenades.[722]

But the unique part of the Appalachian Trail story in terms of institutional bioregionalism has been the use of three separate institutions to achieve its program objectives. A true working partnership has emerged between the

ATC, the Project Office, and ANSTAC over the years, with three distinct but independent groups of constituents – the private Trail clubs, the federal agencies, and the states – assured of an equal and meaningful role in the Trail protection program. While there have been the inevitable overlaps, participants have tended to define their principal roles functionally: management for the ATC, acquisition for the Project Office, and policy articulation for ANSTAC. Put another way, ATC has served as the advocate for program changes, ANSTAC as the mediating ground, and the Project Office as the implementing agency. There is little question that ATC's relationship with the National Park Service, the really critical axis of the Trail program,[723] has been made more workable with ANSTAC in the wings.[724] The advantage of the troika, as one observer has noted, is that there is bound to be at least one part alive and breathing at any given moment.[725] With all three of the institutions active, and the chemistry just right, an effective program balance can be maintained. One can have a crisis without a catastrophe. The future, however, is not quite so certain.

For example, ANSTAC's ten-year authorization is scheduled to expire in 1988. Legislative reauthorization is always difficult, and the present climate for a continuation of ANSTAC administratively is not promising.[726] Similarly, the AT Project Office is nearing the end of its major acquisition assignment and will be winding down shortly. Now that the management responsibilities have been assigned by cooperative agreement to the ATC, the need for a formal Project Office and a project manager may be open to question.[727] Privately constituted, the ATC is in no danger of elimination, but since much of its program vitality is derived from the support it receives from its other two partners, their abolition could affect ATC significantly. And ATC's five-year management agreement for the Trail will be up for renewal in 1989. In the years remaining, a number of options should be explored by the parties concerned.

The first would be an extension of the existing ANSTAC for an additional period of time. The simplest route would be another ten-year authorization, supplied by special legislation or by amendment inserted in a companion bill or appropriations measure. Trail proponents would have to find sponsors, navigate the shoals of legislative jurisdiction and privilege, and persuade a reluctant bureaucracy to take the necessary steps to constitute the advisory council. All of this has been done before. Alternately, the Trail community might seek to persuade Congress to exempt the Appalachian Trail from the purview of the Federal Advisory Committee Act on the grounds that the intergovernmental nature of the Trail requires an advisory apparatus in perpetuity. Reauthorization of ANSTAC without term would be the end result. This would still leave extant the cumbersome matter of action by the Department of the Interior to appoint members and constitute the Council in a timely manner, but the future of ANSTAC would at least be assured.

A second option would be a conversion of ANSTAC from an advisory council into the organization governmentally responsible for the Trail. Federal-interstate compact legislation would be necessary, and consent would be required at both state and federal levels. Model language would have to be drafted and entered as amendments to the existing state Appalachian Trail acts. Companion federal legislation would be required no later than 1988. Alternately, the provisions of existing advance-consent legislation, such as the Interstate Environment Compact Act,[728] might be found to apply. Converting ANSTAC into the agency with oversight responsibility for the Trail would not materially alter present arrangements. When the present management delegation agreement with the Appalachian Trail Conference came up for renewal in 1988, ANSTAC would simply replace the National Park Service as the governmental signator.

The third option would be to allow ANSTAC expire and see what happened. In the past, the opportunistic approach has been the one that seemed to work the best. An advisory apparatus might arise of its own volition and in its own form. The Appalachian Trail Conference would be the most likely sponsoring organization. The earlier and successful partnership committee could be taken out of mothballs. Any such arrangements would enjoy maximum flexibility and ease of operation, but they would lack official credentials. This might translate into an unwillingness of the states and federal agencies to commit senior personnel and travel funds to such an informal advisory structure, and it might make the ATC Trail managers suspect by seeming to have an in-house board of advisers. But none of these potential problems is insurmountable. Subregional advisory bodies could be formed to mirror the present management regions, and the groups could be convened in plenary session at each biennial Trail Conference to look at the Trail as a whole. The successful precedent of the previous "partnership committee," created as an informal working mechanism at a time when ANSTAC was due to lapse, indicates that even informal advisory bodies can work well if there is a willingness and a demonstrated need.

Finally, what is there about the Appalachian Trail experience that might presage other regional natural resource and environmental issues? Much of it, regrettably, is just not a negative from which other prints can be made.[729] The constituency for the Trail is clearly unique, the product of six decades of conviction and concerted attention by thousands of committed volunteers. As one participant put it, "the concept of a permanent green corridor two thousand miles long is just fantastic."[730] And another—"it is hard to believe that the same folks who fought the Civil War found themselves sitting down together to discuss a project barely three feet wide."[731] Despite the advocacy of other long trails—the North Country Trail in the Midwest, for example—

the same supportive citizen constituencies have thus far failed to emerge. The tradition of volunteer involvement, so central to the success of the Appalachian Trail, has not proved readily replicable in other park, forest, and recreation settings.[732] The Appalachian Mountain Club's fine National Volunteer Project notwithstanding, professional land managers remain largely unconvinced that volunteers can be counted upon to perform regular management services.[733]

Yet, there are aspects of the Appalachian Trail experience where the question of precedent does appear to be relevant. Other corridor-type projects — such as trailways for pedestrian, equestrian, and all-terrain vehicle users; routes for waterway travel; recycled utility and railroad rights-of-way; marginal farm lands; or wild and scenic rivers — manifest some of the same characteristics as the Appalachian Trail. Linear projects of this sort are beginning to crop up at both state and national levels, and Congress is reportedly considering a set of generic hearings for corridor parks in general.[734]

Another facet of the Appalachian Trail directly relevant to other conservation projects has been its experience in land acquisition, notably its experimentation with less-than-fee protection measures — easements, development rights, life interest and special use reservations, term estates, purchase and leaseback arrangements and, occasionally, purchase and sellback provisions. In its absence of fixed boundaries, its diversified approaches to land acquisition, the flexibility employed in obtaining the interests to be acquired, and its use of volunteers to assist with negotiations,[735] the Trail project has clearly broken new ground; in the words of one observer, "it is the greatest experiment we have going today".[736] Overall, approximately 20 percent of the property transactions have been in the form of easements tailor-made to the landowner, resulting in a savings of at least twenty cents on the dollar. The device of fee interests with reserved uses has proved to be especially creative, reducing costs to the government and enabling landowners to remain fully protected from liability from public use. But even more important than the cost reductions has been the flexibility employed to meet a given landowner's needs, timetable, and objectives, not only in the interests to be acquired but in the project manager's freedom to adjust boundaries. Ten years after the passage of the National Trails System Act, less than 4 percent of the transactions have involved unwilling sellers, and no more than half a dozen of these have been adversary beyond the question of price.[737]

A special problem has been the case of publicly held properties that can only be acquired with the consent of the owner. Here, creativity has been applied again in the form of easements and cooperative agreements with the status of de facto protection for the Trail's route and corridor. A further unique feature has been the use of nongovernmental representatives (e.g., Trail club members) to help determine and negotiate for the tracts to be acquired.[738]

The risk of misrepresentation has been more than offset by the heightened local credibility afforded the NPS's acquisition efforts. The net result has been, in Charles Rinaldi's words, "the most complex acquisition project I know about – a project whose flexibility encourages new things – every acquisition is a challenge."[739]

Related directly to the special arrangements with landowners along the Trail are the pioneering efforts of the Appalachian Trail community with respect to the future of adjacent lands. The absence of a legislated park boundary has removed barriers to involvement in local zoning and land use decisions, but little guidance is available as to the appropriate role of a manager in matters indirectly related to his area of responsibility. In fact, some senior land managers have been frankly horrified by the prospect.[740] Harking back to Benton MacKaye's advocacy of "a project in regional planning,"[741] and Interior's later case study conclusion that long-term protection rests in "nourishing relationships and fostering responsibilities among the communities through which the Trail passes,"[742] the ATC has called for a number of demonstration "countryside" projects to build local support and cooperation in selected areas near the Appalachian Trail corridor.[743] For research has indicated that the quality of naturalness, as represented by an open, countryside environment, is the major contributor to the quality of the user experience.[744] If the necessary funds can be found, the Trail community stands to break important new ground in what William K. Reilly has termed "the rising emphasis on humanism" within the park movement."[745]

Last but not least, of course, is the precedent represented by the Appalachian Trail in a pluralistic sense, a manifestation likely to happen again but only in more modest proportions.[746] Although there have been identifiable heroes in the course of its history, the Trail has proved bigger than any one individual.[747] In a sense, it has been a microcosm of what it takes to get something done in our society.[748] A truly staggering array of actors and interests has been involved for more than half a century in the Trail protection program. They have ranged from entrenched, conservative, governmental bureaucracies to private groups determined to bring about major changes in the nation's social agenda. Participants have run the philosophical gamut from ultraliberal to reactionary. Forging a common alliance has not been easy, but, astonishingly, the movement has had room for them all. The process of outreach has been cumbersome at times – agonizingly slow at others – but as an experiment in effective networking, the Appalachian Trail has been a shining success. The right people always seemed to be there, wanting it, at the right time.[749]

A large part of the reason has been the steady, personal commitment of the Trail's own leadership, the low-key, trusting way of going at the program, and its prior history of volunteerism.[750] The early Trail, in particular, was like a string of pearls—a voluntary masterpiece.[751] Throughout its history, the degree of citizen involvement and commitment has made the Appalachian Trail, as the *Christian Science Monitor* so aptly editorialized, "a trail truly worth following."[752] But the institutional realities have helped too. No one entity has ever had the full capacity to accomplish the Trail protection job by itself. Since the private sector historically controlled the resource, it had to participate and contribute to the solutions.[753] Since it could not achieve full protection itself, government had to be called upon to help. The dependency upon others has necessitated and sustained the idea of a true working partnership. But there has been something innate in the concept, too, which has encouraged such cooperation. As one veteran ATC participant put it, "The Trail has a way of becoming an icon, making a true believer of you, a force that sometimes acts out of all proportion to rational expectations."[754] That mystique has served it well in times past, and should for many years to come. On the Appalachian Trail, seemingly anything is possible.[755]

APPENDIX A

Chronological Summary

THE EARLY YEARS

1876 – Appalachian Mountain Club founded
1908 – Pres. Theodore Roosevelt's Conference of Governors
1909 – Dartmouth Outing Club founded
1910 – Green Mountain Club (Vermont) founded
1911 – Passage of Weeks Act authorizing establishment of eastern national forests
1915 – First Forest Service appropriation for recreation
1916 – Passage of Organic Act establishing National Park Service
1920 – New York-New Jersey Trail Conference founded
October, 1921 – Publication of Benton MacKaye's article, "An Appalachian Trail: A Project in Regional Planning," *Journal of American Institute of Architects.*
1922 – First mile of Appalachian Trail cut and marked (Palisades Interstate Park, New York)
March 2-3, 1925 – First Appalachian Trail Conference held in Washington, D.C.
1927 – Potomac Appalachian Trail Club founded
1930 – Georgia Appalachian Trail Club founded
1930-1940 – Civilian Conservation Corps (CCC) active
– Blue Ridge Parkway constructed
1936 – Passage of Parks, Parkway, and Recreation Act assigning primary responsibility for recreation planning on federal lands to National Park Service
August 14, 1937 – Last mile of Appalachian Trail opened (Mount Sugarloaf, Maine)
1937 – Appalachian Trail Conference, Gatlinburg, Tennessee; Appalachian Trailway proposed
1938 – Appalachian Trailway Agreements signed with National Park Service and Forest Service
– Hurricane damages Appalachian Trail in New England
1940 – Appalachian Trailway Agreements in effect with all states but Maine
1941 – Last Appalachian Trail Conference before World War II
1944 – Passage of Federal-Aid Highway Act
– Extension of Blue Ridge Parkway into Georgia under consideration by Congress
February 13, 1945 – Congressman D. K. Hoch (Pennsylvania) introduces National System of Foot Trails bill
October 24, 1945 – Hearings of the House Committee on Roads on the Hoch bill

January, 1946 – Myron Avery editorial, *Appalachian Trailway News*, advocating public ownership of the Appalachian Trail

May, 1948 – Congressman Francis Walter (Pennsylvania) introduces National System of Foot or Horse Trails bill

1959 – Outdoor Recreation Resources Review Commission (ORRRC) established

1961 – Stanley A. Murray begins fourteen-year service as chairman of the Appalachian Trail Conference

1962 – ORRRC Report issued

1963 – Passage of Outdoor Recreation Program Act

August 20, 1963 – Stanley Murray meeting, Chairback Mountain Camps (Maine) to discuss need for federal legislation

October, 1963 – Washington meeting called by ATC to determine legislative strategy

June, 1964 – Sen. Gaylord Nelson (Wisconsin) introduces Appalachian Trail bill

February 8, 1965 – Pres. Lyndon B. Johnson issues special message on natural beauty

September 16, 1965 – Hearings of the Senate Subcommittee on Parks and Recreation on Appalachian Trail legislation, Washington, D.C.

December, 1966 – *Trails for America* report issued by Bureau of Outdoor Recreation

1967 – National Trails System bills introduced for the administration by Sen. Henry B. Jackson (Washington) and Rep. Roy Taylor (North Carolina)

March 15-16, 1967 – Hearings of the Senate Subcommittee on Parks and Recreation on national trails legislation, Washington, D.C.

October 2, 1968 – National Trails System Act (P.L. 90-543) signed by Pres. Lyndon B. Johnson

October 9, 1968 – Extension of Blue Ridge Parkway from Beech Gap, North Carolina to Kennesaw Mountain, Georgia, authorized by Congress

September 1, 1969 – Col. Lester R. Holmes appointed part-time executive director of Appalachian Trail Conference

November 3, 1969 – Inaugural meeting of Appalachian National Scenic Trail Advisory Council (ANSTAC), Washington, D.C.; Robert Moore, chairman

May 13, 1970 – Master National Park Service/Appalachian Trail Conference cooperative agreement signed

May 29, 1970 – ANSTAC executive committee meeting, Washington, D.C

1971 – National park Service/State cooperative agreements signed

February 9, 1971 – Publication of proposed Appalachian Trail route in Federal Register

June 1, 1971 – ANSTAC meeting, Washington, D.C.

September, 1971 – Richard L. Stanton succeeds Robert Moore as ANSTAC chairman

April, 1972 – Edgar Gray succeeds Richard Stanton as new ANSTAC chairman

June 19, 1972 – ANSTAC meeting, Plymouth, New Hampshire
October 19, 1972 – Publication of official Appalachian Trail route in Federal Register
November 11-12, 1972 – ATC Board of Managers authorizes Appalachian Greenway study
April 27, 1973 – ANSTAC meeting, Harpers Ferry, West Virginia
September 28, 1973 – ANSTAC executive committee meeting, Washington, D.C.
October 19, 1973 – Chairman's report (ANSTAC); Trail program complete
1973 – Passage of Federal Advisory Committee Act (P.L. 92-463)
1974 – Initial five-year terms of ANSTAC members expire

THE TRANSITION YEARS

October, 1974 – Appalachian greenway report issued by Appalachian Trail Conference
December, 1974 – David A. Richie assigned part time to Appalachian Trail project
February 24, 1975 – New ANSTAC charter signed
May 21, 1975 – First non-governmental ANSTAC chairman (Charles H.W. Foster) appointed
June 20, 1975 – ANSTAC meeting, Boone, North Carolina
June 23, 1975 – Appalachian Trail Conference, Boone, North Carolina
July 1, 1975 – Paul C. Pritchard appointed full-time executive director of Appalachian Trail Conference
July 21, 1975 – Follow-up meeting with National Park Service director Gary Everhardt
July 30, 1975 – Follow-up meeting with Interior's Interagency Task Force on Trails to discuss contingency reserve allocation
July, 1975 – Individual state visits begin
October, 1975 – ANSTAC chairman's report to Potomac Appalachian Trail Club
December 13, 1975 – Death of Benton MacKaye at age ninety-six
January 30, 1976 – Meeting of southern regional Council, Great Smoky Mountains National Park, Tennessee
February, 1976 – Meeting of mid-Atlantic regional Council, Washington, D.C.
February 23, 1976 – Interior secretary Thomas Kleppe signs ANSTAC charter amendments permitting expense reimbursement
March 1, 1976 – David A. Richie appointed full-time Appalachian Trail project manager
March 6, 1976 – $1 million in contingency reserve funds made available by Interior secretary Thomas Kleppe
March 11-12, 1976 – Oversight hearings, House Subcommittee on National Parks and Recreation, Washington, D.C.
March 19-20, 1976 – Appalachian greenway workshop, Arlington, Virginia
April 2, 1976 – Meeting of New England regional Council, Worcester, Massachusetts

April 15, 1976 – Appalachian Trail Project Office opened at former Charlestown Navy Yard, Boston

May 24, 1976 – ANSTAC meeting, Bear Mountain Park, New York

1976 – Meetings of Pennsylvania Appalachian Trail Task Force initiated by Assistant Secretary William Eichbaum

January, 1977 – Carter administration assumes office; all advisory committees under review

– Congressman Phillip Burton (California) becomes chairman of House Subcommittee on National Parks and Recreation

January 22, 1977 – Meeting of southern regional Council, Asheville, N.C.

February 4, 1977 – Meeting of mid-Atlantic regional Council, Ringwood State Park, New Jersey

March 4, 1977 – Meeting of New England regional Council, Boston, Massachusetts

May 27, 1977 – ANSTAC meeting, Shepherdstown, West Virginia

May 28, 1977 – Appalachian Trail Conference hears Interior assistant secretary Robert Herbst's commitment to three-year, $90 million, Appalachian Trail protection program

May 30, 1977 – Henry Lautz replaces Paul Pritchard as executive director of Appalachian Trail Conference

October 25, 1977 – House passes Appalachian Trail legislative amendments

March 18, 1978 – Senate passes Appalachian Trail legislative amendments

March 21, 1978 – Appalachian Trail legislative amendments (P.L. 95-248) signed into law by Pres. Jimmy Carter

THE PROTECTION YEARS

January, 1978 – Appalachian Trail Project Office moves to Harpers Ferry, West Virginia

February 4, 1978 – Meeting of southern regional Council, Roanoke, Virginia

March 10, 1978 – ANSTAC meeting, Washington, D.C.

April, 1978 – Forest Service's Lawrence Henson joins Appalachian Trail Project staff on special assignment

April 13, 1978 – Meeting of mid-Atlantic regional Council, Boiling Spring, Pennsylvania

May 22, 1978 – Meeting of New England regional Council, Hanover, New Hampshire

July 31, 1978 – New ANSTAC charter issued under terms of legislative amendments; Robert Herbst succeeds Charles Foster as ANSTAC chairman

August 10, 1979 – ANSTAC meeting, Carrabassett, Maine

September, 1979 – Separate land acquisition office for Appalachian Trail established under Charles Rinaldi

February 15, 1980 – Meeting of southern regional Council, Johnson City, Tennessee

March 29, 1980 – Meeting of New England regional Council, Kent, Connecticut

May 9, 1980 – Meeting of mid-Atlantic regional Council, Bethel, Pennsylvania

May 18, 1980 – Master Forest Service/Appalachian Trail Conference cooperative agreement signed

July 24, 1980 – New ANSTAC charter filed

August 23, 1980 – ANSTAC meeting, Mountain Lake, Virginia

January 19, 1981 – ANSTAC chairman Herbst resigns; Thomas S. Deans appointed ANSTAC chairman by Interior secretary Cecil Andrus

January, 1981 – Reagan administration assumes office

THE MANAGEMENT YEARS

February, 1981 – Laurence Van Meter succeeds Henry Lautz as executive director of Appalachian Trail Conference

March 6, 1981 – ANSTAC meeting, Harpers Ferry, West Virginia

May, 1981 – Establishment of Interior Land Policy Group under Ric Davidge

May 5, 1981 – First meeting of "partnership committee" established by Appalachian Trail Conference

June, 1981 – Comprehensive plan draft circulated to ANSTAC for approval

June, 1981 – New ANSTAC charter issued; Arthur W. Brownell succeeds Thomas S. Deans as ANSTAC chairman

September, 1981 – Interior case-study team for Appalachian Trail established

May 14, 1982 – ANSTAC meeting, Harpers Ferry, West Virginia

August 4, 1982 – Hearings of Senate Subcommittee on Public Lands and Reserved Water on National Trails System Act amendments, Washington, D.C.

September 24, 1982 – Special meeting to discuss management delegation, Pipestem State Park, West Virginia

February 5, 1983 – Meeting of special committee on management delegation, Appalachian Trail Conference, Washington, D.C.

February, 1983 – Draft land protection plan issued by National Park Service for Appalachian Trail

March 19, 1983 – Board of Managers meeting (Appalachian Trail Conference), Shepherdstown, West Virginia; vote to anticipate management delegation

March 28, 1983 – Additional National Trails System Act amendments (P.L. 98-11) signed by Pres. Ronald Reagan

April 11, 1983 – Pennsylvania state forester Richard Thorpe circularizes ANSTAC state members in favor of management delegation

April 22, 1983 – ANSTAC meeting, Harpers Ferry, West Virginia; management delegation approved in principle

May 20, 1983 – National park Service agrees in principle with management delegation

May 27, 1983 – Board of Managers meeting (Appalachian Trail Conference), New Paltz, New York; authorization to enter into cooperative agreement for management of Appalachian Trail

July, 1983 — Draft statement of management policy prepared by Laurence Van Meter

November 19, 1983 — Board of Managers meeting (Appalachian Trail Conference), Harpers Ferry, West Virginia draft cooperative agreement for management approved

January 26, 1984 — Signing ceremonies for execution of Amendment No. 8, National Park Service Cooperative Agreement No. 0631-81-01, Washington, D.C.

Individuals Interviewed

Stanley T. Albright, National Park Service, Washington, D.C.
Laura C. Beaty, National Parks and Conservation Association, Washington, D.C.
C. Francis Belcher, Appalachian Mountain Club, Boston, Massachusetts
Ruth E. Blackburn, Appalachian Trail Conference, Washington, D.C.
Christopher N. Brown, American Rivers Conservation Council, Washington, D.C.
Arthur W. Brownell, International Paper Company, Washington, D.C.
Charles S. Cushman, National Inholder Association, Sonoma, California
Thomas S. Deans, Appalachian Mountain Club, Boston, Massachusetts
William M. Eichbaum, Maryland Department of Health and Mental Hygiene, Baltimore, Maryland
Dr. Sally K. Fairfax, Department of Conservation and Resource Studies, University of California Berkeley, California
Steven Golden, National Park Service, Boston, Massachusetts
George T. Hamilton, Bank East, Concord, New Hampshire
Lawrence R. Henson, U.S. Forest Service, Milwaukee, Wisconsin
Robert L. Herbst, Trout Unlimited, Vienna, Virginia
Raymond F. Housley, U.S. Forest Service, Washington, D.C.
Henry W. Lautz, Trust Company of Georgia, Atlanta, Georgia
Stanley A. Murray, Appalachian Trail Conference, Kingsport, Tennessee
Cleveland F. Pinnix, Washington Department of Natural Resources, Olympia, Washington
Paul C. Pritchard, National Parks and Conservation Association, Washington, D.C.
David A. Richie, National Park Service, Harpers Ferry, West Virginia
Charles R. Rinaldi, National Park Service, Martinsville, West Virginia
David M. Sherman, National Park Service, Washington, D.C.
Charles W. Sloan, Attorney at Law, Vienna, Virginia
Richard L. Stanton, National Park Service, Sharpsburg, Maryland
Laurence R. Van Meter, Appalachian Trail Conference, Harpers Ferry, West Virginia
George M. Zoebelein, KMG Main Hurdman, New York, New York

Charter

APPALACHIAN NATIONAL SCENIC TRAIL ADVISORY COUNCIL

1. The official designation of the committee is the Appalachian National Scenic Trail Advisory Council.

2. The purpose of the committee is to advise the Secretary of the Interior in regard to matters relating to the trail, including the selection of rights-of-way, standards for the erection and maintenance of markers along the trail, and the administration of the trail.

3. The statutory life of the committee will extend through March 20, 1988. The committee will, however, be reviewed biennially as required by Section 14 of the Federal Advisory Committee Act (P.L. 92-463).

4. The committee reports to the Project Manager, Appalachian Trail Project, National Park Service.

5. Support for the committee is provided by the National Park Service, Department of the Interior.

6. The duties of the committee are solely advisory and are as stated in paragraph 2 above.

7. The estimated annual operating cost of this committee is $15,000 which includes the cost of 1/4 person year of staff support.

8. The committee meets approximately twice a year.

9. The committee will terminate on March 20, 1988.

10. The members of the committee shall not exceed 35 in number and shall serve for a term of 2-years. The committee shall consist of the following:

    a. the head of each Federal department and independent agency administering lands through which the trail route passes, or his designee;

    b. a member appointed by the Secretary to represent each State through which the trail passes, and such appointments shall be made from recommendations of the Governors of such states;

    c. one of more members appointed to represent private organizations, including corporate and individual landowners and land users, that, in the opinion of the Secretary, have an established and recognized interest in the trail and such appointments shall be made from recommendations of the heads of such organizations; provided, that the Appalachian Trail Conference shall be represented by a sufficient number of persons to represent the various sections of the country through which the trail passes.

The Chairman is designated by the Secretary of the Interior.

The members shall serve without compensation, but the Secretary may pay, upon vouchers signed by the Chairman of the Council, the expenses reasonably incurred by the Council and its members in carrying out their responsibilities.

11. The Council is not composed of, but may include, formal subcommittees or subgroups and, in addition, there may be ad hoc committees formed for special purposes. Meetings of these groups are subject to the same requirements of the Federal Advisory Committee Act as are meetings of the full committee.

12. The Appalachian National Scenic Trail Advisory Council was established by Section 5(a)(3) of Public Law 90-543 (82 Stat. 920; 16 U.S.C. 1244), as amended by Public Law 95-248 of March 21, 1978.

_____

William P. Clark
Secretary of the Interior

Date Signed: _____July 3, 1984_____

Date Charter Filed: _____July 13, 1984_____

Appalachian National Scenic Trail Advisory Council Members (1968-1985)

FEDERAL AGENCY

Interior

Stanley T. Albright
Edgar L. Gray
Robert L. Herbst
Robert B. Moore
David A. Richie
Richard L. Stanton

Agriculture

Richard F. Droege
Roy Feuchter
Raymond F. Housley
Russell P. McRorey

Other Federal

Terry Chilcoat
Susan Martell
John Paulk
Thomas H. Ripley

NEW ENGLAND STATES

Maine

Herbert Hartman
George L. Smith
Austin H. Wilkins

New Hampshire

George T. Hamilton
David Hartman
Arthur A. Morrill
David C. Neville
Ronald Poltak

Vermont

Edward Koeneman
Forrest E. Orr
Stephen Sease
Robert B. Williams

Massachusetts

Arthur W. Brownell
William Hicks
Richard Kendall
George S. Wislocki

Connecticut

Joseph N. Gill
Joseph E. Hickey, Jr.
Dan W. Lufkin

MID-ATLANTIC STATES

New York

Harold J. Dyer
Orin Lehman
Ivan P. Vamos

New Jersey

Helen Fenske
Donald Graham
Alfred T. Guido
Daniel O'Hern
Robert A. Roe

Pennsylvania

Ralph Abele
Samuel S. Cobb
William M. Eichbaum
Caren E. Glotfelty
Conrad R. Lickel
Richard Thorpe

Maryland

Torrey Brown
Goodloe E. Byron
Goodloe E. Byron, Jr.
Spencer P. Ellis
Fred L. Eskew

SOUTHERN STATES

Virginia

Dennis R. Baker
Ben H. Bolen
Ira S. Latimer, Jr.

West Virginia

David Callaghan
Arthur P. Foley
Kermit McKeever

North Carolina

James B. Hallsey
Howard Lee

Tennessee

B.R. Allison
James M. Callaway
David Charpio
Joe R. Gaines
Timothy McCall
Ann Tuck

Georgia

Sara Davis
Margaret Drummond
Kurt Fanstill
Robin Jackson
James O. Oates
David M. Sherman

APPALACHIAN TRAIL CONFERENCE

C. Francis Belcher
Ruth E. Blackburn
James L. Botts
David Burwell
Thomas H. Campbell
Stephen Clark
Grant Conway
Walter L. Criley
William Curnett
Thomas S. Deans
A. Lionel Edney
David B. Field
Maurice J. Forrester

Edward B. Garvey
Norman A. Greist
Thurston Griggs
Lester L. Holmes
Raymond F. Hunt
Earl Jette
Richard Kimmel
Arthur R. Koerber
Henry W. Lautz
Charley A. McLaugherty, III
Henry B. Morris
Stanley A. Murray
Harry F. Nees

William Nelson
Arch Nichols
Charles L. Pugh
David L. Raphael
Edwin J. Seiferle
Charles W. Sloan
George M. Stephens
Jean Stephenson
Joseph Truncer
Laurence R. Van Meter
Samuel N. Wilkinson
George M. Zoebelein

AT LARGE

Gerald Allen
Frank Armstrong
Decorsey Bolden
Arthur W. Brownell
Peter Burr
Richard Carbin
D.O. Davies
Roger R. Fischer

Charles H.W. Foster
George T. Hamilton
Destry Jarvis
Peter Kirby
C. David Loeks
John T. Maines
Joanne Mantikos
John Marchesi

Jacob Myers
Patrick F. Noonan
Catherine M. Nowicki
Linwood E. Palmer, Jr.
Jeffrey Rieves
Jean W. Roesser
Nicholas Schaus
George C. Williams

APPENDIX E

Dates, Locations, and Officers of the Appalachian Trail Conferences

CONFERENCE DATES AND LOCATIONS (1925-85)

(1925)	Washington, D.C.	(1958)	Mountain Lake, VA
(1928)	Washington, D.C.	(1961)	Delaware Water Gap, PA
(1929)	Easton, PA	(1964)	Stratton Mountain, VT
(1930)	Skyland, VA	(1967)	Cashiers, NC
(1931)	Gatlinburg, TN	(1970)	Shippensburg, PA
(1934)	Long Trail Lodge, VT	(1972)	Plymouth, NH
(1935)	Skyland, VA	(1975)	Boone, NC
(1937)	Gatlinburg, TN	(1977)	Shepherdstown, WV
(1939)	Daicey Pond, ME	(1979)	Carrabassett, ME
(1941)	Bear Mountain, NY	(1981)	Cullowhee, NC
(1948)	Fontana Village, NC	(1983)	New Paltz, NY
(1952)	Skyland, VA	(1985)	Poultney, VT
(1955	Mt. Moosilauke, NH		

CONFERENCE OFFICERS (1968-85)

#*Ruth E. Blackburn	xSadye Giller	xWilliam R. Nelson
#James L. Botts	+Raymond P. Gingrick	#*Charles L. Pugh
#Thomas H. Campbell	+Norman A. Greist	#David L. Raphael
#Stephen Clark	+#Thurston Griggs	xLois N. Shores
#Margaret Drummond	+Herbert S. Hiller	+Charles W. Sloan
+David B. Field	*Raymond F. Hunt	*Murray H. Stevens
xArthur P. Foley	#Earl Jette	+Shirley J. Strong
xMaurice J. Forrester, Jr.	#Arthur R. Koerber	#Samuel N. Wilkinson
#Edward B. Garvey	*Stanley A. Murray	#*George M. Zoebelein

* Chairman and/or chairman emeritus

Vice-chairman

x Treasurer

+ Secretary and/or corresponding secretary

Amendment No. 8 Cooperative Agreement No.: 0631-81-01

MEMORANDUM OF AGREEMENT BETWEEN THE NATIONAL PARK SERVICE AND THE APPALACHIAN TRAIL CONFERENCE CONCERNING THE APPALACHIAN TRAIL

Purpose and Authority

This Agreement between the National Park Service (NPS) and the Appalachian Trail Conference (ATC) is for the purpose of delegating management responsibility to ATC for certain lands NPS has acquired, as further provided herein. This delegation is authorized by Section 7(h) of the National Trails System Act (the Act) and is encouraged by the March 28, 1983, amendment to the Act, which states in part: "...it is further the purpose of this Act to encourage and assist volunteer citizen involvement in the planning, development, maintenance, and management where appropriate, of trails." This Agreement is based upon and extends the existing Memorandum of Agreement between NPS and ATC as executed on May 13, 1970, and is Amendment Number 8 thereto.

Explanation

The Appalachian Trail began as a volunteer project in the 1920's. It continues as a unique partnership among private groups and state and federal agencies. Within this partnership ATC plays a leadership role in defining policies and practices that are consistent with Trail traditions and in coordinating the work of over 30 Trail clubs which perform much of the essential maintenance and operations for the Trail. NPS administers the Trail under the Act on behalf of the Secretary of the Interior and in cooperation with the Secretary of Agriculture.

Understandings between NPS and ATC for cooperation in the administration of the Trail were set forth in the Memorandum of Agreement signed in May 1970. These understandings were supplemented by a Comprehensive Plan for the Protection, Management, Development and Use of the Appalachian National Scenic Trail, which was approved by the Director, NPS and the Chief, USDA Forest Service in August 1981 and endorsed by the Secretary of the Interior in September 1981. The cooperative management system set forth in the Comprehensive Plan has been implemented through cooperation and agreement among private and state partners.

The concept of a formal delegation of responsibility by NPS to ATC for management of lands acquired by NPS for the Trail was recommended to the Secretary of the Interior by the Appalachian National Scenic Trail Advisory Council in April 1983 and was endorsed by the Secretary in a memorandum to the Director, NPS, dated

June 7, 1983. It was also endorsed by the Board of Managers of ATC on May 27, 1983. Under this concept, NPS and ATC expect that most land acquired by NPS for the Appalachian Trail will be managed by ATC and its member Trail clubs either under this Agreement or under agreements with the Forest Service or the Massachusetts Department of Environmental Management, in the event NPS enters into delegation agreements with one or both of those organizations. The manner in which ATC intends to meet its responsibilities is described in this Agreement and in a concept document entitled Management of Residual NPS-Acquired A.T. Lands by the Appalachian Trail Conference dated November 9, 1983, which shall be included as Attachment A to this Agreement.

Responsibilities

NPS delegates and ATC accepts responsibility for management of certain lands, easements and other interests acquired for the Appalachian Trail outside of the proclaimed or designated boundaries of National Forests and existing units of the National Park System. These lands, easements and interests will be defined more specifically in supplemental agreements between the NPS Project Manager for the Appalachian Trail and the Executive Director, ATC, and included with this agreement as Attachment B. These supplemental agreements will exclude tracts that are found to be more suitable for direct management by adjacent NPS areas or which require management actions by NPS before coming under this Agreement. Decisions on which lands, easements and interests to include will be made after consultation with affected NPS Superintendents.

ATC will manage these designated lands in a manner consistent with the purposes for which the Trail was established and as further described herein and in the concept document entitled Management of Residual NPS-Acquired A.T. Lands, Attachment A. This concept document may be amended to reflect experience under this Agreement by the Executive Director, ATC, with the written concurrence of the Project Manager, NPS, subject to the following limitations. The Project Manager, NPS, is not authorized to delegate NPS responsibility with regard to law enforcement; transfers of title or use and occupancy to any lands or interests therein; authority to relocate the overall Trail right-of-way (as distinguished from the Trail route within the existing Trail right-of-way); land acquisition on behalf of the United States; and authority to charge any fee or cost or otherwise utilize any proceeds from the management of the Trail.

ATC will serve as guarantor to NPS that the Trail and corridor included under this agreement will be adequately managed.

NPS will continue to provide limited technical, material and financial assistance to ATC to facilitate the ability of ATC to meet these responsibilities, as provided by the May 13, 1970, Memorandum of Agreement, as amended, subject to the availability of appropriations.

Assignment

Consistent with the Comprehensive Plan for the Protection, Management, Development and Use of the Appalachian National Scenic Trail, the responsibilities delegated to the ATC by NPS pursuant to the terms of this Agreement may be further delegated to ATC member clubs and organizations. The Executive Director, ATC, will notify the Project Manager, NPS, of such assignments. No other delegation assignment or transfer of the terms of this Agreement is authorized.

Title

All right, title and interest in and to the lands subject to the terms of this Agreement remain in the United States; neither ATC nor its member clubs and organizations may encumber these lands in any way.

Non-Discrimination

ATC and those member organizations which participate in this Agreement will abide by the provisions of Executive Orders 11246 and 11375; will not discriminate in the selection of participants for any program on the grounds of race, creed, color, sex or national origin; and will observe all the provisions of Title VI of the Civil Rights Act of 1964 (78 Stat. 252; 42 U.S.C. 2000(d)).

Officials Not to Benefit

No member of or delegate to Congress, or resident Commissioner, shall be admitted to any share or part of this Agreement, or to any benefit that may arise therefrom; but this provision shall not be construed to extend to this Agreement if made with a corporation for its general benefit.

Term of Agreement

This Agreement shall continue for terms of five years from the last date of signing. At the end of each term, the parties may assess the benefits of the Agreement and either reaffirm it for an additional term or amend it.

Termination and Revision

This Agreement may be terminated upon written notice given by one of the parties to the other party and may be revised at any time by agreement of both parties.

November 18, 1983	Richard M. Briceland
date	Acting Director; NPS
November 10, 1983	Raymond F. Hunt
date	Chairman, ATC

Attachment A

Management of "Residual" NPS-Acquired A.T. Lands By the Appalachian Trail Conference

I. Introduction

II. Rationale

III. The Delegation Agreement

IV. Management Construct

V. Specific Management Responsibilities

A. Trail Maintenance/Management
B. Public Information
C. Corridor Monitoring
D. Structure Utilization
E. Special Use Permits
F. Boundary Marking/Maintenance
G. Law Enforcement
H. Search & Rescue
I. Liability
J. Fire Suppression
K. Active Land Management
L. NEPA Compliance
M. Costs

* properties, located outside established/proclamation boundaries, which have been acquired by the National Park Service for protection of the Appalachian Trail; referred to as "NPS-acquired" lands hereafter.

Appalachian Trail Conference
Harpers Ferry, West Virginia
November 9, 1983

MANAGEMENT OF NPS-ACQUIRED LANDS BY
THE APPALACHIAN TRAIL CONFERENCE

I. *Introduction*

The National Park Service has now acquired more than 35,000 acres in eight states to help provide permanent protection for the Appalachian Trail. Although dimensions vary greatly, on average the corridor is about 1000' wide (125 acres per Trail mile). Although aggregate acreage is substantial and may double before the NPS protection program is completed, from a broader management standpoint the corridor, with few exceptions, constitutes a relatively narrow band of publicly-owned land surrounded by private property.

The Appalachian Trail Conference recognizes that management of these lands is a formidable task which will require a great deal of planning, cooperation, and just plain hard work. The Conference, with the support of the National Park Service, U.S. Forest Service, and state governments (through ANSTAC), is being provided, under the provisions of Section 7(h) of the 1968 National Trail System Act, a broad delegation of management responsibility for those NPS-acquired lands not transferred to the Secretary of Agriculture under 7(a) of P.L. 98-11, or assigned or transferred to another organizational unit within the Department of the Interior.

II. *Rationale*

Without volunteer leadership it is unlikely that the Appalachian Trail would exist today. The steadfast support of state and federal agencies from the outset has been essential to the A.T., but leadership in the Trail's construction, management, and protection, as well as in public education, has come largely from volunteers in ATC and the trail clubs.

The rationale for a broad delegation of management responsibility to ATC is consistent with this tradition, and is particularly appropriate considering that most of the NPS-acquired lands were, until recently, private properties on which the clubs managed the Trail without agency assistance.

There are other reasons for private management of NPS-acquired lands. Today there is widespread support for the concept of increased volunteer involvement in National Parks and Forests. A delegation of management responsibility to ATC fits neatly with this national priority.

Thus the rationale for the delegation concept is based largely on the appropriateness of such action—from the standpoint of historical traditions, current national policy, and specific legislative direction. It would be difficult to find a project better suited than the A.T. to serve as an experiment in expanded volunteer responsibility.

III. *The Delegation of Management Responsibility to ATC*

In simple terms the agreement between NPS and ATC would transfer *responsibility* on NPS-acquired lands for those functions that the Park Service can legally delegate, including trail and shelter maintenance, corridor monitoring, and structure utilization. Functions that cannot be delegated, according to the Interior Solicitor's Office, are law enforcement; transfers of title or use and occupancy to any lands or interests therein; authority to relocate the overall Trail right-of-way (as distinguished from the Trail route within the existing Trail right-of-way); land acquisition on behalf of the United States; and authority to charge any fee or cost or otherwise utilize any proceeds from the management of the Trail.

It is important to stress that the National Park Service would retain overall *authority* for the properties it has acquired along Trail. No transfer of title or any interest land is contemplated or authorized. ATC will report periodically to the Service on the status of management, and the delegation agreement would be revocable with due notice. As noted elsewhere in this paper, NPS would retain responsibility for initial boundary survey, structure removal, NEPA compliance and budgeting. The Park Service would also retain an oversight function for policy compliance and, in the end, be accountable to the public for the quality of ATC management just as the Conference will be accountable to NPS for the quality of trail club management.

Since the ability of the U.S. Forest Service to take action outside its proclamation boundaries will be very important in some areas, an agreement is being developed which will assign management authority on some NPS-acquired lands located near National Forests to USFS under the provisions of 7(a) of P.L. 98-11. Section 11 of P.L. 98-11 permits the Forest Service to provide assistance at the request of the Trail club manager on those lands not assigned to USFS.

IV. *Management Construct*

Under an NPS delegation to ATC, the clubs will deal not only with what happens on the Trail, but with what happens within the corridor as well. In some places, where the corridor is narrow and remote, the difficulties may not be great. In more complicated settings, however, concerns about corridor stewardship may outweigh traditional trail maintenance worries. In addition, public ownership of these properties requires a commitment on the part of the private Trail community to live up to a high standard of care consistent with the public trust.

For most trail clubs the transition to land management will not occur overnight. Although clubs have made great progress over the past 5 to 10 years, it will take time for them to learn land management skills. It is ATC's view that with the Conference serving as facilitator and coordinator, and with support from local state and federal agency partners, the trail clubs can and will be able to take a leadership role in the management of these lands.

Just as agency programs fluctuate from year to year depending on funding and staffing, trail clubs have their cyclical ups and downs based on participation and leadership. The role of the ATC Board and staff is to even out these fluctuations, provide support in "down" periods, and most importantly, provide oversight of the entire volunteer management program. ATC will serve as guarantor to the National Park Service that the Trail and corridor are being adequately managed. If there is a problem with a trail club's performance, ATC will be accountable to NPS in rectifying the problem. When a club is unable to keep up with its responsibilities, ATC will work with the club to stimulate activity and provide assistance, both volunteer and professional, to be sure that management responsibilities are met.

This rationale answers the question of how ATC, with a professional staff of only ten, can accept responsibility from the Park Service for 35,000+/− acres of land: the management will be done by volunteers within a reasonable framework developed locally with professional agency and ATC involvement.

The basic building blocks of volunteer management are the local management plans which are guided by the Appalachian Trail *Comprehensive Plan*. All 31 trail clubs from Maine to Georgia have made progress in this continuous process. These plans are being developed in consultation with agency partners and ATC, and deal with larger management philosophy issues as well as with specific management activities. Normally this process will represent a consensus of the partners—club, agency, ATC, and ATPO. The Conference, with assistance from its regional management committees, will review and endorse each local management plan. The plan will then represent an agreement between the club and Conference on how to meet management responsibilities. In the case of responsibilities that a club feels it cannot meet, ATC and the agency partner will work with the club to provide assistance in getting the job done.

If there are issues of regional concern, or if there is a lack of consensus among local partners, the regional management committees will serve as a forum for further discussion and resolution. These committees are made up of ATC regional board members and representatives from the clubs and public agencies in the region.

Issues of Trailwide significance or on which there is no regional consensus will be referred to the ATC Board of Managers. It is assumed that issues coming to the Board will be relatively few, and that the appropriate Board committee will study issues carefully before making recommendations to the full Board of Managers.

A good example of how this process works occurred in 1982 when a New England club proposed harvesting timber within the NPS-corridor, a possibility that would require legislation to implement. This proposal was reviewed and endorsed by the New England Regional Management Committee. The Committee, however, noted the Trailwide significance of the proposal and referred it for final approval to the Board of Managers.

The Board requested that the Mid-Atlantic and Southern regions also develop recommendations for timber harvesting in the corridor. After the drafting of the regional policy statements, key people from each region got together to prepare a Trailwide policy and procedure statement.

The result was a detailed policy recommendation to NPS, endorsed by the ATC Board of Managers, which would permit harvesting in the corridor, but only under highly prescribed circumstances, including a plan drawn up by a professional forester and a transfer of proceeds to the federal government. NPS is now considering that proposal.

In this case, a highly controversial management issue was handled with calmness and careful deliberation. It provides a prototype for the resolution of other issues of Trailwide significance.

It is possible that some issues cannot be resolved even on the Board level. In such cases the Park Service, which retains management authority, would make the final judgement.

V. *Specific Management Responsibilities*

A. *Trail Maintenance/Management* (light and heavy maintenance, shelters, signs, etc.): When the newly-acquired NPS lands were in private ownership, the trail clubs were wholly responsible for maintenance of the trail and shelters. Despite some unevenness of performance, maintenance quality was generally satisfactory.

In recent years, the Conference and many clubs have made concerted efforts to upgrade the consistency and quality of maintenance, particularly in heavily-used or fragile areas. ATC's *Trail Design, Construction, and Maintenance*, a 166-page book, serves as a basic document to guide these efforts. Trail maintenance workshops and an inexpensive, illustrated handbook summarizing basic trail maintenance techniques help stimulate greater club enthusiasm toward high quality work.

Several clubs have used paid trail crews in addition to volunteer workers for many decades. Recently, ATC has begun a cooperative program with the U.S. Forest Service to sponsor and run a volunteer work and training center at Camp Konnarock in southwest Virginia. The purposes of the Konnarock program are several: (1) to develop skills of trail club volunteers in doing heavy maintenance (erosion control, sidehill construction, trail hardening, etc.), (2) to give the clubs a boost on major, labor-intensive projects, and (3) to provide an opportunity for volunteers not associated with a club to contribute to the improvement of the A.T.

Trail quality is monitored by ATC through reports submitted by hikers and by a growing "self-assessment" program in which clubs are encouraged by ATC's regional committees to take a step back and evaluate, by themselves or with volunteer assistance from other clubs, the quality of the Trail in their assigned area. This information is used to identify problem areas and take steps to make needed improvements.

Construction of new shelters has always required the permission of the landowner. As recipient of the NPS management delegation, the ATC Board will approve the construction of new shelters and other facilities on NPS corridor lands, in accordance with A.T. traditions, the overnight use management principles (approved in 1977 by ANSTAC), categorical exclusions to NEPA (published in the Federal Register 1/5/81), and any state or local laws.

B. *Public Information*: The Conference and clubs have long worked together to produce accurate, up-to-date guidebooks and maps for the entire Trail. The task is one of staggering detail made still more complicated by constant Trail relocations resulting from the land acquisition program. All guides are now reasonably current, and are on a 2-3 year revision cycle to keep information up to date. The Conference and clubs also put out numerous educational materials on the Trail and on hiking.

C. *Corridor Monitoring*: Unlike Trail management and public information, corridor monitoring is a new function for ATC and the clubs. Protecting government lands from encroachment and abuse requires regular watchfulness. An ATC task force recently developed guidelines for monitoring, including inspection, reporting, and follow-up. The most important recommendations are for a system of ranking properties by priority based on the perceived threat of incursions, and for a procedure whereby the trail club will report to ATC at least once annually on its monitoring activities. A compilation of these reports will be sent to NPS by the Conference on a regular basis.

Corridor monitoring will sometimes involve road closures and other active steps to reduce encroachment problems. Where possible, the trail clubs will undertake such projects with the assistance of one or more local agency partners. ATC is prepared to provide financial assistance if contractors must be engaged to erect gates, build tank traps, etc.

A newly created standing committee on Corridor Management will review the task force's recommendations, and help foster implementation through workshops and publications. It is anticipated, for example, that the next title in the ATC Stewardship Series will deal with corridor monitoring and management.

ATC Headquarters in Harpers Ferry will become a central repository for monitoring information currently on the NPS Management Information System computer program. Information on easement terms, administrative determinations, etc. will continue to be distributed to clubs for use in the field, but ATC will retain permanent records on microfiche.

D. *Structure Utilization:* In the process of acquiring land for the A.T. corridor, the National Park Service has sometimes found itself buying houses, barns, and other structures. Decisions on the removal or retention of structures are based on agreement between club, local agency, ATC, and ATPO as part of local management planning. Normally, the local trail club, with assistance where needed from ATC, will be responsible for interim management before decisions are made, and for longer term management of structures that are retained from some Trail-related use. Such structures will be managed only for purposes consistent with written understandings between the Park Service and ATC.

If structures are to be removed, the club and agency partner will make every effort to arrange for demolition and clean-up locally at minimal cost. If local efforts fail, however, it is a Park Service responsibility to see that structures are removed in a timely fashion.

Where structures are to be retained for non Trail-related purposes, resale with restrictions and other permanent solutions are preferred over those that require constant oversight and administration (e.g. leases). All such sales or leases shall be executed by the National Park Service. Where structures must be leased or rented, the clubs and ATC will do all they can to serve as managers for the "landlord" (NPS), but will not be the recipient of lease or rent payments.

In rare cases structures may be retained for A.T. visitor use on a fee-paying basis. Such arrangements will comply with the existing ATC/NPS Concessions Permit Agreement, which is reflected in Concessions Permit ATPO-1.

E. *Special Use Permits:* As used here, "special use permits" are for small projects not requiring NEPA documentation. There is a technical legal question as to whether administration of such special use permits can be delegated by NPS. On the assumption that further research will find that it can be delegated, ATC is prepared to take on this function. Such permits would allow limited and revocable non-public use of NPS-acquired lands so long as that use would not be inconsistent with the purposes for which the Trail was established by Congress.

There are two major risks in private administration of a special use permit program: appearances of conflict of interest and inadequate oversight of permit compliance. The latter problem is endemic to special use permit administration; terms are sometimes unclear and constant field-checking is time-consuming. ATC is encouraged by the realization that there are relatively few special use permits on the A.T., and that most have been subject to wide review by NPS and trail clubs. New permits should be granted only for uses that will clearly enhance trail quality.

The potential for conflict of interest is strong when a private organization administers public land and there is a fee involved. For that reason, all special use permit fees would be sent directly to the National Park Service, and terms of agreements would comply with carefully written guidelines jointly developed by NPS and ATC. Any fees or proceeds arising from such special use permits must be paid directly to NPS.

F. *Boundary Survey and Maintenance*: Initial monumenting and marking of the exterior boundaries of the NPS corridor will be an ATPO responsibility. ATC will continue to assist in the refinement of contract specifications that will result in easily monitored boundary lines.

Land management professionals can't seem to agree on whether or not it is feasible to have volunteers maintain boundaries. Given such uncertainties and the warnings of some that boundary maintenance involves potential liability and may require a substantial commitment of professional time, it is prudent for ATC to take a position similar to the one it takes on structure removal: the Conference and clubs will do all they reasonably can to assist in the maintenance of boundaries, but if unable to meet this task, the cost of remonumenting and renewing boundary lines should be considered one of the few ongoing costs the National Park Service will incur in management of its lands along the A.T.

G. *Law Enforcement*: Despite recent incidents of crime on the Trail, an ATC task force made up of law enforcement professionals, volunteers, hikers, and ATC, NPS, USFS staffers recently studied the incidents and determined that the trail is relatively safe. Concern that some hikers may have inadvertently brought trouble on themselves by careless or insensitive actions in small towns has led to preparation of a series of guidelines for hikers that will include some basic common sense pointers on avoiding trouble in rural communities.

The Comprehensive Plan cites the goal of minimal regulation on the A.T. ATC and the trail clubs have a basic commitment to education as a means of preventing public behavior problems on the Trail. Some problems (accidental trespass, shelter vandalism, littering) can be alleviated by improved trail and facility design and maintenance. Others eventually respond to repeated messages in guidebooks and on signs. But some problems do not improve with subtle approaches.

Because the NPS-acquired lands have proprietary jurisdiction, local law enforcement officials should be prepared to enforce state and local laws as they would on private property. Strong relationships between trail clubs and local and state police are important if the constabulary is to have enough interest in and information about the Trail to be of assistance where there are problems. ATC and the Trail clubs should work for such a constructive relationship.

In some cases the local laws may be insufficient or the police uninterested in pursuing minor but nagging problems on the Trail. To help deal with such situations, ATC will be reviewing with the National Park Service the newly published 36 CFR general regulations for NPS-administered areas. ATC expects to recommend "special regulations" that would substantially amend the applicability of 36 CFR to the Trail, but would seek to retain those rules that might be useful. The nature of these "special regulations" will be especially important to neighboring units of the National Park System. Decisions on hunting in particular will require careful consideration of historical uses and close cooperation with state game commissions and federal partners.

H. *Search and Rescue*: Most of the especially popular places along the A.T. are located in state or national forests/parks (Katahdin, the Presidentials, the Smokies, etc.). Search and rescue operations are most likely to be needed in these heavily used, high elevation areas, and local managers normally have procedures well in place. Despite a lesser probability of trouble, procedures for search and rescue are also necessary on the NPS-acquired lands.

Search and rescue in a proprietary jurisdiction is the responsibility of local authorities. Experience has shown, however, that local police and rescue squads are often ignorant of access points and of trail and shelter locations. It is important for clubs to work closely with local authorities to supply maps, advice, and actual search assistance when called upon. Where NPS land lies near a National Forest, it would be highly desirable to have an arrangement which would permit Forest Service personnel to participate in search and rescue operations regardless of land ownership.

Wherever possible, ATC and the clubs will attempt to avoid the need for search and rescue by marking the Trail clearly, and by designing and maintaining as safe a footpath as possible. Educational materials produced by the Conference also stress the need for hikers to exercise proper care to avoid becoming lost or getting hurt on the Trail.

I. *Liability*: Court awards to people claiming injury on hiking trails are rare. But the concern is great enough to lead many A.T. clubs, and the Conference itself to hold extensive liability insurance policies with private carriers. Additional protection is provided by the Volunteers in the Parks (VIP) and Volunteers in the Forests (VIF) programs. Under VIP, volunteer A.T. workers on NPS, state, and private lands are protected by the federal government from tort claims consistent with amendment #1 to Cooperative Agreement #0631-81-01. VIF provides similar coverage on National Forest land. P.L. 98-11 provides authority to extend liability protection to the trail clubs themselves as well as to individual volunteers, and this change is reflected in the NPS/ATC Agreement for Sponsored Voluntary Services.

Additional protection is provided by "proceed at your own risk"-type disclaimers in ATC guidebooks, and by state laws designed to protect people who volunteer their services for the public benefit.

J. *Fire Suppression*: Although incidents of campfires getting away from hikers are relatively rare, they have occurred. Lightning, cigarettes, and even arson can also lead to fires in the corridor. In the typical situation where the Trail corridor is narrow and is surrounded by private land, fire suppression is a local responsibility. Again, a close relationship with the local club can help firefighters (who also are often the search and rescue people) find access points. Since fires do not often pay attention to boundary lines, most firefighters respond first and ask questions about ownership and responsibility later. Where the corridor is near USFS land, support from the Forest Service will also be important. Where it is located near private land, protection of private landowners is an important consideration.

In some areas, government agencies are expected to reimburse local communities for firefighting costs incurred on public lands. If a local community can substantiate that a fire started in the corridor, then regular federal channels for handling such claims will be followed.

Education by ATC and the clubs can help prevent forest fires. Hikers are encouraged to use gas campstoves rather than campfires for cooking. Where state laws and local ordinances permit the use of open fires, they should be confined to designated permanent fireplaces at the campsite.

K. *Resource Management*: In most cases the NPS corridor is too narrow to make active resource management worthwhile. In addition, the land was purchased to protect the remote qualities of the Trail, and management activities that might detract from this purpose would be inappropriate.

A relatively low-key attitude towards resource management on NPS lands does not mean that a hands-off policy is desirable. As the ATC timber policy recognizes, there may be some larger parcels on which limited sawtimber and firewood harvesting would meet a public need yet not be detrimental to the Trail. This policy is under review by NPS at this time. Extreme cases of insect infestation or disease may obviously require action.

There are also cases, e.g. open fields and highland balds, where a failure to act might result in reforestation and a loss of views and overall scenic quality intended to be retained under the provisions of the National Trails System Act. These areas should be identified early in local management planning, and specific steps outlined to ensure that management goals are met.

It may be desirable to allow some fields and balds to return to woodland, but only after careful consideration and consultation. Where balds are to be kept open, professional advice is needed to help decide on the scientifically appropriate means, be it mowing, prescribed burning, etc. The ATC-sponsored Balds Management Symposium in 1980 showed that there is no consensus on the best way to preserve balds, and wide involvement of professional researchers and managers will be necessary before action is taken in the field.

L. *NEPA Compliance*: The National Environmental Policy Act (NEPA) provides guidelines for assessing the impact of proposed activity on the NPS corridor. Categorical exclusions have already been established that address possible NEPA concerns for most trail management activities.

New development such as highway building, powerline construction, extensive pest control, and other projects having a significant impact on NPS corridor lands would involve NEPA. Such decisions relating to NEPA compliance on NPS land remain an NPS responsibility.

M. *Costs*: The cost of A.T. management on NPS-acquired land is difficult to calculate. Volunteer leadership will reduce overall costs substantially, but ATC will incur additional expenses, as will some agency partners — mostly for staff time spent assisting local clubs.

In the case of ATC, the Board of Managers has made a commitment to embark on an aggressive fundraising program to help meet new responsibilities with a minimal amount of financial assistance from the federal government. Until that program is fully functioning, however, partial support for management through the NPS cooperative agreement will continue. ATC does not anticipate major expansion of the Harpers Ferry staff.

In the case of the back-up agencies it is still more difficult to estimate costs. Some partners may never be called upon for help in the field while others may have a fairly constant involvement on NPS lands. Time will be needed to learn from experience what sorts of costs are involved and how to meet them.

Overall, it is important to stress that the cost of corridor management by ATC should constitute a much smaller drain on the taxpayer than would direct NPS or other public agency management. Most of the burden is being borne by the private sector, either through volunteer commitment or through private financial support for ATC professional staff and other expenses.

Appalachian National Scenic Trail

Memorandum of Agreement
between
The National Park Service,
Department of the Interior
and
The Forest Service,
U.S. Department of Agriculture
concerning
Appalachian National Scenic Trail

This memorandum of agreement is made and entered into by and between the National Park Service and the Forest Service, in furtherance of the Act of October 2, 1968 (82 Stat. 919; 16 U.S.C. 1241).

WHEREAS the aforesaid act provides that the "Appalachian Trail shall be administered primarily as a footpath by the Secretary of the Interior, in consultation with the Secretary of Agriculture"; and

WHEREAS an agreement was entered into in May 1969 between the Departments of Agriculture and Interior (1) to establish mutual understandings on general matters pertaining to all operations of the National Trails System involving both Departments and (2) to provide for utilization of an Interagency Task Force to assist in the planning, coordination, development, and administration of that System; and

WHEREAS the said agreement recognizes the need and makes provision for supplemental agreements to cover development and management of specific Trails where two or more agencies are involved; and

WHEREAS significant portions of the Appalachian National Scenic Trail traverse lands under the separate administrative jurisdictions of the National Park Service and the Forest Service, as well as privately owned lands within the exterior boundaries of units administered by those Services; and

WHEREAS, it is the desire of the National Park Service and Forest Service to cooperate fully with each other, the Appalachian Trail Conference, the Advisory Council for the Appalachian National Scenic Trail, the affected States, political subdivisions thereof, and private owners in matters relating to administration and development, operation and maintenance of the said Trail (referred to herein as the Trail):

NOW, THEREFORE, the parties hereto mutually agree:

1. To cooperate with each other in developing uniform policies as to the location of the Trail corridor across private lands and as to the nature and extent of the interest in lands to be acquired.

It is further understood and agreed that all acquisitions of lands and interests in lands which are undertaken by the Forest Service for Trail purposes shall be reported to the National Park Service. General guidelines or criteria will be developed by those two agencies to determine the amount or proportion of such acquisition costs chargeable to the $5,000,000 limitation contained in section 10 of the aforesaid Act of October 2, 1968. The National Park Service shall compile and maintain a record of all appropriated funds expended by Federal agencies for the acquisition of lands or interests in lands for Trail purposes under that act, so that information will be available at all times as to the amounts expended and remaining available under the said statutory limitation.

2. For the purpose of enhancing the Trail environment, to designate zones for segments of the Trail which traverse areas under their separate administration, which zones will range from a minimum width of one hundred feet on each side of the Trail to any greater width necessary to assure maximum retention of the outdoor recreation experience for which the Trail was established. The determinations as to width of these zones will take into account variations in terrain, land cover, land management, scenic and historic points of interests, natural features, cultural qualities, recreational values and other factors that may affect operation, development and maintenance of the Trail. Said zones shall be planned and designated on development or management plans prepared in consultation with the Appalachian Trail Conference. Changes may be made in such zones for the purpose of enhancing the Trail environment, on the basis of the variations referred to above, and such changes shall be subject to consultation with the Conference.

3. To relocate wherever desirable—to the extent that the parties hereto have funds available for this purpose, and after consultation with the Appalachian Trail Conference—those portions of the Trail located on lands under their jurisdiction which lie within one mile of paralleling routes for the passage of motorized transportation.

All relocations of the Trail, including adjustments or alterations of the footpath which do not change either the officially described route of the Trail or the published maps of the Trail, as described and published in the "Federal Register," should be reported to the National Park Service and the Appalachian Trail Conference so that descriptions and maps of the Trail and guidebooks may be revised as necessary. However, if the ultimate change is of such a trivial nature as not to deviate more than 20 feet from the location established at the time of publication of the official Trail route, it need not be so reported.

4. To maintain—to the extent that available funds permit—the portions of the Trail which pass through areas under their separate jurisdiction, in cooperation with the Appalachian Trail Conference.

5. Each party to this agreement shall afford the other party thereto opportunities to review and comment on development plans with a view to harmonizing each others use and development programs for the Trail. Both parties hereto will cooperate with and encourage States, political subdivisions thereof, landowners, private organizations and individuals, to operate, develop, and maintain portions of the Trail and related Trail facilities. The parties will especially encourage the Appalachian Trail Conference, through local member clubs, to actively participate in the maintenance of the Trail and in the operation, development and maintenance of facilities along the Trail.

6. To erect at appropriate points on lands administered or controlled by them along the Trail, the uniform markers established for the Trail, and to maintain such markers. The erection and maintenance of these markers shall be in accordance with the standards established therefor.

7. To encourage local governments which have the authority to zone private lands adjacent to the Trail rights-of-way within the boundaries of areas under their separate jurisdictions, to control the uses of such properties, offering technical advice and assistance.

8. To cooperate in developing uniform regulations, insofar as possible, for the management, protection, development, administration, and use of segments of the Trail located on Federal lands under their separate jurisdictions, enforcement of which will be carried out by the agency administering the lands through which the Trail passes; and to encourage the adoption and enforcement of such uniform regulations by other Federal agencies for segments of the Trail they administer, and by States and local agencies for nonfederally owned portions of it.

9. To correlate and coordinate their interpretive activities and programs to avoid duplication in these matters and to assure that the interpretive efforts of each agency will complement those of the other. The National Park Service, as administering agency, will be responsible for developing and publishing any needed maps, brochures, press releases, etc., of a general nature for the entire Trail.

10. To meet from time to time for a discussion of matters of mutual concern affecting administration, development and use of the Trail so as to arrive at ways and means for furthering their cooperative efforts in these matters. Such meetings shall be held between persons or officials at comparable administrative levels.

Nothing in this agreement shall affect or interfere with fulfillment of the obligations and rights of the parties hereto to manage the lands and programs administered by them in accordance with their other basic land management responsibilities.

Either party may terminate this agreement by giving six months advance notice in writing to the other and either party may by similar notice to the other seek a modification of the agreement. It is subject to termination or modification at any time without prior notice, by mutual agreement.

This agreement supersedes "The Appalachian Trailway Agreement" entered into between the National Park Service and the Forest Service on October 15, 1938.

Date: Sep. 29, 1970   Edward A. Hummel
Acting Director, National Park Service   _____
U.S. Department of the Interior

Date: Oct. 6, 1970   M.M. Nelson
Acting Chief, Forest Service   _____
U.S. Department of Agriculture

The Appalachian Trailway Agreement

The Appalachian Trailway Agreement is the basic and controlling policy with respect to the Trail on Federal or State-owned lands. The Federal Appalachian Trailway Agreement follows:

MEMORANDUM OF AGREEMENT
between
THE NATIONAL PARK SERVICE
and
THE UNITED STATES FOREST SERVICE
for the Promotion of
THE APPALACHIAN TRAILWAY

WHEREAS, The Appalachian Trail is recognized as a regional project involving specialized forms of recreational land use; and

WHEREAS, Certain portions of the Trail traverse public lands under the separate jurisdictions of the National Park Service and the United States Forest Service; and

WHEREAS, The Federal Government is committed to the policy of fostering and promoting recreation in the public interest; and

WHEREAS, It is the desire of the respective Services to cooperate with the Appalachian Trail Conference and with the States through which the Trail passes in its protection and perpetuation;

NOW, THEREFORE, The National Park Service and the United States Forest Service do hereby mutually agree to carry out the following program, looking towards the creation of the Appalachian Trailway, insofar as consistent with their established policies, and subject to appropriate authority under Acts of Congress and the availability of funds therefor:

I

To designate a zone extending for a minimum width of one mile on each side of those portions of The Appalachian Trail which pass through areas under their separate jurisdiction, except in those localities where it descends into the main valleys, within which zone there will be constructed no new paralleling routes for the passage of motorized transportation and no developments which in the judgment of the administering agency are incompatible with the existence of said zone: Provided, that this agreement shall not be construed to effect the location of the Blue Ridge Parkway: Provided, further, that this shall not prevent logging and the construction of logging roads not open to the general public where the Trail crosses areas under management for the production of timber: Provided, further, that within 200 feet of the Trail no cutting primarily for timber production will take place.

II

To relocate wherever desirable and as rapidly as the agencies administering the land have available funds which can be devoted to these purposes and are not necessary for work of higher priority, and after agreement with the Appalachian Trail Conference, those portions of The Appalachian Trail which lie within one mile of paralleling routes for the passage of motorized transportation.

III

To maintain as well as available funds permit all other portions of The Appalachian Trail which pass through areas under their separate jurisdictions.

IV

To develop and maintain campsites with simple fireplace, water, sanitation and in most cases lean-to or other simple shelter facilities along or near the route of The Appalachian Trail wherever it passes through areas under their separate jurisdictions, and to locate such facilities so that they will not be more than a comfortable day's journey apart.

V

To cooperate with the several States and their political subdivisions in the gradual extension of public holdings along the general route of The Appalachian Trail, wherever the most justifiable forms of land use indicate such acquisition to be desirable, and as rapidly as the agencies administering the land have available funds which can be devoted to these purposes and are not necessary for work of higher priority.

VI

To encourage the acquisition of scenic easements along The Appalachian Trail or land use regulation through rural zoning, which ever appears to be the more feasible and economical means of protecting the scenic values of those portions of the Trailway which are not in public ownership.

VII

It is understood and agreed that this understanding may be terminated or modified in whole or in part upon six months' advance notice in writing given by either party hereto to the other.

Signed this 15th day of October, 1938.

By Arno B. Cammerer,
Director,
National Park Service.

By C. L. Forsling,
Acting Chief,
U.S. Forest Service.

* * * *

The Agreement with the States, to which all except Maine have adhered, differs in that the area is one-fourth mile on each side of the Trail. This limitation arises out of the limited area of the reservations in State ownership, which make the width in the Federal area, one mile, unworkable on the State-owned lands.

National Trails System Act

Public Law 90-543
(16 U.S.C. 1241 et seq.)
as amended
through P.L. 98-405, August 28, 1984

AN ACT

To establish a national trails system, and for other purposes.

Be it enacted by the Senate and House of Representatives of the United States of America in Congress assembled,

SHORT TITLE

SECTION 1. This Act may be cited as the "National Trails System Act".

STATEMENT OF POLICY

SEC. 2. (a) In order to provide for the ever-increasing outdoor recreation needs of an expanding population and in order to promote the preservation of, public access to, travel within, and enjoyment and appreciation of the open-air, outdoor areas and historic resources of the Nation, trails should be established (i) primarily, near the urban areas of the Nation, and (ii) secondarily, within scenic areas and along historic travel routes of the Nation which are often more remotely located.

(b) The purpose of this Act is to provide the means for attaining these objectives by instituting a national system of recreation, scenic and historic trails, by designating the Appalachian Trail and the Pacific Crest Trail as the initial components of that system, and by prescribing the methods by which, and standards according to which, additional components may be added to the system.

(c) The Congress recognizes the valuable contributions that volunteers and private, nonprofit trail groups have made to the development and maintenance of the Nation's trails. In recognition of these contributions, it is further the purpose of this Act to encourage and assist volunteer citizen involvement in the planning, development, maintenance, and management, where appropriate, of trails.

NATIONAL TRAILS SYSTEM

SEC. 3. (a) The national system of trails shall be composed of the following:

(1) National recreation trails, established as provided in section 4 of this Act, which will provide a variety of outdoor recreation uses in or reasonably accessible to urban areas.

(2) National scenic trails, established as provided in section 5 of this Act, which will be extended trails so located as to provide for maximum outdoor recreation potential and for the conservation and enjoyment of the nationally significant scenic, historic, natural, or cultural qualities of the areas through which such trails may pass. National scenic trails may be located so as to represent desert, marsh, grassland, mountain, canyon, river, forest, and other areas, as well as landforms which exhibit significant characteristics of the physiographic regions of the Nation.

(3) National historic trails, established as provided in section 5 of this Act, which will be extended trails which follow as closely as possible and practicable the original trails or routes of travel of national historic significance. Designation of such trails or routes shall be continuous, but the established or developed trail, and the acquisition thereof, need not be continuous on-site. National historic trails shall have as their purpose the identification and protection of the historic route and its historic remnants and artifacts for public use and enjoyment. Only those selected land and water based components of a historic trail which are on federally owned lands and which meet the national historic trail criteria established in this Act are included as Federal protection components of a national historic trail. The appropriate Secretary may certify other lands as protected segments of a historic trail upon application from State or local governmental agencies or private interests involved if such segments meet the national historic trail criteria established in this Act and such criteria supplementary thereto as the appropriate Secretary may prescribe, and are administered by such agencies or interests without expense to the United States.

(4) Connecting or side trails, established as provided in section 6 of this Act, which will provide additional points of public access to national recreation, national scenic or national historic trails or which will provide connections between such trails.

The Secretary of the Interior and the Secretary of Agriculture, in consultation with appropriate governmental agencies and public and private organizations, shall establish a uniform marker for the national trails system.

(b) For purposes of this section, the term 'extended trails' means trails or trail segments which total at least one hundred miles in length, except that historic trails of less than one hundred miles may be designated as extended trails. While it is desirable that extended trails be continuous, studies of such trails may conclude that it is feasible to propose one or more trail segments which, in the aggregate, constitute at least one hundred miles in length.

(c) On October 1, 1982, and at the beginning of each odd numbered fiscal year thereafter, the Secretary of the Interior shall submit to the Speaker of the United States House of Representatives and to the President of the United States Senate, an initial and revised (respectively) National Trails System plan. Such comprehensive plan shall indicate the scope and extent of a completed nationwide system of trails, to include (1) desirable nationally significant scenic and historic components which are considered necessary to complete a comprehensive national system, and (2) other trails which would balance out a complete and comprehensive nationwide system of trails. Such plan, and the periodic revisions thereto, shall be prepared in full consultation with the Secretary of Agriculture, the Governors of the various States, and the trails community.

NATIONAL RECREATION TRAILS

SEC. 4. (a) The Secretary of the Interior, or the Secretary of Agriculture where lands administered by him are involved, may establish and designate national recreation trails, with the consent of the Federal agency, State, or political subdivision having jurisdiction over the lands involved, upon finding that—

(i) such trails are reasonably accessible to urban areas, and, or

(ii) such trails meet the criteria established in this Act and such supplementary criteria as he may prescribe.

(b) As provided in this section, trails within park, forest, and other recreation areas administered by the Secretary of the Interior or the Secretary of Agriculture or in other federally administered areas may be established and designated as "National Recreation Trails" by the appropriate Secretary and, when no Federal land acquisition is involved—

(i) trails in or reasonably accessible to urban areas may be designated as "National Recreation Trails" by the appropriate Secretary with the consent of the States, their political subdivision, or other appropriate administering agencies;

(ii) trails within park, forest, and other recreation areas owned or administered by States may be designated as "National Recreation Trails" by the appropriate Secretary with the consent of the State; and

(iii) trails on privately owned lands may be designated 'National Recreation Trails' by the appropriate Secretary with the written consent of the owner of the property involved.

NATIONAL SCENIC AND NATIONAL HISTORIC TRAILS

SEC. 5. (a) National scenic and national historic trails shall be authorized and designated only by Act of Congress. There are hereby established the following National Scenic and National Historic Trails:

(1) The Appalachian National Scenic Trail, a trail of approximately two thousand miles extending generally along the Appalachian Mountains from Mount Katahdin, Maine, to Springer Mountain, Georgia. Insofar as practicable, the right-of-way for such trail shall comprise the trail depicted on the maps identified as "Nationwide System of Trails, Proposed Appalachian Trail, NST-AT-101-May 1967", which shall be on file and available for public inspection in the office of the Director of the National Park Service. Where practicable, such rights-of-way shall include lands protected for it under agreements in effect as of the date of enactment of this Act, to which Federal agencies and States were parties. The Appalachian Trail shall be administered primarily as a footpath by the Secretary of the Interior, in consultation with the Secretary of Agriculture.

(2) The Pacific Crest National Scenic Trail, a trail of approximately two thousand three hundred fifty miles, extending from the Mexican-California border northward generally along the mountain ranges of the west coast States to the Canadian-Washington border near Lake Ross, following the route as generally depicted on the map, identified as "Nationwide System of Trails, Proposed Pacific Crest Trail, NST-PC-103-May 1967" which shall be on file and available for public inspection in the office of the Chief of the Forest Service. The Pacific Crest Trail shall be administered by the Secretary of Agriculture, in consultation with the Secretary of the Interior.

(3) The Oregon National Historic Trail, a route of approximately two thousand miles extending from near Independence, Missouri, to the vicinity of Portland, Oregon, following a route as depicted on maps identified as 'Primary Route to the Oregon Trail 1841-1848', in the Department of the Interior's Oregon Trail study report dated April 1977, and which shall be on file and available for public inspection in the office of the Director of the National Park Service. The trail shall be administered by the Secretary of the Interior.

(4) The Mormon Pioneer National Historic Trail, a route of approximately one thousand three hundred miles extending from Nauvoo, Illinois, to Salt Lake City, Utah, following the primary historical route of the Mormon Trail as generally depicted on a map, identified as, 'Mormon Trail Vicinity Map, figure 2'
in the Department of the Interior Mormon Trail study report dated March 1977, and which shall be on file and available for public inspection in the office of the Director, National Park Service, Washington, D.C. The trail shall be administered by the Secretary of the Interior.

(5) The Continental Divide National Scenic Trail, a trail of approximately thirty-one hundred miles, extending from the Montana-Canada border to the New Mexico-Mexico border, following the approximate route depicted on the map, identified as 'Proposed Continental Divide National Scenic Trail' in the Department of the Interior Continental Divide Trail study report dated March 1977 and which shall be on file and available for public inspection in the office of the Chief, Forest Service, Washington, D.C. The Continental Divide National Scenic Trail shall be administered by the Secretary of Agriculture in consultation with the Secretary of the Interior. Notwithstanding the provisions of section 7(c), the use of motorized vehicles on roads which will be designated segments of the Continental Divide National Scenic Trail shall be permitted in accordance with regulations prescribed by the appropriate Secretary.

(6) The Lewis and Clark National Historic Trail, a trail of approximately three thousand seven hundred miles, extending from Wood River, Illinois, to the mouth of the Columbia River in Oregon, following the outbound and inbound routes of the Lewis and Clark Expedition depicted on maps identified as, 'Vicinity Map, Lewis and Clark Trail' study report dated April 1977. The map shall be on file and available for public inspection in the office of the Director, National Park Service, Washington, D.C. The trail shall be administered by the Secretary of the Interior.

(7) The Iditarod National Historic Trail, a route of approximately two thousand miles extending from Seward, Alaska, to Nome, Alaska, following the routes as depicted on maps identified as 'Seward-Nome Trail', in the Department of the Interior's study report entitled 'The Iditarod Trail (Seward-Nome Route) and other Alaskan Gold

Rush Trails' dated September 1977. The map shall be on file and available for public inspection in the office of the Director, National Park Service, Washington, D.C. The trail shall be administered by the Secretary of the Interior.

(8) The North County National Scenic Trail, a trail of approximately thirty-two hundred miles, extending from eastern New York State to the vicinity of Lake Sakakawea in North Dakota, following the approximate route depicted on the map identified as 'Proposed North Country Trail-Vicinity Map' in the Department of the Interior 'North Country Trail Report', dated June 1975. The map shall be on file and available for public inspection in the office of the Director, National Park Service, Washington, District of Columbia. The trail shall be administered by the Secretary of the Interior.

(9) The Overmountain Victory National Historic Trail, a system totaling approximately two hundred seventy-two miles of trail with routes from the mustering point near Abingdon, Virginia, to Sycamore Shoals (near Elizabethton, Tennessee); from Sycamore Shoals to Quaker Meadows (near Morganton, North Carolina); from the mustering point in Surry County, North Carolina, to Quaker Meadows; and from Quaker Meadows to Kings Mountain, South Carolina, as depicted on the map identified as Map 3—Historic Features—1780 in the draft study report entitled 'Overmountain Victory Trail' dated December 1979. The map shall be on file and available for public inspection in the Office of the Director, National Park Service, Washington, District of Columbia. The trail shall be administered by the Secretary of the Interior.

(10) The Ice Age National Scenic Trail, a trail of approximately one thousand miles, extending from Door County, Wisconsin, to Interstate Park in Saint Croix County, Wisconsin, generally following the route described in "On the Trail of the Ice Age—A Hiker's and Biker's Guide to Wisconsin's Ice Age National Scientific Reserve and Trail", by Henry S. Reuss, Member of Congress, dated 1980. The guide and maps shall be on file and available for public inspection in the Office of the Director, National Park Service, Washington, District of Columbia. Overall administration of the trail shall be the responsibility of the Secretary of the Interior pursuant to section 5(d) of this Act. The State of Wisconsin, in consultation with the Secretary of the Interior, may, subject to the approval of the Secretary, prepare a plan for the management of the trail which shall be deemed to meet the requirements of section 5(e) of this Act. Notwithstanding the provisions of section 7(c), snowmobile use may be permitted on segments of the Ice Age National Scenic Trail where deemed appropriate by the Secretary and the managing authority responsible for the segment.

[NOTE: the indented portion that follows was included in the legislation adding the Ice Age National Scenic Trail to the System (P.L. 96-370), but not as an amendment to P.L. 90-543.]

SEC. 2. Authorizations of moneys to be appropriated under this Act shall be effective on October 1, 1981. Notwithstanding any other provision of this Act, authority to enter into contracts, to incur obligations, or to make payments under this Act shall be effective only to the extent, and in such amounts, as are provided in advance in appropriation Acts.

(11) The Potomac Heritage National Scenic Trail, a corridor of approximately seven hundred and four miles following the route as generally depicted on the map identified as 'National Trails System, Proposed Potomac Heritage Trail' in 'The Potomac Heritage Trail', a report prepared by the Department of the Interior and dated

December 1974, except that no designation of the trail shall be made in the State of West Virginia. The map shall be on file and available for public inspection in the office of the Director of the National Park Service, Washington, District of Columbia. The trail shall initially consist of only those segments of the corridor located within the exterior boundaries of federally administered areas. No lands or interests therein outside the exterior boundaries of any federally administered area may be acquired by the Federal Government for the Potomac Heritage Trail. The Secretary of the Interior may designate lands outside of federally administered areas as segments of the trail, only upon application from the States or local governmental agencies involved, if such segments meet the criteria established in this Act and are administered by such agencies without expense to the United States. The trail shall be administered by the Secretary of the Interior.

(12) The Natchez Trace National Scenic Trail, a trail system of approximately six hundred and ninety-four miles extending from Nashville, Tennessee, to Natchez, Mississippi, as depicted on the map entitled 'Concept Plan, Natchez Trace Trails Study' in 'The Natchez Trace', a report prepared by the Department of the Interior and dated August 1979. The map shall be on file and available for public inspection in the office of the Director of the National Park Service, Department of the Interior, Washington, District of Columbia. The trail shall be administered by the Secretary of the Interior.

(13) The Florida National Scenic Trail, a route of approximately thirteen hundred miles extending through the State of Florida as generally depicted in 'The Florida Trail', a national scenic trail study draft report prepared by the Department of the Interior and dated February 1980. The report shall be on file and available for public inspection in the office of the Chief of the Forest Service, Washington, District of Columbia. No lands or interests therein outside the exterior boundaries of any federally administered area may be acquired by the Federal Government for the Florida Trail except with the consent of the owner thereof. The Secretary of Agriculture may designate lands outside of federally administered areas as segments of the trail, only upon application from the States or local governmental agencies involved, if such segments meet the criteria established in this Act and are administered by such agencies without expense to the United States. The trail shall be administered by the Secretary of Agriculture.

(b) The Secretary of the Interior, through the agency most likely to administer such trail, and the Secretary of Agriculture where lands administered by him are involved, shall make such additional studies as are herein or may hereafter be authorized by the Congress for the purpose of determining the feasibility and desirability of designating other trails as national scenic or national historic trails. Such studies shall be made in consultation with the heads of other Federal agencies administering lands through which such additional proposed trails would pass and in cooperation with interested interstate, State, and local governmental agencies, public and private organizations, and landowners and land users concerned. The feasibility of designating a trail shall be determined on the basis of an evaluation of whether or not it is physically possible to develop a trail along a route being studied, and whether the development of a trail would be financially feasible. The studies listed in subsection (c) of this section shall be completed and submitted to the Congress, with recommendations as to the suitability of trail designation, not later than three complete fiscal years from the date of enactment of their addition to this subsection, or from the date of enactment of this sentence, whichever is later. Such studies, when submitted, shall be printed as a House or Senate document, and shall include, but not be limited to:

(1) the proposed route of such trail (including maps and illustrations);

(2) the areas adjacent to such trails, to be utilized for scenic, historic, natural, cultural, or developmental, purposes;

(3) the characteristics which, in the judgment of the appropriate Secretary, make the proposed trail worthy of designation as a national scenic or national historic trail; and in the case of national historic trails the report shall include the recommendation of the Secretary of the Interior's National Park System Advisory Board as to the national historic significance based on the criteria developed under the Historic Sites Act of 1935 (40 Stat. 666; 16 U.S.C. 461);

(4) the current status of land ownership and current and potential use along the designated route;

(5) the estimated cost of acquisition of lands or interest in lands, if any;

(6) the plans for developing and maintaining the trail and the cost thereof;

(7) the proposed Federal administering agency (which, in the case of a national scenic trail wholly or substantially within a national forest, shall be the Department of Agriculture);

(8) the extent to which a State or its political subdivisions and public and private organizations might reasonably be expected to participate in acquiring the necessary lands and in the administration thereof;

(9) the relative uses of the lands involved, including: the number of anticipated visitor-days for the entire length of, as well as for segments of, such trail; the number of months which such trail, or segments thereof, will be open for recreation purposes; the economic and social benefits which might accrue from alternate land uses; and the estimated man-years of civilian employment and expenditures expected for the purposes of maintenance, supervision, and regulation of such trail;

(10) the anticipated impact of public outdoor recreation use on the preservation of a proposed national historic trail and its related historic and archeological features and settings, including the measures proposed to ensure evaluation and preservation of the values that contribute to their national historic significance; and

(11) to qualify for designation as a national historic trail, a trail must meet all three of the following criteria;

(A) It must be a trail or route established by historic use and must be historically significant as a result of that use. The route need not currently exist as a discernible trail to qualify, but its location must be sufficiently known to permit evaluation of public recreation and historical interest potential. A designated trail should generally accurately follow the historic route, but may deviate somewhat on occasion of necessity to avoid difficult routing through subsequent development, or to provide some route variations offering a more pleasurable recreational experience. Such deviations shall be so noted on site. Trail segments no longer possible to travel by trail due to subsequent development as motorized transportation routes may be designated and marked onsite as segments which link to the historic trail.

(B) It must be of national significance with respect to any of several broad facets of American history, such as trade and commerce, exploration, migration and settlement, or military campaigns. To qualify as nationally significant, historic use of the trail must have had a far-reaching effect on broad patterns of American culture. Trails significant in the history of native Americans may be included.

(C) It must have significant potential for public recreational use or historical interest based on historic interpretation and appreciation. The potential for such use is generally greater along roadless segments developed as historic trails and at historic sites associated with the trail. The presence of recreation potential not related to historic appreciation is not sufficient justification for designation under this category.

(c) The following routes shall be studies in accordance with the objectives outlined in subsection (b) of this section.

(1) Continental Divide Trail, a three-thousand-one-hundred-mile trail extending from near the Mexican border in southwestern New Mexico northward generally along the Continental Divide to the Canadian border in Glacier National Park.

(2) Potomac Heritage Trail, an eight-hundred-and-twenty-five-mile trail extending generally from the mouth of the Potomac River to its sources in Pennsylvania and West Virginia including the one-hundred-and-seventy-mile Chesapeake and Ohio Canal towpath.

(3) Old Cattle Trails of the Southwest from the vicinity of San Antonio, Texas, approximately eight hundred miles through Oklahoma via Baxter Springs and Chetopa, Kansas to Fort Scott, Kansas, including the Chisholm Trail, from the vicinity of San Antonio or Cuero, Texas, approximately eight hundred miles north through Oklahoma to Abilene, Kansas.

(4) Lewis and Clark Trail, from Wood River, Illinois, to the Pacific Ocean in Oregon, following both the outbound and inbound routes of the Lewis and Clark Expedition.

(5) Natchez Trace, from Nashville, Tennessee, approximately six hundred miles to Natchez, Mississippi.

(6) North Country Trail, from the Appalachian Trail in Vermont, approximately three thousand two hundred miles through the States of New York, Pennsylvania, Ohio, Michigan, Wisconsin, and Minnesota, to the Lewis and Clark Trail in North Dakota.

(7) Kittanning Trail from Shirleysburg in Huntingdon County to Kittanning, Armstrong County, Pennsylvania.

(8) Oregon Trail, from Independence, Missouri, approximately two thousand miles to near Fort Vancouver, Washington.

(9) Santa Fe Trail, from Independence, Missouri, approximately eight hundred miles to Santa Fe, New Mexico.

(10) Long Trail extending two hundred and fifty-five miles from the Massachusetts border northward through Vermont to the Canadian border.

(11) Mormon Trail, extending from Nauvoo, Illinois, to Salt Lake City, Utah, through the States of Iowa, Nebraska, and Wyoming.

(12) Gold Rush Trails in Alaska.

(13) Mormon Battalion Trail, extending two thousand miles from Mount Pisgah, Iowa, through Kansas, Colorado, New Mexico, and Arizona to Los Angeles, California.

(14) El Camino Real from St. Augustine to San Mateo, Florida, approximately 20 miles along the southern boundary of the St. Johns River from Fort Caroline National Memorial to the St. August National Park Monument.

(15) Bartram Trail, extending through the States of Georgia, North Carolina, South Carolina, Alabama, Florida, Louisiana, Mississippi, and Tennessee.

(16) Daniel Boone Trail, extending from the vicinity of Statesville, North Carolina, to Fort Boonesborough State Park, Kentucky.

(17) Desert Trail, extending from the Canadian border through parts of Idaho, Washington, Oregon, Nevada, California, and Arizona, to the Mexican border.

(18) Dominguez-Escalante Trail, extending approximately two thousand miles along the route of the 1776 expedition led by Father Francisco Atanasio Dominguez and Father Silvestre Velez de Escalante, originating in Sante Fe, New Mexico; proceeding northwest along the San Juan, Dolores, Gunnison, and White Rivers in Colorado, thence westerly to Utah Lake; thence southward to Arizona and returning to Santa Fe.

(19) Florida Trail, extending north from Everglade National Park, including the Big Cypress Swamp, the Kissimme Prairie, the Withlacoochee State Forest, Ocala National Forest, Osceola National Forest, and Black Water River State Forest, said completed trail to be approximately one thousand three hundred miles along, of which over four hundred miles of trail have already been built.

(20) Indian Nations Trail, extending from the Red River in Oklahoma approximately two hundred miles northward through the former Indian nations to the Oklahoma-Kansas boundary line.

(21) Nez Perce Trail extending from the vicinity of Wallowa Lake, Oregon, to Bear Paw Mountain, Montana.

(22) Pacific Northwest Trail, extending approximately one thousand miles from the Continental Divide in Glacier National Park, Montana, to the Pacific Ocean beach of Olympic National Park, Washington, by way of —

(A) Flathead National Forest and Kootenai National Forest in the State of Montana;

(B) Kaniksu National Forest in the State of Idaho; and

(C) Colville National Forest, Okanogan National Forest, Pasayten Wilderness Area, Ross Lake National Recreation Area, North Cascades National Park, Mount Baker, the Skagit River, Deception Pass, Whidbey Island, Olympic National Forest, and Olympic National Park in the State of Washington.

(23) Overmountain Victory Trail, extending from the vicinity of Elizabethton, Tennessee, to Kings Mountain National Military Park, South Carolina.

(24) Juan Bautista de Anza Trail, following the overland route taken by Juan Bautista de Anza in connection with his travels from the United Mexican States to San Francisco, California.

(25) Trail of Tears, including the associated forts and specifically, Fort Mitchell, Alabama, and historic properties, extending from the vicinity of Murphy, North Carolina, through Georgia, Alabama, Tennessee, Kentucky, Illinois, Missouri, and Arkansas, to the vicinity of Tahlequah, Oklahoma.

(26) Illinois Trail, extending from the Lewis and Clark Trail at Wood River, Illinois to the Chicago Portage National Historic Site, generally following the Illinois River and the Illinois and Michigan Canal.

(27) Jedediah Smith Trail, to include the routes of the explorations led by Jedediah Smith —

(A) during the period 1826-1827, extending from the Idaho-Wyoming border, through the Great Salt Lake, Sevier, Virginia and Colorado River Valleys, and the Mojave Desert, to the San Gabriel Mission, California; thence through the Tehachapi Mountains, San Joaquin and Stanislaus River Valleys, Ebbetts Pass, Walker River Valley, Bald Mount, Mount Grafton, and Great Salt Lake to Bear Lake, Utah; and

(B) during 1828, extending from the Sacramento and Trinity River Valleys along the Pacific coastline, through the Smith and Willamette River Valleys to the Fort Vancouver National Historic Site, Washington, on the Columbia River.

(28) General Crook Trail, extending from Prescott, Arizona, across the Mogollon Rim to Fort Apache.

(29) Beale Wagon Road, within the Kaibab and Cononino National Forests in Arizona; *Provided*, Such study may be prepared in conjunction with ongoing planning processes for these National Forests to be completed before 1990.

(30) Pony Express Trail, extending from Saint Joseph, Missouri, through Kansas, Nebraska, Colorado, Wyoming, Utah, Nevada, to Sacramento, California, as indicated on a map labeled "Potential Pony Express Trail", dated October 1983 and the California Trail extending from the vicinity of Omaha, Nebraska, and Saint Joseph, Missouri, to various points in California, as indicated on a map labeled "Potential California Trail" and dated August 1, 1983. Notwithstanding subsection (b) of this section, the study under this paragraph shall be completed and submitted to the Congress no later than the end of two complete fiscal years beginning after the date of the enactment of this paragraph. Such study shall be separated into two portions, one relating to the Pony Express Trail and one relating to the California Trail.

(d) The Secretary charged with the administration of each respective trail shall, within one year of the date of the addition of any national scenic or national historic trail to the system, and within sixty days of the enactment of this sentence for the Appalachian and Pacific Crest National Scenic Trails, establish an advisory council for each such trail, each of which councils shall expire ten years from the date of its establishment. If the appropriate Secretary is unable to establish such an advisory council because of the lack of adequate public interest, the Secretary shall so advise the appropriate committees of the Congress. The appropriate Secretary shall consult with such council from time to time with respect to matters relating to the trail, including the selection of rights-of-way, standards for the erection and maintenance of markers along the trail, and the maintenance of markers along the trail, and the administration of the trail. The members of each advisory council, which shall not exceed thirty-five in number, shall serve for a term of two years and without compensation as such, but the Secretary may pay, upon vouchers signed by the chairman of the council, the expenses reasonably incurred by the council and its members in carrying out their responsibilities under this section. Members of each council shall be appointed by the appropriate Secretary as follows:

(1) the head of each Federal department or independent agency administering lands through which the trail route passes, or his designee;

(2) a member appointed to represent each State through which the trail passes, and such appointments shall be made from recommendations of the Governors of such States;

(3) one or more members appointed to represent private organizations, including corporate and individual landowners and land users, which in the opinion of the Secretary, have an established and recognized interest in the trail, and such appointments shall be made from recommendations of the heads of such organizations: *Provided*, That the Appalachian Trail Conference shall be represented by a sufficient number of persons to represent the various sections of the country through which the Appalachian Trail passes; and

(4) the Secretary shall designate one member to be chairman and shall fill vacancies in the same manner as the original appointment.

(e) Within two complete fiscal years of the date of enactment of legislation designating a national scenic trail, except for the Continental Divide National Scenic Trail and the North Country National Scenic Trail as part of the system, and within two complete fiscal years of the date of enactment of this subsection for the Pacific Crest and Appalachian Trails, the responsible Secretary shall, after full consultation with affected Federal land managing agencies, the Governors of the affected States, the relevant advisory council established pursuant to section 5(d), and the Appalachian Trail Conference in the case of the Appalachian Trail, submit to the Committee on Interior and Insular Affairs of the House of Representatives and the Committee on Energy and Natural Resources of the Senate, a comprehensive plan for the acquisition, management, development, and use of the trail, including but not limited to, the following items:

(1) specific objectives and practices to be observed in the management of the trail, including the identification of all significant natural, historical, and cultural resources to be preserved (along with high potential historic sites and high potential route segments in the case of national historic trails), details of anticipated cooperative agreements to be consummated with other entities, and an identified carrying capacity of the trail and a plan for its implementation;

(2) an acquisition or protection plan, by fiscal year, for all lands to be acquired by fee title or lesser interest, along with detailed explanation of anticipated necessary cooperative agreements for any lands not to be acquired; and

(3) general and site-specific development plans including anticipated costs.

(f) Within two complete fiscal years of the date of enactment of legislation designating a national historic trail or the Continental Divide National Scenic Trail or the North Country National Scenic Trail as part of the system, the responsible Secretary shall, after full consultation with affected Federal land managing agencies, the Governors of the affected States, and the relevant Advisory Council established pursuant to section 5(d) of this Act, submit to the Committee on Interior and Insular Affairs of the House of Representatives and the Committee on Energy and Natural Resources of the Senate, a comprehensive plan for the management; and use of the trail, including but not limited to, the following items:

(1) specific objectives and practices to be observed in the management of the trail, including the identification of all significant natural, historical, and cultural resources to be preserved, details of any anticipated cooperative agreements to be consummated with State and local government agencies or private interests, and for national scenic or national historic trails an identified carrying capacity of the trail and a plan for its implementation;

(2) the process to be followed by the appropriate Secretary to implement the marking requirements established in section 7(c) of this Act;

(3) a protection plan for any high potential historic sites or high potential route segments; and

(4) general and site-specific development plans, including anticipated costs.

CONNECTING AND SIDE TRAILS

SEC. 6. Connecting or side trails within park, forest, and other recreation areas administered by the Secretary of the Interior or Secretary of Agriculture may be established, designated, and marked by the appropriate Secretary as components of a national recreation, national scenic or national historic trail. When no Federal land acquisition is involved, connecting or side trails may be located across lands administered by interstate, State, or local governmental agencies with their consent, or, where the appropriate Secretary deems necessary or desirable, on privately owned lands with the consent of the landowners. Applications for approval and designation of connecting and side trails on non-Federal lands shall be submitted to the appropriate Secretary.

ADMINISTRATION AND DEVELOPMENT

SEC. 7. (a)(1)(A) The Secretary charged with the overall administration of a trail pursuant to section 5(a) shall, in administering and managing the trail, consult with the heads of all other affected State and Federal agencies. Nothing contained in this Act shall be deemed to transfer among Federal agencies any management responsibilities established under any other law for federally administered lands which are components of the National Trails System. Any transfer of management responsibilities may be carried out between the Secretary of the Interior and the Secretary of Agriculture only as provided under subparagraph (B).

(B) The Secretary charged with the overall administration of any trail pursuant to section 5(a) may transfer management of any specified trail segment of such trail to the other appropriate Secretary pursuant to a joint memorandum of agreement containing such terms and conditions as the Secretaries consider most appropriate to accomplish the purposes of this Act. During any period in which management responsibilities for any trail segment are transferred under such an agreement, the management of any such segment shall be subject to the laws, rules, and regulations of the Secretary provided with the management authority under the agreement except to such extent as the agreement may otherwise expressly provide.

(2) Pursuant to section 5(a), the appropriate Secretary shall select the rights-of-way for national scenic and national historic trails and shall publish notice thereof of the availability of appropriate maps or descriptions in the Federal Register; *Provided,* That in selecting the rights-of-way full consideration shall be given to minimizing the adverse effects upon the adjacent landowner or user and his operation. Development and management of each segment of the National Trails System shall be designed to harmonize with and complement any established multiple-use plans for the specific area in order to insure continued maximum benefits from the land. The location and width of such rights-of-way across Federal lands under the jurisdiction of another Federal agency shall be by agreement between the head of that agency and the appropriate Secretary. In selecting rights-of-way for trail purposes, the Secretary shall obtain the advice and assistance of the States, local governments, private organizations, and landowners and land users concerned.

(b) After publication on notice of the availability of appropriate maps or descriptions in the Federal Register, the Secretary charged with the administration of a national scenic or national historic trail may relocate segments of a national scenic or national historic trail right-of-way, with the concurrence of the head of the Federal agency having jurisdiction over the lands involved, upon a determination that: (i) such a relocation is necessary to preserve the purposes for which the trail was established, or (ii) the relocation is necessary to promote a sound land management program in accordance with established multiple-use principles: *Provided,* That a substantial relocation of the rights-of-way for such trail shall be by Act of Congress.

(c) National scenic or national historic trails may contain campsites,shelters, and related-public-use facilities. Other uses along the trail, which will not substantially interfere with the nature and purposes of the trail, may be permitted by the Secretary charged with the administration of the trail. Reasonable efforts shall be made to provide sufficient access opportunities to such trails and, to the extent practicable, efforts be made to avoid activities incompatible with the purposes for which such trails were established. The use of motorized vehicles by the general public along any national scenic trail shall be prohibited and nothing in this Act shall be construed as authorizing the use of motorized vehicles within the natural and historical areas of the national park system, the national wildlife refuge system, the national wilderness preservation system where they are presently prohibited or on other Federal lands where trails are designated as being closed to such use by the appropriate Secretary: *Provided,* That the Secretary charged with the administration of such trail shall establish regulations which shall authorize the use of motorized vehicles when, in his judgment, such vehicles are necessary to meet emergencies or to enable adjacent landowners and land users to have reasonable access to their lands or timber rights: *Provided further,* That private lands included in the national recreation, national scenic, or national historic trails by cooperative agreement of a landowner shall not preclude such owner from using motorized vehicles on or across such trails or adjacent lands from time to time in accordance with regulations to be established by the appropriate Secretary. Where a national historic trail follows existing public roads, developed rights-of-way or waterways, and similar features of man's nonhistorically related development, approximating the original location of a historic route, such segments may be marked to facilitate retracement of the historic route, and where a national historic trail parallels an existing public road, such road may be marked to commemorate the historic route. Other uses along the historic trails and the Continental Divide National Scenic Trail, which will not substantially interfere with the nature and purposes of the trail, and which, at the time of designation, are allowed by administrative regulations, including the use of motorized vehicles, shall be permitted by the Secretary charged with administration of the trail. The Secretary of the Interior and the Secretary of Agriculture, in consultation with appropriate governmental agencies and public and private organizations, shall establish a uniform marker, including thereon an appropriate and distinctive symbol for each national recreation, national scenic, and national historic trail. Where the trails cross lands administered by Federal agencies such markers shall be erected at appropriate points along the trails and maintained by the Federal agency administering the trail in accordance with standards established by the appropriate Secretary and where the trails cross non-Federal lands, in accordance with written cooperative agreements, the appropriate Secretary shall provide such uniform markers to cooperating agencies and shall require such agencies to erect and maintain them in accordance with the standards established. The appropriate Secretary may also provide for trail interpretation sites, which shall be located at historic sites along the route of any national scenic or national historic trail, in order to present information to the public about the trail, at the lowest possible cost, with emphasis on the portion of the trail passing through the State in which the site is located. Wherever possible, the sites shall be maintained by a State agency under a cooperative agreement between the appropriate Secretary and the State agency.

(d) Within the exterior boundaries of areas under their administration that are included in the right-of-way selected for a national recreation, national scenic, or national historic trail, the heads of Federal agencies may use lands for trail purposes and may acquire lands or interests in lands by written cooperative agreement, donation, purchase with donated or appropriated funds or exchange.

(e) Where the lands included in a national scenic or national historic trail right-of-way are outside of the exterior boundaries of federally administered areas, the Secretary charged with the administration of such trail shall encourage the States or local governments involved (1) to enter into written cooperative agreements with landowners, private organizations, and individuals to provide the necessary trail right-of-way, or (2) to acquire such lands or interests therein to be utilized as segments of the national scenic or national historic trail: *Provided,* That if the State or local governments fail to enter into such written cooperative agreements or to acquire such lands or interests therein after notice of the selection of the right-of-way is published, the appropriate Secretary, may (i) enter into such agreements with landowners, States, local governments, private organizations, and individuals for the use of lands for trail purposes, or (ii) acquire private lands or interests therein by donation, purchase with donated or appropriated funds or exchange in accordance with the provisions of subsection (f) of this section: *Provided further,* That the appropriate Secretary may acquire lands or interests therein from local governments or governmental corporations with the consent of such entities. The lands involved in such rights-of-way should be acquired in fee, if other methods of public control are not sufficient to assure their use for the purpose for which they are acquired: *Provided,* That if the Secretary charged with the administration of such trail permanently relocates the right-of-way and disposes of all title or interest in the land, the original owner, or his heirs or assigns, shall be offered, by notice given at the former owner's last known address, the right of first refusal at the fair market price.

(f)(1) The Secretary of the Interior, in the exercise of his exchange authority, may accept title to any non-Federal property within the right-of-way and in exchange therefor he may convey to the grantor of such property any federally owned property under his jurisdiction which is located in the State wherein such property is located and which he classifies as suitable for exchange or other disposal. The values of the properties so exchanged either shall be approximately equal, or if they are not approximately equal the values shall be equalized by the payment of cash to the grantor or to the Secretary as the circumstances require. The Secretary of Agriculture, in the exercise of his exchange authority, may utilize authorities and procedures available to him in connection with exchanges of national forest lands.

(2) In acquiring lands or interests therein for a National Scenic or Historic Trail, the appropriate Secretary may, with consent of a landowner, acquire whole tracts notwithstanding that parts of such tracts may lie outside the area of trail acquisition. In furtherance of the purposes of this act, lands so acquired outside the area of trail acquisition may be exchanged for any non-Federal lands or interests therein within the trail right-of-way, or disposed of in accordance with such procedures or regulations as the appropriate Secretary shall prescribe, including: (i) provisions for conveyance of such acquired lands or interests therein at not less than fair market value to the highest bidder, and (ii) provisions for allowing the last owners of record a right to purchase said acquired lands or interests therein upon payment or agreement to pay an amount equal to the highest bid price. For lands designated for exchange or disposal, the appropriate Secretary may convey these lands with any reservations or covenants deemed desirable to further the purposes of this Act. The proceeds from any disposal shall be credited to the appropriation bearing the costs of land acquisition for the affected trail.

(g) The appropriate Secretary may utilize condemnation proceedings without the consent of the owner to acquire private lands or interests, therein pursuant to this section only in cases where, in his judgment, all reasonable efforts to acquire such lands or interest therein by negotiation have failed, and in such cases he shall acquire only such title as, in his judgment, is reasonably necessary to provide passage across such lands: *Provided,* That condemnation proceedings may not be utilized to acquire fee title or lesser interests to more than an average of one hundred and twenty-five acres per mile. Money appropriated for Federal purposes from the land and water conservation fund shall, without prejudice to appropriations from other sources, be available to Federal departments for the acquisition of lands or interests in lands for the purposes of this Act. For national historic trails, direct Federal acquisition for trail purposes shall be limited to those areas indicated by the study report or by the comprehensive plan as high potential route segments or high potential historic sites. Except for designated protected components of the trail, no land or site located along a designated national historic trail or along the Continental Divide National Scenic Trail shall be subject to the provisions of section 4(f) of the Department of Transportation Act (49 U.S.C. 1653(f)) unless such land or site is deemed to be of historical significance under appropriate historical site criteria such as those for the National Register of Historic Places.

(h)(1) The Secretary charged with the administration of a national recreation, national scenic, or national historic trail shall provide for the development and maintenance of such trails within federally administered areas and shall cooperate with and encourage the States to operate, develop, and maintain portions of such trails which are located outside the boundaries of federally administered areas. When deemed to be in the public interest, such Secretary may enter written cooperative agreements with the States or their political subdivisions, landowners, private organizations, or individuals to operate, develop, and maintain any portion of such a trail either within or outside a federally administered area. Such agreements may include provisions for limited financial assistance to encourage participation in the acquisition, protection, operation, development, or maintenance of such trails, provisions providing volunteer in the park or volunteer in the forest status (in accordance with the Volunteers in the Parks Act of 1969 and the Volunteers in the Forests Act of 1972) to individuals, private organizations, or landowners participating in such activities, or provisions of both types. The appropriate Secretary shall also initiate consultations with affected States and their political subdivisions to encourage—

(A) the development and implementation by such entities of appropriate measures to protect private landowners from trespass resulting from trail use and from unreasonable personal liability and property damage caused by trail use, and

(B) the development and implementation by such entities of provisions for land practices, compatible with the purposes of this Act,

for property within or adjacent to trail rights-of-way. After consulting with States and their political subdivisions under the preceding sentence, the Secretary may provide assistance to such entities under appropriate cooperative agreements in the manner provided by this subsection.

(2) Whenever the Secretary of the Interior makes any conveyance of land under any of the public land laws, he may reserve a right-of-way for trails to the extent he deems necessary to carry out the purposes of this Act.

(i) The appropriate Secretary, with the concurrence of the heads of any other Federal agencies administering lands through which a national recreation, national scenic, or national historic trail passes, and after consultation with the States, local governments, and organizations concerned, may issue regulations, which may be revised from time to time, governing the use, protection, management, development, and administration of trails of the national trails system. In order to maintain good conduct on and along the trails located within federally administered areas and to provide for the proper government and protection of such trails, the Secretary of the Interior and the Secretary of Agriculture shall prescribe and publish such uniform regulations as they deem necessary and any person who violates such regulations shall be guilty of a misdemeanor, and may be punished by a fine of not more than $500, or by imprisonment not exceeding six months, or by both such fine and imprisonment. The Secretary responsible for the administration of any segment of any component of the National Trails System (as determined in a manner consistent with subsection (a)(1) of this section) may also utilize authorities related to units of the national park system or the national forest system, as the case may be, in carrying out his administrative responsibilities for such component.

(j) Potential trail uses allowed on designated components of the national trails system may include, but are not limited to, the following: bicycling, cross-country skiing, day hiking, equestrian activities, jogging or similar fitness activities, trail biking, overnight and long-distance back-packing, snowmobiling, and surface water and underwater activities. Vehicles which may be permitted on certain trails may include, but need not be limited to, motorcycles, bicycles, four-wheel drive or all-terrain off-road vehicles.

In addition, trail access for handicapped individuals may be provided. The provisions of this subsection shall not supersede any other provisions of this Act or other Federal laws, or any State or local laws.

(k) For the conservation purpose of preserving or enhancing the recreational, scenic, natural, or historical values of components of the national trails system, and environs thereof as determined by the appropriate Secretary, landowners are authorized to donate or otherwise convey qualified real property interests to qualified organizations consistent with section 170(h)(3) of the Internal Revenue Code of 1954, including, but not limited to, right-of-way, open space, scenic, or conservation easements, without regard to any limitation on the nature of the estate or interest otherwise transferable within the jurisdiction where the land is located. The conveyance of any such interest in land in accordance with this subsection shall be deemed to further a Federal conservation policy and yield a significant public benefit for purposes of section 6 of Public Law 96-541.

STATE AND METROPOLITAN AREA TRAILS

SEC. 8. (a) The Secretary of the Interior is directed to encourage States to consider, in their comprehensive statewide outdoor recreation plans and proposals for financial assistance for State and local projects submitted pursuant to the Land and Water Conservation Fund Act, needs and opportunities for establishing park, forest, and other recreation and historic trails on lands owned or administered by States, and recreation and historic trails on lands in or near urban areas. The Secretary is also directed to encourage States to consider, in their comprehensive statewide historic preservation plans and proposals for financial assistance for State, local, and private projects submitted pursuant to the Act of October 15, 1966 (80 Stat. 915), as amended, needs and opportunities for establishing historic trails. He is further directed in accordance with the authority contained in the Act of May 28, 1963 (77 Stat. 49), to encourage States, political subdivisions, and private interests, including nonprofit organizations, to establish such trails.

(b) The Secretary of Housing and Urban Development is directed, in administering the program of comprehensive urban planning and assistance under section 701 of the Housing Act of 1954, to encourage the planning of recreation trails in connection with the recreation and transportation planning for metropolitan and other urban areas. He is further directed, in administering the urban openspace program under title VII of the Housing Act of 1961, to encourage such recreation trails.

(c) The Secretary of Agriculture is directed, in accordance with authority vested in him, to encourage States and local agencies and private interests to establish such trails.

(d) The Secretary of Transportation, the Chairman of the Interstate Commerce Commission, and the Secretary of the Interior, in administering the Railroad Revitalization and Regulatory Reform Act of 1976, shall encourage State and local agencies and private interests to establish appropriate trails using the provisions of such programs. Consistent with the purposes of that Act, and in furtherance of the national policy to preserve established railroad rights-of-way for future reactivation of rail service, to protect rail transportation corridors, and to encourage energy efficient transportation use, in the case of interim use of any established railroad rights-or-way pursuant to donation, transfer, lease, sale, or otherwise in a manner consistent with the National Trails System Act, if such interim use is subject to restoration or reconstruction for railroad purposes, such interim use shall not be treated, for purposes of any law or rule of law, as an abandonment of the use of such rights-of-way for railroad purposes. If a State, political subdivision, or qualified private organization is prepared to assume full responsibility for management of such rights-of-way and for any legal liability arising out of such transfer or use, and for the payment of any and all taxes that may be levied or assessed against such rights-of-way, then the Commission shall impose such terms and conditions as a requirement of any transfer or conveyance for interim use in a manner consistent with this Act, and shall not permit abandonment or discontinuance inconsistent or disruptive of such use.

(e) Such trails may be designated and suitably marked as parts of the nationwide system of trails by the States, their political subdivisions, or other appropriate administering agencies with the approval of the Secretary of the Interior.

RIGHTS-OF-WAY AND OTHER PROPERTIES

SEC. 9. (a) The Secretary of the Interior or the Secretary of Agriculture as the case may be, may grant easements and rights-of-way upon, over, under, across, or along any component of the national trails system in accordance with the laws applicable to the national park system and the national forest system, respectively: *Provided*, That any conditions contained in such easements and rights-of-way shall be related to the policy and purposes of this Act.

(b) The Department of Defense, the Department of Transportation, the Interstate Commerce Commission, the Federal Communications Commission, the Federal Power Commission, and other Federal agencies having jurisdiction or control over or information concerning the use, abandonment, or disposition of roadways, utility rights-of-way, or other properties which may be suitable for the purpose of improving or expanding the national trails system shall cooperate with the Secretary of the Interior and the Secretary of Agriculture in order to assure, to the extent practicable, that any such properties having values suitable for trail purposes may be made available for such use.

AUTHORIZATION OF APPROPRIATIONS

SEC. 10. (a)(1) There are hereby authorized to be appropriated for the acquisition of lands or interests in lands not more than $5,000,000 for the Appalachian National Scenic Trail and not more than $500,000 for the Pacific Crest National Scenic Trail. From the appropriations authorized for fiscal year 1979 and succeeding fiscal years pursuant to the Land and Water Conservation Fund Act (78 Stat. 897), as amended, not more than the following amounts may be expended for the acquisition of lands and interests in lands authorized to be acquired pursuant to the provisions of this Act: for the Appalachian National Scenic Trail, not to exceed $30,000,000 for fiscal year 1979; $30,000,000 for fiscal year 1980, and $30,000,000 for fiscal year 1981, except that the difference between the foregoing amounts and the actual appropriations in any one fiscal year shall be available for appropriation in subsequent fiscal years.

(2) It is the express intent of the Congress that the Secretary should substantially complete the land acquisition program necessary to insure the protection of the Appalachian Trail within three complete fiscal years following the date of enactment of this sentence. Until the entire acquisition program is completed, he shall transmit

in writing at the close of each fiscal year the following information to the Committee on Energy and Natural Resources of the Senate and the Committee on Interior and Insular Affairs of the House of Representatives:

(A) the amount of land acquired during the fiscal year and the amount expended therefor:

(B) the estimated amount of land remaining to be acquired; and

(C) the amount of land planned for acquisition in the ensuing fiscal year and the estimated cost thereof.

(b) For the purposes of Public Law 95-42 (91 Stat. 211), the lands and interests therein acquired pursuant to this section shall be deemed to qualify for funding under the provisions of section 1, clause 2, of said Act.

(c)(1) There is hereby authorized to be appropriated such sums as may be necessary to implement the provisions of this Act relating to the trails designated by paragraphs 5(a)(3), (4), (5), (6), (7), (8), (9) and (10): *Provided*, That no such funds are authorized to be appropriated prior to October 1, 1978: *And provided further*, That notwithstanding any other provisions of this Act or any other provisions of law, no funds may be expended by Federal agencies for the acquisition of lands or interests in lands outside the exterior boundaries of existing Federal areas for the Continental Divide National Scenic Trail, the North Country National Scenic Trail, The Ice Age National Scenic Trail, the Oregon National Historic Trail, the Mormon Pioneer National Historic Trail, the Lewis and Clark National Historic Trail, and the Iditarod National Historic Trail, except that funds may be expended for the acquisition of lands or interests therein for the purpose of providing for one trail interpretation site, as described in section 7(c), along with such trail in each State crossed by the trail.

(2) There is hereby authorized to be appropriated for fiscal year 1983 and subsequent fiscal years such sums as may be necessary to implement the provisions of this Act relating to the trails designated by paragraphs (9) through (13) of section 5(a) of this Act. Not more than $500,000 may be appropriated for the purposes of acquisition of land and interests therein for the trail designated by section 5(a)(12) of this Act, and not more than $2,000,000 may be appropriated for the purposes of the development of such trail. The administrating agency for the trail shall encourage volunteer trail groups to participate in the development of the trail.

VOLUNTEER TRAILS ASSISTANCE

SEC. 11. (a)(1) In addition to the cooperative agreement and other authorities contained in this Act, the Secretary of the Interior, the Secretary of Agriculture, and the head of any Federal agency administering Federal lands, are authorized to encourage volunteers and volunteer organizations to plan, develop, maintain, and manage, where appropriate, trails throughout the Nation.

(2) Wherever appropriate in furtherance of the purposes of this Act, the Secretaries are authorized and encouraged to utilize the Volunteers in the Parks Act of 1969, the Volunteers in the Forests Act of 1972, and section 6 of the Land and Water Conservation Fund Act of 1965 (relating to the development of Statewide Comprehensive Outdoor Recreation Plans).

(b) Each Secretary or the head of any Federal land managing agency, may assist volunteers and volunteer organizations in planning, developing, maintaining, and managing trails. Volunteer work may include, but need not be limited to—

(1) planning, developing, maintaining, or managing (A) trails which are components of the national trails system, or (B) trails which, if so developed and maintained, could qualify for designation as components of the national trails system; or

(2) operating programs to organize and supervise volunteer trail building efforts with respect to the trails referred to in paragraph (1), conducting trail-related research projects, or providing education and training to volunteers on methods of trails planning, construction, and maintenance.

(c) The appropriate Secretary or the head of any Federal land managing agency may utilize and make available Federal facilities, equipment, tools, and technical assistance to volunteers and volunteer organizations, subject to such limitations and restrictions as the appropriate Secretary or the head of any Federal land managing agency deems necessary or desirable.

DEFINITIONS

SEC. 12. As used in this Act:

(1) The term 'high potential historic sites' means those historic sites related to the route, or sites in close proximity thereto, which provide opportunity to interpret the historic significance of the trail during the period of its major use. Criteria for consideration as high potential sites include historic significance, presence of visible historic remnants, scenic quality, and relative freedom from intrusion.

(2) The term 'high potential route segments' means those segments of a trail which would afford high quality recreation experience in a portion of the route having greater than average scenic values or affording an opportunity to vicariously share the experience of the original users of a historic route.

(3) The term 'State' means each of the several States of the United States, the District of Columbia, the Commonwealth of Puerto Rico, the Virgin Islands, Guam, American Samoa, the Trust Territory of the Pacific Islands, the Northern Mariana Islands, and any other territory or possession of the United States.

(4) The term 'without expense to the United States' means that no funds may be expended by Federal agencies for the development of trail related facilities or for the acquisition of lands or interest in lands outside the exterior boundaries of Federal areas. For the purposes of the preceding sentence, amounts made available to any State or political subdivision under the Land and Water Conservation Fund Act of 1965 or any other provision of law shall not be treated as an expense to the United States.

Notes

1. Inscriptions on historical buildings and monuments, Shirley Center, Mass., April 2, 1985.
2. Article entitled "The Shirley Influence", in *The Public Spirit* (undated), by Harley P. Holden (ninth generation Shirley resident). Material on file in Gordon T. Banks Shirleyana Room, Hazen Memorial Library, Shirley, Mass.
3. Author's observations, visit to Shirley Center (Mass.), April 2, 1985. Bryant, *The Quality of the Day*, 1965.
4. Lowrey, *Benton MacKaye's Appalachian Trail*, 1981.
5. Bryant, *The Quality of the Day*, 1965.
6. Appalachian Trail Conference, *The Appalachian Trail*, 1973.
7. Benton MacKaye's own term for his home and work environment in Shirley, MA (e.g. Benton MacKaye to Ruth E. Blackburn, March 22, 1967). MacKaye's "Sky Parlor" has been reproduced at the Appalachian Trail Conference's headquarters in Harpers Ferry, W.Va.
8. Holden, "The Shirley Influence", undated.
9. Ibid. Bryant, *The Quality of the Day*, 1965.
10. *New York Times*, May 9, 1971.
11. Holden, "The Shirley Influence", undated.
12. See list of individuals interviewed, Appendix B.
13. Peirce, *The Border South States*, 1975.
14. Description of Appalachians drawn from Connelly, *Discovering the Appalachians*, 1968.
15. Ralph Widner, "Foreword" in ibid.
16. For example, Raitz and Ulack, *Appalachia, a Regional Geography*, 1984; Malcolm J. Rohrbough, *The Trans-Appalachian Frontier: People, Societies, and Institutions, 1775-1850*, 1978; New York Office of Planning Coordination, *The Appalachian Region of New York State: An Atlas of Natural and Cultural Resources*, 1969. Appalachian Trail Conference, *Guides*, various dates.
17. As of June, 1986, 1440 "end-to-enders" were registered with the Appalachian Trail Conference as having hiked the Trail since 1936.
18. Maurice Forrester, "Battle of Endless Mountain", *Appalachian Trailway News*, November 1976.
19. Connelly, *Discovering the Appalachians*, 1968.
20. Farb, *Face of North America*, 1963.
21. Jerry Wyckoff, "Geology Along the Appalachian Trail", *Appalachian Trailway News*, May-June, 1979.
22. Farb, *Face of North America*, 1963.
23. Hunt, *Physiography of the United States*, 1967.
24. "Coves" are described by Raitz and Ulack, *Appalachia*, as areas where overlying metamorphic rock has been eroded away to expose younger sediments and provide a sort of geologic "window".

25. Connelly, *Discovering the Appalachians*, 1968.
26. Appalachian Trail Conference, *Appalachian Trail Guides* (Maine, New Hampshire—Vermont, Massachusetts—Connecticut, New York—New Jersey, Pennsylvania).
27. Connelly, *Discovering the Appalachians*, 1968.
28. Raitz and Ulack, *Appalachia*, 1984.
29. Hunt, *Physiography of the United States*, 1967.
30. Advisory Commission on Intergovernmental Relations, *Multistate Regionalism*, 1972.
31. Ibid.
32. Derthick, *Between State and Nation*, 1974.
33. Peirce, *The Border South States*, 1975; idem, *The New England States*, 1976; Peirce and Barone, *The Mid-Atlantic States of America*, 1977.
34. U.S. Government Manual, 1984-85.
35. Appalachian Trail Conference, *The Appalachian Trail*, 1973.
36. Raitz and Ulack, *Appalachia*, 1984.
37. For example: Howard W. Odum, *An American Epoch*, 1930; idem, *Southern Regions of the United States*, 1936; idem, *In Search of the Regional Balance of America*, 1945; idem, *The Way of the South*, 1947.
38. Raitz and Ulack, *Appalachia*, 1984.
39. Peirce, *The Border South States*, 1975.
40. Raitz and Ulack, *Appalachia*, 1984.
41. Foster, *Cape Cod National Seashore*, 1985.
42. Ibid.
43. Ibid.
44. Planet Drum Foundation, P.O. Box 31251, San Francisco, Calif. 94131.
45. Foster, *Cape Cod National Seashore*, 1985.
46. Ibid.
47. MacKaye, "An Appalachian Trail", 1921.
48. Benton MacKaye to Stanley A. Murray, October 2, 1968. Kocher and Warren, *The Appalachian Trail*, 1979.
49. George H. Dacy, "The Appalachian Trail", *The Mentor*, August 1928: "The princely path of Pedestrianism..."
50. Interview with Laurence R. Van Meter, June 7, 1985.
51. Fairfax, "Federal-State Cooperation", 1973.
52. Interview with George M. Zoebelein, October 1, 1985; Lowrey, "Benton MacKaye's Appalachian Trail", 1981.
53. See Chronological Summary, Appendix A, for actual dates.
54. Appalachian Trail Conference, *The Appalachian Trail*, 1973.
55. Avery was "one of the three central figures in the history of the Appalachian Trail Conference", interview with Henry W. Lautz, March 26, 1986. Perkins was characterized as a "Trail hero" in Kocher and Warren, *The Appalachian Trail*, 1979.
56. Interview with Ruth E. Blackburn, October 31, 1985.
57. Appalachian Trail Conference, "Brief of Proceedings", 1925.
58. Interview with George M. Zoebelein, October 1, 1985.
59. Appalachian Trail Conference, "Proceedings", 1937.
60. Appalachian Trail Conference, Letter Report No. 12, October 1938. Interview with Ruth E. Blackburn, October 31, 1985.
61. Fairfax, "Federal-State Cooperation", 1973.
62. *Appalachian Trailway News*, July 1939.

63. *Appalachian Trailway News*, January 1940.
64. *Appalachian Trailway News*, 1941.
65. Interview with Stanley A. Murray, April 26, 1986.
66. *Appalachian Trailway News*, January 1943.
67. *Appalachian Trailway News*, May 1946.
68. *Appalachian Trailway News*, May 1945.
69. Ibid.
70. *Appalachian Trailway News*, January 1946.
71. *Appalachian Trailway News*, January 1943.
72. Examples were *Life*, October 13, 1941; *Reader's Digest*, July 1949; *National Geographic*, August 1949.
73. Stanley A. Murray to David M. Sherman, November 14, 1985. Interview with Stanley A. Murray, April 26, 1986.
74. Appalachian Trail Conference, *The Appalachian Trail*, 1973. Interview with Stanley A. Murray, April 26, 1986.
75. W. Harley Webster to Lee C. White, special counsel to the president, December 19, 1958.
76. Interview with David M. Sherman, October 30, 1985. Interview with Richard L. Stanton, June 6, 1985. Interview with Ruth E. Blackburn, October 31, 1985.
77. Interview with Gaylord Nelson (Edmund Garvey, David Sherman, Ronald Tipton), December 12, 1983.
78. Stanley A. Murray to David M. Sherman, November 14, 1985. Interview with Stanley A. Murray, April 26, 1986.
79. Hearings of the Subcommittee on Parks and Recreation, Senate Committee on Interior and Insular Affairs, on Senate 622, September 16, 1965. *Appalachian Trailway News*, January 1966.
80. Fairfax, "Federal-State Cooperation", 1973.
81. Interview with Richard L. Stanton, June 6, 1985.
82. Bureau of Outdoor Recreation, *Trails for America*, December 1966.
83. Interview with Stanley A. Murray, April 26, 1986. *Appalachian Trailway News*, September 1967.
84. *Appalachian Trailway News*, May 1966.
85. *Appalachian Trailway News*, September 1967.
86. Interview with Stanley A. Murray, April 26, 1986.
87. *Appalachian Trailway News*, January 1969. Potomac Appalachian Trail Club *Bulletin*, October-December, 1985.
88. Interview with C. Francis Belcher, January 11, 1985.
89. Robert D. Faiss, staff assistant to the president, to Benton MacKaye, October 3, 1968.
90. Public Law 90-543 (as amended), Appendix I.
91. *Appalachian Trailway News*, May 1968.
92. ANSTAC minutes, November 3, 1969.
93. Interview with Richard L. Stanton, June 6, 1985.
94. Interview with Ruth E. Blackburn, October 31, 1985. Interview with Stanley A. Murray, April 26, 1986.
95. Interview with C. Francis Belcher, January 11, 1985. Interview with Stanley A. Murray, April 26, 1986.
96. Produced by the Walter J. Klein Co. of Charlotte, N.C. as a 28 1/2 minute, 16 mm, color film; *Appalachian Trailway News*, May 1969.
97. ANSTAC minutes, November 3, 1969.

98. Ibid.
99. Ibid.
100. Author's personal recollections as Massachusetts commissioner of natural resources from 1959 to 1966.
101. Benton MacKaye to Stanley A. Murray, April 25, 1970.
102. Interview with C. Francis Belcher, January 11, 1985. "A Message from the Chairman", *Appalachian Trailway News*, January 1970.
103. Interview with Arthur W. Brownell, June 6, 1985.
104. Interview with C. Francis Belcher, January 11, 1985.
105. ANSTAC Executive Committee minutes, May 29, 1970.
106. Ibid.
107. Ibid.
108. Ibid.
109. Ibid.
110. Interview with George M. Zoebelein, October 1, 1985.
111. ANSTAC minutes, June 1, 1971.
112. Interview with Richard L. Stanton, June 6, 1985.
113. ANSTAC minutes, June 1, 1971.
114. Ibid. Interview with George T. Hamilton, June 5, 1985. *Manchester* (N.H.) *Sunday News*, August 1, 1971.
115. Potomac Appalachian Trail Club *Bulletin*, January-March, 1971, describes successful campaign for Virginia trails legislation.
116. ANSTAC minutes, June 1, 1971.
117. Ibid.
118. Interview with Stanley A. Murray, April 26, 1986.
119. ANSTAC minutes, June 1, 1971.
120. The National Park Service did explore the matter of adverse possession (E.V. Buschman file memorandum, June 15, 1970). So also did Georgetown University's National Law Center (Prof. Arnold W. Reitze, Jr. to Paula Strain, president, Potomac Appalachian Trail Club, December 9, 1970).
121. ANSTAC minutes, June 1, 1971. The National Park Service had encountered a similar issue at Cape Cod (Foster, *The Cape Cod National Seashore*, 1985).
122. In later years, representatives of other conservation organizations were appointed to ANSTAC (e.g. Nature Conservancy, National Parks and Conservation Association, National Wildlife Federation), and joint lobbying activities were undertaken by the Appalachian Trail Conference and the Wilderness Society.
123. ANSTAC minutes, June 19, 1972.
124. Robert B. Moore (January 1969-August 1971), Richard L. Stanton (September 1971-March 1972), Edgar L. Gray (April 1972-October 1973) as reported by Director Gary Everhardt, National Park Service, to Congressman Roy A. Taylor, March 10, 1976.
125. Interview with Stanley A. Murray, April 26, 1986. Interview with Ruth E. Blackburn, October 31, 1985. Interview with Richard L. Stanton, June 6, 1985. Interview with Sally K. Fairfax, May 30, 1985.
126. National Environmental Policy Act, Public Law 91-190, 1970.
127. Edgar L. Gray to assistant director, National Park Service, August 14, 1972. Edgar L. Gray to directors, Northeast and Southeast Regional Offices, National Park Service, August 14, 1972. Edgar L. Gray to deputy associate director, National Park Service, September 28, 1972. Richard L. Stanton to chief, Division of land Acquisition, National Park Service, July 30, 1974.

128. Gov. Thomas B. Salmon (VT) to Director James G. Watt, Bureau of Outdoor Recreation, August 20, 1974.
129. Fairfax, "Federal-State Cooperation", 1973. Interview with Sally K. Fairfax, May 30, 1985.
130. ANSTAC minutes, June 19, 1972.
131. The matter of expense reimbursement was not pursued vigorously until 1975 (e.g. deputy regional director, North Atlantic Region, to deputy associate director, Legislation, July 14, 1975; deputy assistant secretary for fish and wildlife and parks to J.P. Crumrine, Office of Policy Analysis, November 11, 1975; director, National Park Service, to secretary of the interior, January 7, 1976).
132. ANSTAC minutes, June 19, 1972.
133. ANSTAC minutes, April 27, 1973.
134. Thomas Jefferson, "Notes on Virginia", 1782, as quoted in Potomac Appalachian Trail Club, *Guide to the Appalachian Trail* (Susquehanna River to the Shenandoah National Park), 1974.
135. Potomac Appalachian Trail Club, *Guide to the Appalachian Trail*.
136. Extension authorized by Congress, October 9, 1968, as reported in *Appalachian Trailway News*, May 1969.
137. ANSTAC minutes, April 27, 1973.
138. See n. 131.
139. Interview with Stanley A. Murray, April 26, 1986.
140. ANSTAC minutes, April 27, 1973.
141. ANSTAC Executive Committee minutes, September 28, 1973.
142. Interview with Paul C. Pritchard, June 6, 1985.
143. ANSTAC Executive Committee minutes, September 28, 1973.
144. Ibid.
145. The Eastern Wilderness Act would pass the Senate on May 31, 1974.
146. Interview with C. Francis Belcher, January 11, 1985. Interview with Thomas S. Deans, July 25, 1985.
147. ANSTAC Executive Committee minutes, September 28, 1973.
148. Ibid.
149. Public Law 88-578, 1964.
150. ANSTAC Executive Committee minutes, September 28, 1973.
151. The Appalachian "greenway" was proposed in part as a Bicentennial project (interviews with George M. Zoebelein, October 1, 1985, and Stanley A. Murray, April 26, 1986).
152. Public Law 92-463, 1972.
153. Appalachian National Scenic Trail *Anniversary Report*, October 1973. "All concerned, at this time, believe that all initial objectives set by Congress have been achieved" (final paragraph).
154. For example, Grant Conway, John L. Oliphant, and Edward B. Garvey to Congressman Roy A. Taylor, April 22, 1974. Grant Conway and Edward B. Garvey, Chronology of efforts to determine reasons for failure of National Park Service and other related agencies to implement their responsibilities for A.T. under National Trails System Act of 1968 (Public Law 90-543), May 5, 1974.
155. Interview with Henry W. Lautz, March 26, 1986. Popular articles (e.g. James B. Steele, "Is the Appalachian Trail Endangered?", *Frontiers*, Summer 1973; Peter H. Dunning, "Appalachian Trail–Through Wilderness and Real Estate", *National Parks and Conservation Magazine*, July 1972; "Use of Appalachian Trail Restricted", *New York Times*, July 4, 1972).

156. Interview with David A. Richie, June 7-8, 1985.
157. Personal recollections of the author.
158. Stanley A. Murray to Secretary of the Interior Rogers C.B. Morton, February 13, 1975.
159. *Appalachian Trailway News*, May 1975. Deputy regional director (NAR) to director, National Park Service, April 17, 1975.
160. ANSTAC minutes, June 20, 1975.
161. Ibid.
162. Ibid.
163. Ibid.
164. Ibid.
165. This was the case in New Hampshire, Connecticut, New York, and Pennsylvania, among others.
166. C. Francis Belcher and Stanley A. Murray were among the original members of ANSTAC.
167. ANSTAC minutes, June 20, 1975.
168. Deputy regional director (NAR) David A. Richie to deputy regional directors (MAR and SER) and assistant director (Visitor Services), National Park Service, July 25, 1975.
169. ANSTAC minutes, June 20, 1975.
170. Stanley A. Murray to Russell P. McRorey, U.S. Forest Service, June 6, 1975.
171. ANSTAC minutes, June 20, 1975.
172. Public Law 90-543, 1968, Appendix I.
173. This was never done, however.
174. Ad hoc committee of the Potomac Appalachian Trail Club to David A. Richie, May 15, 1975.
175. See n. 131. An amendment to the administrative ANSTAC charter finally resolved the matter.
176. In later correspondence (Edward B. Garvey to David A. Richie, November 22, 1980), Garvey observed that his original motion (modified before submission) had included possible transfer of responsibility for the Appalachian Trail from the secretary of the interior to the secretary of agriculture.
177. Charles H.W. Foster, Special Address, "The Appalachian Trail Conference: Reflections and Retrospections", June 23, 1975.
178. For example, Grant Conway, John L. Oliphant, and Edward B. Garvey to Congressman Roy A. Taylor, April 22, 1974. Interview with Cleveland F. Pinnix, May 10, 1985.
179. Interview with David M. Sherman, October 30, 1985.
180. June 27, 1975, was the date of the meeting.
181. Personal notes of the author, July 21, 1975.
182. David A. Richie, memorandum to the files, July 29, 1975.
183. Ibid.
184. David A. Richie to William Rennebohm, Bureau of Outdoor Recreation, July 15, 1975; agenda and background information for July 30 meeting.
185. Personal recollections of the author.
186. Personal notes of the author from the July 30 meeting.
187. ANSTAC minutes, June 20, 1975.
188. Fairfax, "Federal-State Cooperation", 1973.
189. Charles H.W. Foster to David A. Richie, August 7, 1975.
190. Interview with Steven Golden, January 11, 1985.

191. October 17, 1975.
192. David A. Richie to Board of Managers, Appalachian Trail Conference, June 18, 1975.
193. John L. Oliphant to Charles H.W. Foster, October 22, 1975.
194. Ben H. Bolen to David Gaines, National Park Service, November 18, 1975.
195. Charles H.W. Foster to Ben H. Bolen, July 31, 1975.
196. Southern regional Council minutes, January 30, 1976.
197. Stanley A. Murray to Edward J. Seiferle, November 12, 1975. Stanley A. Murray to David A. Richie, December 10, 1975.
198. Southern regional Council minutes, January 30, 1976.
199. Mid-Atlantic regional Council minutes, February 13, 1976.
200. Personal footnote on copy of letter to David A. Richie, December 17, 1975.
201. Regional Director (NAR) Jerry D. Wagers to associate director (legislation), National Park Service, February 12, 1976. Interview with David A. Richie, June 7-8, 1985.
202. Interview with Steven Golden, January 11, 1985.
203. C. Francis Belcher to Charles H.W. Foster, August 20, 1975. Northern regional Council minutes, April 2, 1976.
204. Northern regional Council minutes, April 2, 1976.
205. Interview with Cleveland F. Pinnix, May 10, 1985.
206. Personal notes of the author, January 19, 1976. Deputy regional director (NAR) to regional director (NE), Bureau of Outdoor Recreation, January 19, 1976.
207. Regional director (NE) to director, Bureau of Outdoor Recreation, January 28, 1976.
208. Personal notes of the author, February 5, 1976.
209. February 5, 1976.
210. Interview with Paul C. Pritchard, June 6, 1985.
211. See n. 201.
212. News release, Office of the Secretary, Department of the Interior, March 6, 1976.
213. *Appalachian Trail Conference Newsletter*, January 1976. Frederick Blackburn of the Potomac Appalachian Trail Club coordinated a moving "Tribute to Benton MacKaye" held at the Cosmos Club, Washington, D.C., on March 24, 1976. Harley P. Holden et al., "Benton MacKaye: A Tribute", *Living Wilderness* 39 (1976): 132.
214. Interview with Cleveland F. Pinnix, May 10, 1985.
215. Ibid.
216. Congressman Roy A. Taylor to Director Gary Everhardt, National Park Service, February 27, 1976.
217. Interview with Richard L. Stanton, June 6, 1985.
218. Hearings of the House Subcommittee on National Parks and Recreation, March 11, 1976.
219. June 21-23, 1975. Among other attributes, Rep. Byron was the sponsor of the first state Appalachian Trail legislation ever enacted (Maryland).
220. Interview with Cleveland F. Pinnix, May 10, 1985.
221. See n. 154.
222. Interview with Paul C. Pritchard, June 6, 1985.
223. Hearings of the House Subcommittee on National Parks and Recreation, March 11, 1976.
224. The office opened on April 15, 1976.
225. Appalachian Trail Conference, "Appalachian Greenway" brochure, 1975.
226. Interview with Paul C. Pritchard, June 6, 1985.

227. Interview with Stanley A. Murray, April 26, 1986. Philip Hanes and Ann Satterthwaite to "Members of Brainstorming Session", September 9, 1975.
228. "Progress on the Appalachian Greenway", a report of a workshop on the Appalachian Greenway, April 1976.
229. Interview with George M. Zoebelein, October 1, 1985.
230. ANSTAC minutes, May 24, 1976.
231. Subsequent approaches to both regional agencies failed. A personal approach by ANSTAC member Helen Fenske (NJ) to Appalachian Regional Commission federal cochairman Donald Whitehead elicited the suggestion of sponsorship by an Appalachian Trail governor, but the state selected—North Carolina—did not respond.
232. Paul C. Pritchard to Ben H. Bolen, February 25, 1976.
233. ANSTAC minutes, May 24, 1976.
234. Ibid.
235. Arnold, *The Appalachian Trail*, 1977.
236. "Protecting the Appalachian Trail in Maine", Allagash Environmental Institute, Center for Research and Advanced Study, University of Maine (Portland-Gorham), 1976.
237. ANSTAC minutes, May 24, 1976.
238. Raymond F. Housley to David A. Richie, May 12, 1976: "A trail should lay lightly on the land..."
239. Interview with Raymond F. Housley, March 12, 1986.
240. ANSTAC minutes, May 24, 1976.
241. Ibid.
242. "David Richie to State ANSTAC representatives", April 6, 1976. Status report format developed from pilot sessions in New Jersey, Connecticut, and New York.
243. There is no evidence that further representations were made.
244. The Shirley (Mass.) Historical Society subsequently took the lead.
245. Project manager to advisory council members, June 11, 1976.
246. Interview with William M. Eichbaum, July 18, 1985.
247. Ibid.
248. Interview with David A. Richie, June 7-8, 1985.
249. Interview with William M. Eichbaum, July 18, 1985. The first meeting occurred on July 28, 1975; subsequent sessions were scheduled at bimonthly intervals.
250. Ibid.
251. Interview with David A. Richie, June 7-8, 1985.
252. Interview with William M. Eichbaum, July 18, 1985.
253. Arnold, *At the Eye of the Storm*, 1982.
254. Interview with Cleveland F. Pinnix, May 10, 1985.
255. Ibid.
256. Southern regional Council minutes, January 22, 1977.
257. Ibid.
258. Ibid.
259. Mid-Atlantic regional Council minutes, February 4, 1977.
260. Ibid.
261. New England regional Council minutes, March 4, 1977.
262. Ibid.
263. A forerunner of topics to come later.
264. Interview with Steven Golden, January 11, 1985.
265. Interview with Henry W. Lautz, March 26, 1986.

266. Interview with Steven Golden, January 11, 1985.
267. Interview with Henry W. Lautz, March 26, 1986.
268. Interview with Thomas S. Deans, July 25, 1985.
269. Interview with Paul C. Pritchard, June 6, 1985.
270. Interview with Robert L. Herbst, October 29, 1985.
271. ANSTAC minutes, May 27, 1977.
272. Appalachian Trail Conference, May 28, 1977.
273. Robert L. Herbst, "The Appalachian Trail: A Model for a National Trails System", May 28, 1977. Hank Burchard, *Washington Post*, June 9, 1977.
274. Billie Jeppesen, executive assistant to Interior secretary Cecil Andrus, to Robert Herbst, March 28, 1977, transmitting invitation to Shepherdstown meeting: "This is one that we believe you should attend." Handwritten note on margin of Herbst's draft text from Andrus: "You may express this as your proposal." Interview with Robert L. Herbst, October 29, 1985.
275. ANSTAC minutes, May 27, 1977.
276. Robert M. Landau, National Park Service, to Norman A. Greist, May 6, 1977.
277. This created problems in some states, e.g., Connecticut, where state and federal procedures/requirements were different.
278. Wislocki's modifying language was designed to accommodate Massachusetts' pursuit of a two-hundred-foot, rather than a one-thousand-foot, corridor.
279. ANSTAC minutes, May 27, 1977.
280. Ibid.
281. Ibid.
282. Ibid.
283. Ibid.
284. The deductibility of gifts of conservation easements was a matter of importance to many private conservation organizations.
285. This measure was adopted despite Bureau of Outdoor Recreation regional director Maurice Arnold's advice that a second contingency allocation was unlikely.
286. ANSTAC minutes, May 27, 1977.
287. Interview with William M. Eichbaum, July 18, 1985.
288. Interview with Henry W. Lautz, March 26, 1986.
289. Ibid.
290. Interview with Paul C. Pritchard, June 6, 1985.
291. Interview with Laura C. Beaty, October 30, 1985.
292. Ibid. Interview with Cleveland F. Pinnix, May 10, 1985.
293. Interview with Henry W. Lautz, March 26, 1986.
294. Interview with Laura C. Beaty, October 30, 1985. Interview with George T. Hamilton, June 5, 1985, who recalled visiting former New Hampshire governor Sherman Adams, and was asked: "Is the Trail really worth the $90 million being spent to protect it?"
295. Interview with Henry W. Lautz, March 26, 1986.
296. Interview with Laura C. Beaty, October 30, 1985.
297. Ibid.
298. Ibid. Interview with Thomas S. Deans, July 25, 1985.
299. David A. Richie to "ANSTAC members and friends", November 21, 1977.
300. Interview with Robert L. Herbst, October 29, 1985.
301. Interview with David A. Richie, June 7-8, 1985.
302. David A. Richie to "ANSTAC members and friends", November 21, 1977.
303. Project manager to "Participants, April 8 meeting", April 25, 1977, entitled

"Progress report" on corridor definition project.

304. Personal notes from the author's files.
305. ANSTAC minutes, March 10, 1978.
306. Ibid. Interior secretary Cecil Andrus was invited personally by ANSTAC Chairman Foster but could not attend.
307. Interview with Charles R. Rinaldi, June 7, 1985.
308. ANSTAC minutes, March 10, 1978.
309. Ibid.
310. David N. Startzell to David Richie, March 14, 1978.
311. Southern regional Council minutes, February 4, 1978.
312. Interview with Lawrence R. Henson, March 12, 1986.
313. Interview with Thomas S. Deans, July 25, 1985.
314. Southern regional Council minutes, February 4, 1978.
315. Interview with Stanley A. Murray, April 26, 1986.
316. Benton MacKaye Trail Concept Plan, July 1980. Benton MacKaye Trail Association, P.O. Box 53271, Atlanta, Ga. 30305.
317. Draft memorandum of agreement, William M. Eichbaum, August 24, 1977.
318. Palmer, *Perceptual Research*, 1979.
319. Southern regional Council minutes, February 4, 1978.
320. Mid-Atlantic regional Council minutes, April 13, 1978.
321. Caren Glotfelty had replaced William Eichbaum as the Pennsylvania ANSTAC representative, a fitting selection given her earlier involvement in the Pennsylvania State University corridor study.
322. New England regional Council minutes, May 22, 1978.
323. Interview with Charles R. Rinaldi, June 7, 1985.
324. Interview with Lawrence R. Henson, March 12, 1986.
325. Project manager, Appalachian Trail, to ANSTAC members, July 27, 1978.
326. Edwin J. Seiferle to Sen. Henry M. Jackson/Rep. Morris K. Udall, July 10, 1978.
327. Charles Pugh succeeded George Zoebelein as chairman of the Appalachian Trail Conference, an individual Zoebelein described as having been given "short shrift" in the light of his insistence of the ATC "needing to look down the road to see where it was going" (interview with George Zoebelein, October 1, 1985).
328. Charles L. Pugh, "Working Together", address at the Appalachian Trail Conference, Carrabassett, Maine, August 10-13, 1979.
329. ANSTAC minutes, August 10, 1979.
330. Interview with Robert L. Herbst, October 29, 1985.
331. Interview with David A. Richie, June 7-8, 1985.
332. Interview with Steven Golden, January 11, 1985.
333. "From the Chairman", *Appalachian Trailway News*, November-December 1979.
334. Assistant secretary for fish and wildlife and parks, to secretary of the interior, September 11, 1979.
335. Memorandum to "All ANSTAC members", September 24, 1979.
336. Interview with David M. Sherman, October 30, 1985.
337. Ibid.
338. Memorandum to Members of ANSTAC, January 31, 1980.
339. Interview with Charles S. Cushman, May 24, 1985. Interview with Charles R. Rinaldi, June 7, 1985.
340. Memorandum to "Members of ANSTAC" from David A. Richie, January 31, 1980.
341. Ibid. Pamela Fenicle to David A. Richie, May 5, 1980.
342. Interview with Charles S. Cushman, May 24, 1985.

343. Memorandum to "Members of ANSTAC" from David A. Richie, January 31, 1980.
344. Interview with Charles S. Cushman, May 24, 1985.
345. Ibid.
346. Interview with Arthur W. Brownell, June 6, 1985.
347. Memorandum to "Members of ANSTAC", February 1, 1980.
348. Southern regional Council minutes, February 15-16, 1980.
349. Ibid.
350. New England regional Council minutes, March 29, 1980.
351. Ibid.
352. Van Dyke, "Trail Corridor Design and Protection", 1979.
353. Mid-Atlantic regional Council minutes, May 9, 1980.
354. Interview with David A. Richie, June 7-8, 1985.
355. "Dear Advisory Council Members", July 10, 1980.
356. ANSTAC minutes, August 22-23, 1980.
357. Ibid.
358. Ibid. Personal files of Thomas S. Deans.
359. ANSTAC minutes, August 22-23, 1980. Interview with Christopher N. Brown, October 28, 1985.
360. Arnold, *At the Eye of the Storm*, 1982.
361. *Boston Globe*, March 5, 1981. Comment attributed to Brant Calkin of the Sierra Club.
362. File memorandum of strategy meeting in Harpers Ferry, West Va., on January 9, 1981, attended by Robert L. Herbst, Thomas S. Deans, David M. Sherman, and David A. Richie. Assistant secretary for fish and wildlife and parks to secretary of the interior, approved by Secretary Cecil D. Andrus, January 19, 1981.
363. Interview with Thomas S. Deans, July 25, 1985.
364. Personal files of Thomas S. Deans: handwritten notes ("Talk with Dave Richie", October 16, 1980 and February 20, 1981; "ANSTAC Action Plan next 3 months", January 14, 1981).
365. Ibid. "Dave Richie to Tom Deans, Dave Startzell, Dave Sherman, Chuck Rinaldi, *Appropriations Strategies*", January 14, 1981.
366. David A. Richie to Stanley Albright, August 4, 1981: "There could be a credibility problem with Ric Davidge".
367. Interview with David A. Richie, June 7-8, 1985.
368. Ibid. (Handwritten notes of congressional testimony).
369. Laurence R. Van Meter to "Tom Deans", June 16, 1981, enclosing summaries of ANSTAC subcommittee meetings in Washington with NPS associate director Stanley T. Albright and director Russell Dickenson, June 1, 1981.
370. Draft cover letter (Thomas S. Deans files) suggesting greater use of land trusts and other private sector alternatives.
371. ANSTAC meeting, March 6-7, 1981.
372. David A. Richie to ANSTAC members, February 25, 1981.
373. Handwritten slip of paper (author unknown) in personal files of Thomas S. Deans.
374. Interview with Thomas S. Deans, July 25, 1985.
375. Thomas S. Deans to Secretary of the Interior James G. Watt, March 18, 1981.
376. "Dave Richie to Chuck Rinaldi, Karen Wade, Steve Golden", March 30, 1981. David A. Richie to Charles H.W. Foster, March 12, 1981.
377. "Dave Richie to Chuck, Karen, Steve", March 16, 1981.
378. Despite inquiries made to several national foundations, philanthropy was not

persuaded to make up for the deficiencies in public funds. For example, Charles H.W. Foster to George H. Taber, Richard King Mellon Foundation, May 4, 1981.

379. "Larry Van Meter to Tom Deans, David Richie, Ruth Blackburn", March 12, 1981.
380. "Dave Richie to Tom Deans", April 23, 1981.
381. John L. Bryant, Jr., to David A. Richie, May 27, 1981.
382. In response to an options paper, "Private Protection Alternatives", prepared by Christopher Brown, Les Brewer, and Laurence Van Meter, the ATC Board of Managers acted on April 17, 1982, to establish an affiliated Trust for Appalachian Trail Lands (TATL).
383. Arnold, *At the Eye of the Storm*, 1982.
384. Ibid. "Proposed Land Protection Policy for the Land and Water Conservation Fund" (draft), July 2, 1981.
385. Arnold, *At the Eye of the Storm*, 1982.
386. Interview with Stanley T. Albright, October 28, 1985. Including the Appalachian Trail among the case studies reinforced its suspect status, particularly when two former Heritage Conservation and Recreation Service staffers were put in charge.
387. Arnold, *At the Eye of the Storm*, 1982.
388. Ibid. Interview with Charles S. Cushman, May 24, 1985.
389. Interview with Thomas S. Deans, July 25, 1985.
390. Personal files of Thomas S. Deans.
391. "Creative Conservation", a concept paper distributed by the Division of Federal Lands Planning, Heritage, Conservation and Recreation Service, undated.
392. "Dave Richie to Tom [Deans], Larry [Van Meter], Chuck [Rinaldi], Steve [Golden]", September 15, 1981.
393. Glenn Eugster to AT Case Study Team, November 9, 1981.
394. Interview with Charles S. Cushman, May 24, 1985.
395. "Davie Richie to the files", undated.
396. "Dave Richie to Participants, *Case Study Meeting*, January 27-29", February 1, 1982.
397. Interview with Stanley T. Albright, October 28, 1985.
398. Interview with Laurence R. Van Meter, June 7, 1985.
399. Letter from twenty-five members of the Senate to Sen. James A. McClure, Interior Appropriations Subcommittee chairman, June 11, 1982.
400. Interview with Laurence R. Van Meter, June 7, 1985.
401. ANSTAC Subcommittee minutes, June 1, 1981.
402. Ibid.
403. Project manager, Appalachian Trail, to director, October 27, 1981.
404. Ibid.
405. Interview with Arthur W. Brownell, June 6, 1985.
406. Ibid. Interview with Thomas S. Deans, July 25, 1985. Interview with David A. Richie, June 7-8, 1985.
407. Interview with Arthur W. Brownell, June 6, 1985.
408. ANSTAC minutes, May 14, 1982.
409. Ibid.
410. Ibid.
411. The official opening occurred on October 2, 1982.
412. ANSTAC minutes, May 14, 1982.
413. Subsequently enacted into law as additional amendments to the National Trails System Act (Public Law 98-11, 1983).
414. U.S. Department of the Interior, "Appalachian Scenic Trail Case Study: Final Report", 1982.

415. Interview with George T. Hamilton, June 5, 1985.
416. ANSTAC minutes, May 14, 1982.
417. David A. Richie to ANSTAC members, July 1, 1982.
418. Personal recollections of the author.
419. "David Richie to ANSTAC members", December 20, 1982.
420. Interview with Laurence R. Van Meter, June 7, 1985.
421. Ibid.
422. David A. Richie, "Thoughts on Delegation", undated (probably March of 1981).
423. Handwritten, unsigned note entitled "thoughts" in Appalachian Trail Conference files (probably Laurence Van Meter), March 17, 1981.
424. "Dave Richie to ATPO staff", August 13, 1980.
425. ATC Board of Managers minutes, November 1980.
426. Andrew L. Nichols to David A. Richie, January 8, 1981.
427. Andrew L. Nichols to David A. Richie, March 5, 1981.
428. Interview with Paul C. Pritchard, June 6, 1985.
429. Interview with Charles W. Sloan, October 28, 1985.
430. Interview with George M. Zoebelein, October 1, 1985.
431. Interview with Charles W. Sloan, October 28, 1985. Interview with Stanley T. Albright, October 28, 1985.
432. Interview with Ruth E. Blackburn, October 31, 1985.
433. Charles W. Sloan to ATC Board of Managers, April 10, 1981. He had originally termed it the "management committee".
434. Partnership committee minutes, May 5, 1981.
435. Interview with Charles W. Sloan, October 28, 1985.
436. Thurston Griggs to Ruth E. Blackburn, March 26, 1981.
437. Laurence R. Van Meter to David A. Richie, November 30, 1982. Handwritten, undated response from David A. Richie apologizing for "appearing to rush the delegation strategy".
438. Interview with Charles W. Sloan, October 28, 1985.
439. "David Richie to Partnership Committee", NPS regulations, July 9, 1982: "abdication of responsibility" to exempt A.T. lands from regulation. "Dave Richie to Partnership Committee", September 20, 1982: special regulations may ease effects.
440. Acting assistant solicitor for parks and recreation to Appalachian Trail Project Office, NPS, March 17, 1983.
441. Public Law 98-11, 1983, a measure to authorize new national scenic and historic trails, with a section included further modifying Public Law 90-543 as amended.
442. ANSTAC minutes, March 6-7, 1981.
443. "Steve Clark to Dave Richie", March 4, 1982. Interview with Charles W. Sloan, October 28, 1985.
444. "Dave Richie" to the files, undated.
445. Ibid.
446. David A. Richie to Waynesboro meeting participants, August 22, 1983.
447. Laurence R. Van Meter to Peter Raynor, August 18, 1983.
448. Interview with Charles W. Sloan, October 28, 1985.
449. Interview with Stanley T. Albright, October 28, 1985.
450. "Dave Richie to Stan Albright", December 23, 1982.
451. Stanley T. Albright to Ruth E. Blackburn, May 20, 1983.
452. Secretary of the interior to director, National Park Service, June 7, 1983.
453. Ric Davidge to Laurence R. Van Meter, November 28, 1983. Interview with

Laurence R. Van Meter, June 7, 1985.

454. As reported in ATC executive committee minutes, February 19, 1983.
455. L. Van Meter, "The 'Delegation' Issue, Some Questions and Answers", January 28, 1983.
456. ATC executive committee minutes, February 19, 1983.
457. "Larry Van Meter to Board of Managers, Update on Delegation Issue", March 12, 1983.
458. Partnership committee to ATC Board of Managers, March 18, 1983.
459. ATC Board of Managers minutes, March 18-20, 1983.
460. David A. Richie to ANSTAC members, February 9, 1983.
461. David A. Richie to ANSTAC members, December 20, 1982: transmitted first version of Land Protection Plan.
462. David A. Richie to ANSTAC members, March 15, 1983.
463. Public Law 98-11, 1983.
464. David A. Richie to Ted Kelly, Pennsylvania Division of State Forest Management, March 28, 1983.
465. R.R. Thorpe to state representatives on ANSTAC, April 11, 1983.
466. ATC New England Regional Management Committee meeting, Groton, Mass. April 8, 1978, with all maintaining clubs present, raised questions, for example. Regional Management Committee meeting, Hanover, N.H., on April 23, 1983, revealed no remaining opposition.
467. ANSTAC minutes, April 22, 1983.
468. Interview with Steven Golden, January 11, 1985.
469. For example, an alternative route had finally been agreed upon in western Connecticut.
470. ANSTAC minutes, April 22, 1983.
471. Ibid. George Wislocki (Mass.) abstained from voting.
472. David A. Richie to ANSTAC members, May 18, 1983.
473. Partnership committee minutes, May 17, 1983.
474. Report of Ad Hoc Committee Studying Delegation of Management Responsibility to ATC, April 30, 1983.
475. Partnership committee minutes, May 17, 1983.
476. ATC Board of Managers minutes, May 26-27, 1983.
477. Ibid.
478. Not specified in the minutes but probably Stephen Clark of the Maine Appalachian Trail Club. Interview with Ruth E. Blackburn, October 31, 1985: as the presiding officer, Mrs. Blackburn recalled a few of the Board members as having reservations, but the approach was generally acceptable.
479. Management of NPS-Acquired Lands by the Appalachian Trail Conference (draft), July 1983.
480. Partnership committee minutes, October 4, 1983.
481. David A. Richie to Charles W. Sloan, October 12, 1983.
482. ATC Board of Managers minutes, November 19, 1983.
483. Cooperative Agreement No. 0631-81-01.
484. Public Law 98-11, 1983.
485. ATC Board of Managers minutes, November 19, 1983.
486. Appalachian Trail Conference, *The Register*, March 1984.
487. Ibid.
488. Ibid.
489. Ibid.

490. National Park Service, *Courier*, March 1984.
491. Fairfax, "Federal-State Cooperation", 1973.
492. General description from author's lecture notes, course on "Bioregionalism", Tufts University, 1983-84. Lowrey, "Benton MacKaye's Appalachian Trail", 1981.
493. Lowrey, "Benton MacKaye's Appalachian Trail", 1981.
494. *Appalachian Trailway News*, August 1975. Seven-minute special film, "From a Visit with Benton MacKaye", shown to a "hushed general assembly" at the Boone Appalachian Trail Conference. Interview with Sally K. Fairfax, May 30, 1985: MacKaye was treated at times "like the shroud of Christ".
495. Interview with George M. Zoebelein, October 1, 1985.
496. Interview with C. Francis Belcher, January 11, 1985. Interview with Sally K. Fairfax, May 30, 1985: Belcher was irreverently, but affectionately, referred to as "Foochow" within the Trail community.
497. Interview with Stanley A. Murray, April 26, 1986.
498. Appalachian Trail Conference, "Brief of Proceedings", 1925.
499. Ibid.
500. Interview with Henry W. Lautz, March 26, 1986.
501. 36 Stat. 961, 1911. Ambler, *Activities*, 1931.
502. Interview with Raymond F. Housley, March 12, 1986.
503. Interview with Ruth E. Blackburn, October 31, 1985.
504. Interview with Stanley A. Murray, April 26, 1986.
505. Interview with Steven Golden, January 11, 1985.
506. Interview with Henry W. Lautz, March 26, 1986.
507. Interview with Sally K. Fairfax, May 30, 1985.
508. Interview with Steven Golden, January 11, 1985.
509. Interview with Thomas S. Deans, July 25, 1985.
510. *Appalachian Trailway News*, May 1969.
511. *Appalachian Trailway News*, January 1947. Announcement that Samuel V. Moore had been appointed Corresponding Secretary.
512. Interview with Thomas S. Deans, July 25, 1985.
513. Interview with Stanley A. Murray, April 26, 1986.
514. Ibid.
515. *Appalachian Trailway News*, September 1969. Interview with Sally K. Fairfax, May 30, 1985. Interview with Richard L. Stanton, June 6, 1985. Interview with Ruth E. Blackburn, October 31, 1985.
516. Interview with Henry W. Lautz, March 26, 1986. Interview with Stanley A. Murray, April 26, 1985.
517. A characterization offered by Henry W. Lautz (interview), March 26, 1986.
518. Interview with George M. Zoebelein, October 1, 1985. Interview with Sally K. Fairfax, May 30, 1985. Lowrey, "Benton MacKaye's Appalachian Trail", 1981: quoting Benton MacKaye's address to the seventh Appalachian Trail Conference, June 1935.
519. Interview with Paul C. Pritchard, June 6, 1985. Interview with George Zoebelein, October 1, 1985.
520. Interview with Henry W. Lautz, March 26, 1986.
521. Interview with Charles W. Sloan, October 28, 1985.
522. According to Henry W. Lautz (interview, April 26, 1986), the other major change point was the policy split with wilderness advocates (including Benton MacKaye) at the time of the construction of the Skyline Drive project in Virginia.
523. Interview with George M. Zoebelein, October 1, 1985.

524. Interview with Paul C. Pritchard, June 6, 1985.
525. Interview with Steven Golden, January 11, 1985.
526. Interview with Henry W. Lautz, April 26, 1986.
527. Interview with George M. Zoebelein, October 1, 1985.
528. Interview with Paul C. Pritchard, June 6, 1985.
529. Ibid.
530. Interview with Paul C. Pritchard, June 6, 1985. *Appalachian Trailway News*, May-June 1979.
531. "Reconversion", *Appalachian Trailway News*, January 1946. Report of the Chairman of the Appalachian Trail Conference, May 30, 1952.
532. Interview with David M. Sherman, October 30, 1985.
533. Interview with Laurence R. Van Meter, June 7, 1985.
534. Ibid.
535. *Appalachian Trailway News*, January 1978: report of special meeting of the Board of Managers to discuss the changing status of the Trail.
536. Interview with Laurence R. Van Meter, June 7, 1985.
537. Ibid.
538. *Appalachian Trailway News*, January 1940.
539. Interview with Laurence R. Van Meter, June 7, 1985.
540. Interview with Henry W. Lautz, March 26, 1986.
541. Executive Order 12503 (as amended), Pres. Ronald Reagan, January 28, 1985. Title and reporting date changed August 15, 1985.
542. Conservation Foundation, *National Parks*, 1972 and 1985.
543. *Appalachian Trailway News*, September 1972.
544. Wegman, *Federal Advisory Committees*, 1983.
545. Foster, *Cape Cod National Seashore*, 1985.
546. Interview with Sally K. Fairfax, May 30, 1985.
547. Interview with Arthur W. Brownell, June 6, 1985.
548. Interview with George T. Hamilton, June 5, 1985.
549. Potomac Appalachian Trail Club *Bulletin*, Jan.-March 1969.
550. Fairfax, "Federal-State Cooperation", 1973.
551. Interview with Ruth E. Blackburn, October 31, 1985.
552. Interview with Steven Golden, January 11, 1985.
553. Interview with Laurence R. Van Meter, June 7, 1985.
554. Interview with Steven Golden, January 11, 1985.
555. Interview with Paul C. Pritchard, June 6, 1985.
556. Several comments of this nature (e.g., Deans interview, July 25, 1985; Eichbaum interview, July 18, 1985).
557. Interview with David M. Sherman, October 30, 1985.
558. Interview with Lawrence R. Henson, March 12, 1986.
559. Interview with Steven Golden, January 11, 1985.
560. Ibid. Interview with Arthur W. Brownell, June 6, 1985.
561. Interview with Stanley T. Albright, October 28, 1985.
562. Ibid.
563. Interview with Arthur W. Brownell, June 6, 1985.
564. Interview with Steven Golden, January 11, 1985.
565. Interview with Ruth E. Blackburn, October 31, 1985.
566. Ibid.
567. Interview with David A. Richie, June 7-8, 1985.
568. Ibid. Interview with David M. Sherman, October 30, 1985.

569. Interview with Raymond F. Housley, March 12, 1986.
570. Interview with Thomas S. Deans, July 25, 1985. Interview with George T. Hamilton, June 5, 1985.
571. Interview with David M. Sherman, October 30, 1985.
572. Interview with Thomas S. Deans, July 25, 1985.
573. Interview with C. Francis Belcher, January 11, 1985. Interview with Ruth E. Blackburn, October 31, 1985. Interview with Steven Golden, January 11, 1985. Interview with David A. Richie, June 7-8, 1985.
574. Interview with C. Francis Belcher, January 11, 1985.
575. Interview with Steven Golden, January 11, 1985. Public Law 90-543, section 5(a)(3), 1968.
576. Interview with Laurence R. Van Meter, June 7, 1985.
577. Interview with Steven Golden, January 11, 1985.
578. Interview with Thomas S. Deans, July 25, 1985. Interview with C. Francis Belcher, January 11, 1985.
579. Interview with William M. Eichbaum, July 18, 1985.
580. Interview with Henry W. Lautz, March 26, 1986.
581. Interview with Raymond F. Housley, March 12, 1986.
582. Interview with C. Francis Belcher, January 11, 1985.
583. Interview with Laurence R. Van Meter, June 7, 1985. Interview with David A. Richie, June 7-8, 1985.
584. Interview with Laurence R. Van Meter, June 7, 1985.
585. Interview with David A. Richie, June 7-8, 1985.
586. Ibid. Interview with Ruth E. Blackburn, October 31, 1985. Interview with Thomas S. Deans, July 25, 1985.
587. Interview with David A. Richie, June 7-8, 1985.
588. Interview with Laurence R. Van Meter, June 7, 1985.
589. David A. Richie to Helen Fenske, chairman, Long Range Planning Committee of ANSTAC, October 21, 1985.
590. Interview with Arthur W. Brownell, June 6, 1985.
591. Interview with Steven Golden, January 11, 1985.
592. Interview with David M. Sherman, October 30, 1985. Interview with Stanley T. Albright, October 28, 1985. Interview with C. Francis Belcher, January 11, 1985. Interview with Ruth E. Blackburn, October 31, 1985.
593. David A. Richie to Glen Gessley, Missouri Department of Natural Resources, September 23, 1980.
594. Interview with George T. Hamilton, June 5, 1985.
595. Interview with Arthur W. Brownell, June 6, 1985. Interview with Stanley T. Albright, October 28, 1985. Interview with Ruth E. Blackburn, October 31, 1985.
596. For example, report of Osborne O. Heard, vice-chairman, *Appalachian Trailway News*, January 1940.
597. Appalachian Trail Conference, *The Appalachian Trail*, 1973.
598. Interview with Richard L. Stanton, June 6, 1985.
599. Interview with Raymond F. Housley, March 12, 1986. Fitch and Shanklin, *Bureau of Outdoor Recreation*, 1970.
600. Interview with Robert L. Herbst, October 29, 1985. Ise, *Our National Park Policy*, 1961. Foresta, *America's National Parks*, 1984.
601. Interview with Stanley T. Albright, October 28, 1985. Interview with Richard L. Stanton, June 6, 1985.
602. Foster, *Cape Cod National Seashore*, 1985.

603. Interview with Richard L. Stanton, June 6, 1985.
604. Ibid.
605. Ibid.
606. Ibid.
607. Ibid.
608. Hearings, House Subcommittee on National Parks, 1976.
609. Interview with Sally K. Fairfax, May 30, 1985.
610. Interview with David A. Richie, June 7-8, 1985.
611. Interview with David M. Sherman, October 30, 1985.
612. Interview with David A. Richie, June 7-8, 1985.
613. Interview with Ruth E. Blackburn, October 31, 1985.
614. Interview with David A. Richie, June 7-8, 1985.
615. Interview with Cleveland F. Pinnix, May 10, 1985.
616. Interview with Thomas S. Deans, July 25, 1985.
617. Interview with David A. Richie, June 7-8, 1985.
618. Ibid.
619. Ibid.
620. Interview with Steven Golden, January 11, 1985.
621. Interview with Henry W. Lautz, March 26, 1986.
622. Interview with David A. Richie, June 7-8, 1985.
623. Interview with Ruth E. Blackburn, October 31, 1985.
624. Interview with Stanley T. Albright, October 28, 1985. Interview with Steven Golden, January 11, 1985.
625. Interview with David M. Sherman, October 30, 1985. Interview with Richard L. Stanton, June 6, 1985.
626. Interview with David M. Sherman, October 30, 1985. "Jim Tobin to Cleo Layton", June 4, 1979. Interview with Richard L. Stanton, June 6, 1985. Interview with David A. Richie, June 7-8, 1985.
627. Interview with Charles R. Rinaldi, June 7, 1985.
628. Interview with Cleveland F. Pinnix, May 10, 1985.
629. Citation, Charles R. Rinaldi, Honorary Life Member, Appalachian Trail Conference, New Paltz, N.Y., 1983.
630. Interview with Charles W. Sloan, October 28, 1985. Interview with Richard L. Stanton, June 6, 1985.
631. Interview with Charles R. Rinaldi, June 7, 1985.
632. Interview with Steven Golden, January 11, 1985.
633. Interview with David A. Richie, June 7-8, 1985.
634. Ibid.
635. Ibid.
636. Interview with Charles R. Rinaldi, June 7, 1985.
637. Interview with Arthur W. Brownell, June 6, 1985. Interview with Charles S. Cushman, May 24, 1985.
638. Interview with Christopher N. Brown, October 28, 1985.
639. Ibid.
640. Interview with Charles R. Rinaldi, June 7, 1985.
641. Interview with Stanley A. Murray, April 26, 1986.
642. Interview with William M. Eichbaum, July 18, 1985.
643. Foresta, *America's National Parks*, 1984.
644. Ibid.
645. Ibid.

646. Interview with Raymond F. Housley, March 12, 1986.
647. Pinchot, *Breaking New Ground*, 1947.
648. Interview with Raymond F. Housley, March 12, 1986.
649. Foresta, *America's National Parks*, 1984.
650. ORRRC, *Outdoor Recreation for America*, 1962.
651. Public Law 88-29, 1963. Public Law 88-578, 1964.
652. Interview with Raymond F. Housley, March 12, 1986.
653. Foresta, *America's National Parks*, 1984.
654. Interview with Raymond F. Housley, March 12, 1986. Interview with Lawrence R. Henson, March 12, 1986.
655. Interview with David A. Richie, June 7-8, 1985.
656. Interview with Paul C. Pritchard, June 6, 1985. Interview with Charles W. Sloan, June 6, 1985.
657. For example, resolution of the Georgia House of Representatives, February 26, 1975. In the *Atlanta Journal*, April 28, 1975, Charles Seabrook discusses plans for the Chattahoochee National Forest.
658. Personal recollections of the author.
659. Interview with Stanley A. Murray, April 26, 1986.
660. ANSTAC minutes, June 20, 1975.
661. Interview with Lawrence R. Henson, March 12, 1986.
662. *Appalachian Trailway News*, August 1975.
663. Interview with David A. Richie, June 7-8, 1985.
664. Interview with Raymond F. Housley, March 12, 1986.
665. Personal recollections of the author.
666. Interview with Raymond F. Housley, March 12, 1986.
667. Interview with Cleveland F. Pinnix, May 10, 1985.
668. Interview with Raymond F. Housley, March 12, 1986.
669. Interview with Lawrence R. Henson, March 12, 1986.
670. Interview with Raymond F. Housley, March 12, 1986.
671. Interview with Lawrence R. Henson, March 12, 1986.
672. Interview with Raymond F. Housley, March 12, 1986.
673. Interview with Lawrence R. Henson, March 12, 1986.
674. Ibid. Interview with Raymond F. Housley, March 12, 1986.
675. Interview with Lawrence R. Henson, March 12, 1986.
676. Interview with David A. Richie, June 7-8, 1985.
677. Interview with Lawrence R. Henson, March 12, 1986.
678. Interview with Raymond F. Housley, March 12, 1986.
679. Ibid. Interview with George T. Hamilton, June 5, 1985.
680. Appalachian Trail Conference, *The Appalachian Trail*, 1973.
681. Fairfax, "Federal-State Cooperation", 1973. Interview with Arthur W. Brownell, June 6, 1985.
682. Appalachian Trail Conference, *Appalachian Trail Guide* (Maine), 1983.
683. Appalachian Trail Conference, *Appalachian Trail Guide* (New Hampshire-Vermont), 1983. Interview with Laurence R. Van Meter, June 7, 1985.
684. Fairfax, "Federal-State Cooperation", 1973. Interview with William M. Eichbaum, July 18, 1985.
685. ANSTAC minutes, June 20, 1975.
686. General description of the states from the author's lecture notes, course on "Bioregionalism", Tufts University, 1983-84.
687. The author served in such a capacity as Massachusetts commissioner of natural

resources from 1959 to 1966.

688. Public Law 91-190, 1970.
689. Appalachian Trail Conference, "Brief of Proceedings", 1925.
690. Personal recollections of the author.
691. Blanchard, "Proceedings", 1909.
692. Foresta, *America's National Parks*, 1984.
693. Ibid. Fitch and Shanklin, *Bureau of Outdoor Recreation*, 1970.
694. For example, Georgia was such a state (interview with David M. Sherman, October 30, 1985).
695. New England regional Council minutes, May 22, 1978, reporting New Hampshire Gov. Meldrim Thomson's opposition to the Trail.
696. Fitch and Shanklin, *Bureau of Outdoor Recreation*, 1970.
697. Interview with Stanley T. Albright, October 28, 1985.
698. Interview with Stanley A. Murray, April 26, 1986.
699. Interview with Robert L. Herbst, October 29, 1985.
700. Interview with David A. Richie, June 7-8, 1985.
701. Interview with Steven Golden, January 11, 1985.
702. Interview with David M. Sherman, October 30, 1985.
703. Interview with Steven Golden, January 11, 1985.
704. Interview with Henry W. Lautz, March 26, 1986. Interview with Laurence R. Van Meter, June 7, 1985. Interview with Stanley A. Murray, May 10, 1986.
705. Interview with Henry W. Lautz, March 26, 1986.
706. Lowrey, "Benton MacKaye's Appalachian Trail", 1981.
707. Interview with George M. Zoebelein, October 1, 1985.
708. Interview with David A. Richie, June 7-8, 1985.
709. Interview with Thomas S. Deans, July 25, 1985.
710. Interview with Cleveland F. Pinnix, May 10, 1985.
711. Interview with David A. Richie, June 7-8, 1985.
712. Interview with Henry W. Lautz, March 26, 1986.
713. Interview with David A. Richie, June 7-8, 1985.
714. Mazmanian and Nienaber, *Can Organizations Change?*, 1979.
715. *Appalachian Trailway News*, September-October, 1979: Benton MacKaye's statement "we discover a thing by losing it".
716. Interview with Robert L. Herbst, October 29, 1985.
717. Interview with Sally K. Fairfax, May 30, 1985.
718. Interview with David A. Richie, June 7-8, 1985. Interview with Stanley T. Albright, October 28, 1985. Interview with Arthur W. Brownell, June 6, 1985.
719. Interview with Charles R. Rinaldi, June 7, 1985. Interview with David A. Richie, June 7-8, 1985.
720. Interview with William M. Eichbaum, July 18, 1985. Interview with Richard L. Stanton, June 6, 1985.
721. Interview with Cleveland F. Pinnix, May 10, 1985. Palmer, *Perceptual Research*, 1979.
722. Interview with Sally K. Fairfax, May 30, 1985.
723. Interview with William M. Eichbaum, July 18, 1985.
724. Interview with Thomas S. Deans, July 25, 1985.
725. Interview with Henry W. Lautz, March 26, 1986.
726. The venerable Cape Cod National Seashore Advisory Commission was not rechartered administratively, for example, until special legislation mandated its reactivation.
727. "Dave Richie to Stan Albright", December 23, 1982.

728. Report from Senate Committee on Public Works on S.9, Senate Report 230, June 20, 1972.
729. Interview with Raymond F. Housley, March 12, 1986.
730. Interview with Lawrence R. Henson, March 12, 1986.
731. Interview with Henry W. Lautz, March 26, 1986.
732. Interview with Raymond F. Housley, March 12, 1986.
733. For example, Shenandoah National Park superintendent Robert Jacobsen's speech in April of 1985 to Trail club presidents: "at least half of you will fail in carrying out management" (interview with David A. Richie, June 7-8, 1985).
734. Interview with Laura C. Beaty, October 30, 1985.
735. Interview with Charles R. Rinaldi, June 7, 1985. Interview with Ruth E. Blackburn, October 31, 1985.
736. Interview with Richard L. Stanton, June 6, 1985.
737. Interview with Charles R. Rinaldi, June 7, 1985.
738. Ibid.
739. Ibid.
740. Interview with Stanley T. Albright, October 28, 1985. Interview with Raymond F. Housley, March 12, 1986. Interview with Arthur W. Brownell, June 6, 1985: Brownell characterized the discussions at the 1985 ANSTAC meeting (Carrabassett, Maine) over protecting the entire viewshed of the Trail as "leaving the members aghast".
741. MacKaye, "The Appalachian Trail", 1921.
742. See n. 414.
743. Appalachian Trail Conference, *The Evolution of the Appalachian Trail Protection Program and "Countryside" Conservation*, December 6, 1985.
744. Palmer, *Perceptual Research*, 1979.
745. As quoted in Foresta, *America's National Parks*, 1984. Conservation Foundation, *National Parks*, 1984.
746. Interview with Charles R. Rinaldi, June 7, 1985.
747. Interview with David M. Sherman, October 30, 1985.
748. Interview with Henry W. Lautz, March 26, 1986.
749. Interview with Laura C. Beaty, October 30, 1985. Interview with Ruth E. Blackburn, October 31, 1985.
750. Interview with Stanley A. Murray, April 26, 1986. Interview with Charles R. Rinaldi, June 7, 1985.
751. Interview with Charles S. Cushman, May 24, 1985.
752. *Christian Science Monitor*, June 4, 1980.
753. Interview with Charles W. Sloan, October 28, 1985.
754. Interview with Henry W. Lautz, March 26, 1986.
755. Interview with Charles W. Sloan, October 28, 1985. Interview with Stanley A. Murray, April 26, 1986.

Selected References

PUBLISHED WORKS

Ambler, C. P. 1931. The activities of the Appalachian National Park Association and the Appalachian National Forest Reserve Association, 1899–1906. North Carolina Historical Commission. Raleigh.

Appalachian Trail Conference. Variable dates. Appalachian Trail guides. Harpers Ferry.

_____. 1925. Brief of proceedings of the Appalachian Trail Conference called by the Federated Societies on Planning and Parks. March 2–3, 1925. Hotel Raleigh. Washington, D.C.

_____. 1973. The Appalachian Trail—a mountain footpath—a National Scenic Trail. Publication No. 5 (revised). Harpers Ferry.

Arnold, Hans G., et al. 1976. The Appalachian Trail: Guidelines for preservation. Report of the Appalachian Trail Study Group. Pennsylvania State University. University Park.

Arnold, Ron. 1982. At the eye of the storm: James Watt and the environmentalists. Regnery Gateway. Chicago.

Blanchard, Newton C., ed. The Committee of Governors, 1909. Proceedings of a conference of governors in the White House, May 13–15, 1908. U.S. Government Printing Office. Washington, D.C.

Bryant, Paul T. 1965. The quality of the day: The achievement of Benton MacKaye. Doctoral dissertation. University of Illinois.

Burch, William R., Jr., ed. 1979. Long distance trails: The Appalachian Trail as a guide to future research and management needs. Yale University School of Forestry and Environmental Studies. New Haven.

Clark, Roger W., ed. 1977. The Appalachian Trail: An annotated bibliography. Yale University School of Forestry and Environmental Studies. New Haven.

Connelly, Thomas L. 1968. Discovering the Appalachians. Stackpole Books. Harrisburg.

The Conservation Foundation. 1972. National parks for the future. Washington, D.C.

_____. 1985. National parks for a new generation: Visions, realities, prospects. Executive summary and overview. Washington, D.C.

Fairfax, Sally K. 1973. Federal-state cooperation in outdoor recreation policy formation: The case of the Appalachian Trail. Doctoral dissertation. Duke University.

Farb, Peter. 1963. Face of North America: The natural history of a continent. Harper and Row. New York.

Fitch, Edwin M., and John F. Shanklin. 1970. The Bureau of Outdoor Recreation. Praeger. New York.

Foresta, Ronald A. 1984. America's national parks and their keepers. Resources for the Future. Washington, D.C.

Foster, Charles H. W. 1985. The Cape Cod National Seashore: A landmark alliance. University Press of New England. Hanover, N.H.

Howarth, William. 1982. Thoreau in the mountains. Farrar, Straus and Giroux. New York.

Ise, John. 1961. Our national park policy: A critical history. Johns Hopkins University Press. Baltimore.

Johnson, Hugh B. 1971. The Appalachian Trail and beyond. *Journal of the American Institute of Architects*, October 1971.

Kocher, Sandra and Michael Warren. 1979. *The Appalachian Trail*. Graphic Arts Center Publishing Company. Portland.

Levine, Louis D., ed. 1975. Man in nature: Historical perspectives on man in his environment. Royal Ontario Museum. Toronto.

Lowrey, Gerald B., Jr. 1981. Benton MacKaye's Appalachian Trail as a cultural symbol. Doctoral dissertation. Emory University.

MacKaye, Benton. 1921. The Appalachian Trail: A project in regional planning. *Journal of the American Institute of Architects*, October 1921.

Mazmanian, Daniel A., and Jeanne Nienaber. 1979. *Can organizations change? Environmental protection, citizen participation, and the Corps of Engineers*. Brookings Institution. Washington, D.C.

Outdoor Recreation Resources Review Commission. 1962. *Outdoor recreation for America*. U.S. Government Printing Office. Washington, D.C.

Palmer, James F. 1979. Conducting a wildland visual resources inventory. GTR PSW-35. U.S. Forest Service. Berkeley.

Peirce, Neal R., 1975. *The border South states: People, politics, and power in the border South states*. W. W. Norton. New York.

_____ . 1976. *The New England states: People, politics, and power in the six New England states*. W.W. Norton and Co. New York.

Peirce, Neal R., and Michael Barone. 1977. *The mid-Atlantic states of America: People, politics, and power in the five mid-Atlantic states and the nation's capital*. W. W. Norton. New York.

Pinchot, Gifford. 1947. *Breaking new ground*. Harcourt, Brace and Co. New York.

Raitz, Karl B., and Richard Ulack, with Thomas R. Leinbach. 1984. *Appalachia, a regional geography: Land, people, and development*. Westview Press. Boulder and London.

Robinson, Glen O. 1975. *The Forest Service*. Johns Hopkins University Press. Baltimore.

Ross, John R. 1975. Benton MacKaye: The Appalachian Trail. Journal of the American Institute of Planners, March 1975.

U.S. Department of the Interior, Bureau of Outdoor Recreation. 1966. *Trails for America*. U.S. Government Printing Office. Washington.

_____ , National Park Service. 1972. Part Two of the national park system plan: Natural history. U.S. Government Printing Office. Washington.

_____ . 1981. Comprehensive plan for the protection, management, development, and use of the Appalachian National Scenic Trail. Appalachian Trail Project Office. Harpers Ferry.

Van Dyke, Cornelius. 1979. Trail corridor design and protection: A case study of the Appalachian Trail in New Hampshire. Master's thesis. State University of New York. Syracuse.

Wegman, Richard A. 1983. *The utilization and management of Federal advisory committees: A report of the Charles F. Kettering Foundation*. Dayton.

Wirth, Conrad. 1980. *Parks, politics, and the people*. University of Oklahoma Press. Stillwater.

LEGISLATIVE DOCUMENTS

Hearings of the Subcommittee on Parks and Recreation, Senate Committee on Interior and Insular Affairs, September 16, 1965.

Hearings of the Subcommittee on Parks and Recreation, Senate Committee on Interior and Insular Affairs, March 15–16, 1967.

Senate Report No. 90-1233, Senate Committee on Interior and Insular Affairs, June 13, 1968.

House Report No. 90-1631, Subcommittee on National Parks and Recreation, House Committee on Interior and Insular Affairs, July 3, 1968.

House Report No. 90-1891, Committee of Conference, September 12, 1968.

Public Law 90-543, National Trails System Act, October 2, 1968.

Committee Publication No. 94-50, Subcommittee on National Parks and Recreation, House Committee on Interior and Insular Affairs, March 11–12, 1976.

House Report No. 95-734, House Committee on Interior and Insular Affairs, October 21, 1977.

Committee Publication No. 95-81, Subcommittee on Parks and Recreation, Senate Committee on Energy and Natural Resources, November 1, 1977.

Senate Report No. 95-636, Senate Committee on Energy and Natural Resources, February 10, 1978.

Public Law 95-248, National Trails System Act amendments, March 27, 1978.

House Report 97-267, House Interior and Insular Affairs Committee, October 7, 1981.

Committee Publication No. 97-116, Hearings of the Subcommittee on Public Lands and Reserved Water, Senate Committee on Energy and Natural Resources, August 4, 1982.

Senate Report No. 97-577, Senate Committee on Energy and Natural Resources, September 23, 1982.

Senate Report No. 98-1, Senate Committee on Energy and Natural Resources, January 31, 1983.

House Report No. 98-28, House Committee on Interior and Insular Affairs, March 9, 1983.

Public Law 98-11, National Trails System Act amendments, March 28, 1983.

ADMINISTRATIVE DOCUMENTS

U.S. Department of the Interior, National Park Service, Appalachian Trail Project Office, September 1981. Comprehensive plan for the protection, management, development, and use of the Appalachian National Scenic Trail. Harpers Ferry, West Virginia.

U.S. Department of the Interior, National Park Service, Appalachian Trail Project Office and Mid-Atlantic Regional Office, March 1, 1982. Appalachian National Scenic Trail case study: Final report. Harpers Ferry, West Virginia.

U.S. Department of the Interior, National Park Service, Appalachian Trail Project Office, June 1983 (updated to June 1986). Land protection plan for the Appalachian National Scenic Trail. Harpers Ferry, West Virginia.

Index

219

as vice chairman, 37, 119
Boone Appalachian Trail Conference
(1975), 33-34, 126
Boone meeting of ANSTAC (1975), 33-38,
39, 119, 134
Botts, James, 57
Boy Scouts, use of trail by, 31
Brochure, by Park Service, 30-31
Brown, Christopher, 73-74, 76, 122-123,
128
Brownell, Arthur W., 18
on ANSTAC, 69
as ANSTAC chairman, 84, 97
and Cushman, 73
and Maine landowners, 74
and 1982 meeting, 86
and 1983 meeting, 93
Bryant, John L., Jr., 81
Burch, William R., 48
Bureau of the Budget
and National System of Foot Trails, 14
see also Office of Management and
Budget
Bureau of Outdoor Recreation, 5, 116,
124-125
and contingency funds, 49
and decentralized administration, 126
and Foster/Richie efforts, 42
and LAWCON, 39
at oversight hearings, 44
and Park Service, 132, 133
Pritchard in, 55-56
Bureau of Public Roads, and National
System of Foot Trails, 14
Burns, Robert L., 22
Burton, Phillip, 51-52, 61, 136
Buschman, Elmer V., 18-19, 20, 21, 24,
117
Byron, Goodloe, 44

CANT (Citizens Against the "New"
Trail), 71-72
Cape Cod National Seashore legislation,
116
Carbin, Richard, 79
Carrying capacity, 60
Carter administration, 51, 69, 77, 105,
113, 120
budget by, 71
and Interior Department, 81
and Pritchard and Herbst, 55, 62
Cherokee Indians, "seven sacred trees"
of, 3
Citizen role.*See* Volunteers
Civilian Conservation Corps (CCC), 129,

131, 136
Clark, Steven, 90
Clark, William P., 97
Co-Evolution Quarterly, 8
Cognitive regionalization, 6
Comprehensive plan, 62, 76-77, 122-123
and ANSTAC, 80
and management, 62, 73, 88, 89
Condemnation
Agriculture Department on (1972), 26
authority limited for, 45
delays in (1972), 25
and National Trails Systems Act, 17
Reagan policy on, 83, 93
report on (1982), 85
in Trails Act amendments, 62, 63
see also Acquisition of land
Congress
ANSTAC lobbying of, 110
House vs. Senate operation in, 59-60
Interior appropriations testimony to
(Deans), 78-79
and National Trails System Act, 16-17
and National Trails System Act
amendments, 51
oversight hearings in, 42, 43-45, 108,
118, 120
and Park Service delinquency, 38
Trail clubs needed to campaign in, 76
see also Legislation
Connecticut Forest and Park Association,
130
Connecticut River Valley, connector
across, 49
Connelly, Thomas, 4
Conservation Law Foundation, 53
Conservation movement, 130, 132. *See
also* Environmentalism
Constituency, sense of, 139. *See also*
Partnership
Conway, Grant, 37
Cooperative agreements
and ANSTAC, 19, 21, 28, 46, 47, 58
ATC/NPS (1970), 20, 90
and ATC partnership committee, 89
and hiking-bill amendment, 90
and liability, 22
and management, 67
management delegation through, 94,
95, 96-97, 157-168 (Appendix F)
and Reagan era, 80
Richie prototype of, 73, 74, 77
Richie's use of, 122
with states, 20-21, 25, 31, 134
and Trail Act, 17